Law, Corporate Governance, and Accounting

Routledge Studies in Accounting

Law, Corporate Governance, and Accounting

European Perspectives

Edited by Victoria Krivogorsky

Routledge
Taylor & Francis Group

LONDON AND NEW YORK

First published 2011
by Routledge
Published 2014 by Routledge
711 Third Avenue, New York, NY 10017

Simultaneously published in the UK
by Routledge
2 Park Square, Milton Park, Abingdon, Oxfordshire OX14 4RN

Routledge is an imprint of the Taylor and Francis Group, an informa business

First issued in paperback 2015

Typeset in Sabon by IBT Global.

Library of Congress Cataloging-in-Publication Data
Law, corporate governance, and accounting : European perspectives / edited by Victoria Krivogorsky.
    p. cm. — (Routledge studies in account ; 9)
    Includes bibliographical references and index.
    1.   Corporations—Europe—Accounting.   2.   Accounting—Standards—Europe.
    3.   Corporate governance—Europe.   4.   Financial statements—Standards—
Europe.   I. Krivogorsky, Victoria.
    HF5616.E8L39 2011
    657.094—dc22
    2010039920

ISBN 978-0-415-87186-0 (hbk)
ISBN 978-1-138-95967-5 (pbk)
ISBN 978-0-203-82849-6 (ebk)

Contents

PART III
Analysis of Changing Institutional Environments,
New Accounting Policies, and Corporate Governance
Practices in Selected Countries

Figures

Tables

Acknowledgments

We thank the workshop participants at the American Accounting Association annual meeting, International Section of American Accounting Association midyear meeting, and European Accounting Association annual congress, European Business and Economics Society annual conference, ESSEC Business School in Paris, France, ESCP Europe in Paris, France, Higher School of Economics in Moscow, Russia, for the their helpful comments on Chapters 1 and 3 of this monograph.

We thank the ESSEC School of Business for partial financial support provided for this research.

We offer special thanks to Marina Nacamura and Anton Leonov for their particularly useful editorial and research assistance.

Introduction

Victoria Krivogorsky

The growing internationalization of markets, the relaxation of constraints on capital flows between countries, and the creation of different economic unions (the European Union in particular) has initiated the flow of capital, goods, and services across national borders, the growth and diffusion of shareholding, as well as increasing merger activity among the world's largest stock exchanges. These changes have in turn created interest in understanding the merits of new developments in accounting to a higher qualitative level.

Given the worldwide competition to attract corporate headquarters and investment, it is important to go beyond the analyses of accounting to examine how key aspects of other institutional environments interact with firms' attributes. This research monograph will engage separate strands of literature to advance a more holistic understanding of whether different countries' business environments coincide with accounting convergence. In doing so, it advances a great amount of prior related research by conducting a simultaneous analysis of the fields of accounting, auditing, and corporate governance as the primary means of a much larger economic system, which should be properly developed in order for the system as a whole to operate efficiently.

Several recent occurrences in the world of business are particularly significant for the purposes of this research monograph. First, this monograph provides an analysis of recent efforts in developing integrated formal structures for the formulation of international accounting. The need to develop an international framework of accounting to assess current accounting practices and to encourage the logical development of common accounting principles has long been felt. Current interest in this area was further fostered by the rise of multinational corporations and economic integration among national stock exchanges. In search of a set of robust international accounting principles, the US Financial Accounting Standards Board (FASB) and International Accounting Standards Board (IASB) made specific attempts to set forth some of the bases upon which financial statements rest, evaluate, and/or justify current practices, and develop a conceptual framework that would provide a sound foundation for developing new accounting standards that are principle-based, internally consistent, internationally convergent, and contain the information needed for business decisions. In this regard, this research monograph presents analysis of the new accounting framework and accompanying developments in accounting policies as well as the debate surrounding International Financial Reporting Standards (IFRS) adoption in Europe, focusing mainly on the merits of adoption; such as its effects on the definition, recognition, and measurement of the balance sheet and income statement properties.

Second, in March of 2002, the European Parliament passed a resolution requiring all firms listed on the stock exchanges of European member states to apply IFRS when preparing their group financial statements for fiscal years beginning on or after January 1, 2005.[1] This effort supposedly has a twofold effect. First, it is seen as a stepping-stone toward achieving full European harmonization, following the passing of the fourth and seventh directives decades prior. Second, requiring adoption of IFRS helps to facilitate entry of EU-based listed companies into world stock markets.

Third, corporate scandals in the US and Europe in the early 2000s shook the financial community's confidence in the performance of public companies' boards of directors (BODs) and drew attention to possible flaws in corporate governance practices. As a result, most European countries, that is, members of the European Union, have changed their corporate governance practices to better serve shareholders' interests by emphasizing the accountability and risk management aspects of corporate governance. In this respect, this research monograph performs a comparative country-specific analysis of the latest developments in the corporate governance regulations, and their scope and effectiveness in solving agency problems and promoting and utilizing different control mechanisms depending on country-specific governance requirements.

Fourth, following the Norwolk agreement, the IASB and Securities and Exchange Commission (SEC) have committed themselves toward a path of standards convergence. In this regard, this monograph provides an analysis of the US perspective on implementation of IFRS in the United States.

Finally, in 2008, the International Auditing and Assurance Standards Board (IAASB), operating under the sponsorship of the International Federation of Accountants (IFAC), developed the IAASB Strategy and Work Program 2009–2011. In accordance with this program, IAASB will continue developing auditing, assurance, and quality control standards, as well as facilitating the convergence of international standards to enhance the quality of the practice globally and reinforce public confidence in the global auditing and assurance profession. In this respect, this monograph provides an analysis of the global developments, acting institutions, and status of worldwide adoption of international standards on auditing.

The findings of this study make several contributions that would therefore be of interest to several market sectors. First, the results of (a) the comparative analysis of corporate governance codes will be instrumental in the evaluation of corporate governance differences among European countries, and (b) the analysis on the impact and importance of mandatory adoption of IFRS on EU firms can be used for robust policy prescriptions for future regimes. These findings can therefore help policymakers in fine-tuning their regulatory initiatives.

Second, it is intended that information presented in this monograph and the results of the analyses contained herein can be used for graduate and postgraduate seminars in accounting, corporate governance, management, and finance. The holistic approach used in the analyses of all the issues addressed in this study will be helpful in developing students' understanding of how the economic system as a whole should be used as the object of analysis, rather than focusing on individual components.

Third, this monograph can be instrumental for researchers and practitioners, because it will supply them with information regarding accounting practices and the quality of corporate governance environments in European countries. As of this writing, the IFRS/IAS do not cover the entire spectrum of accounting issues (there are only about fifty IFRS/IAS regulations available), making this book instrumental in the navigation of the "uncharted waters" of international accounting.

NOTES

1. This requirement affected approximately seven thousand firms.

Part I

IFRS as a Global Set of Standards

Conceptual Framework and US Standpoint on them

1 Conceptual Framework for International Financial Reporting Standards

Victoria Krivogorsky

The importance of cross-sectional comparability of financial statements in the facilitation of decision making has been addressed in accounting literature for many years. In this vein, uniformity among financial statements, which implies the presentation of financial statements being invariant among different firms worldwide with regard to several principles, which desirably include accounting procedures, measurements, concepts, classification, and methods of disclosure. It was with this idea in mind that the International Accounting Standards Committee (IASC)[1] was created in 1973 as a body independent of government and pseudo-government control, with the stated purpose of enhancing the accounting profession worldwide and the main goal of generating a single set of international accounting standards. Contemporaneously with these developments the advent of a conceptual framework for international financial reporting became essential; and such a conceptual framework is considered to be an assembled body of interconnected basic accounting principles guiding the formulation of standards on a consistent basis as opposed to the *ad hoc* manner that was often used previously.

The new stage in the development of international accounting standards started in 1995 when IASC entered into an agreement with the International Organization of Securities Commissions (IOSCO) to complete a "core set" of international standards by 1999. In May 2000 IOSCO accepted the completed comprehensive set of "core standards" and recommended them for cross-border use in all global markets, although the US Securities and Exchange Commission (SEC) continued to require reconciliation with US GAAP for all foreign registrants until 2008. In June 2000, immediately following IOSCO acceptance, the European Commission issued a communiqué, stating that all listed companies in the European Union (EU) would be required to prepare their consolidated financial statements using international standards. This tender was later implemented by the launching of EU

Accounting Regulation No. 1606/2002, which required European publicly traded companies to use International Financial Reporting Standards (IAS/IFRS) to prepare their consolidated financial statements starting in 2005 without transposition into national law.

Apparently the acceptance of international standards by the US SEC became a critical element in the IASB's acceptance as the global accounting standard-setting body. In 2002, Financial Accounting Standards Board (FASB) and IASB signed the Norwalk agreement (Memorandum of Understanding—MoU) and began collaboration on a phased program of convergence with an ultimate goal of constructing a single set of standards and a common conceptual framework. MoU was updated in 2008 and again in 2009, when both boards issued a further statement outlining steps for completing their convergence. Consistently with these guidelines, and after thorough discussions with representatives of the European Commission and SEC staff, the FASB and the IASB have agreed to work towards the mutual goal of the development of high-quality common standards. In November 2008 the SEC issued a release that details a "road map" of specific items that should be addressed before US publicly trading companies start their transition to IFRS (in lieu of US GAAP), which is to occur as early as 2014.

In the joint statement of the IASB and the FASB from November 5, 2009, *FASB and IASB Reaffirm Commitment to Memorandum of Understanding*, both boards described their plans for completing the major projects of the MoU. In particular they stated the following:

- "Our commitment to the improvement and convergence of IFRSs and US GAAP is consistent with the strong support for the goal of a single set of high quality global standards recently expressed by the Leaders of the Group of 20 nations at their Pittsburgh Summit, the Financial Crisis Advisory Group of the FASB and IASB, the Monitoring Board of the International Accounting Standards Committee, Foundation, and many others.
- We are redoubling our efforts to achieve a single set of high quality standards within the context of our respective independent standard-setting processes.
- We aim to complete each major project by the end of June 2011, consistent with the milestones established by the 2008 update of the MoU. In establishing target dates, we took into account the fact that several major countries are adopting IFRSs in 2011 and that for some other countries, including the US, continued improvement and convergence is an important consideration in deciding the role of IFRSs in their capital markets.
- We aim to provide a high degree of accountability through appropriate due process, including wide engagement with stakeholders, and oversight conducted in the public interest. We are consulting widely

and will continue to draw on expertise from investors, preparers, auditors, standard-setters, regulators, and others around the world.

- Our efforts to improve IFRS and US GAAP for financial instruments and to achieve their convergence have been complicated by the differing project timetables we established to respond to our respective stakeholder groups and other factors. We are committed to issuing standards by the end of 2010 that represent a comprehensive and improved solution to this complex and contentious area and that provide international comparability. We have developed strategies and plans to deliver on that commitment. As a first step, we reached agreement at our joint meeting last week on a set of core principles designed to achieve comparability and transparency in reporting, consistency in accounting for credit impairments, and reduced complexity of financial instrument accounting.

In issuing this statement, we are also expressing our commitment to:

- The goals and objectives of the 2008 Update of the MoU that set out priorities and milestones to be achieved on major joint projects.
- Fundamental first principles about the purposes of accounting standards and the process by which the standards are determined, as set out in the statement of the Monitoring Board of the International Accounting Standards Committee Foundation, issued on September 22, 2009."

Thus, the IASB and FASB showed their determination to deliver on the commitment to develop high-quality standards accompanied by a conceptual framework, which has for a long time been seen as necessary so as to encourage the logical development of accounting principles and to assess existing practices. Historically, however, it was not until about three decades ago that any real strides were made toward development of a consistent and integrated formal structure for the formulation of accounting principles. Back in 1922, US scholar William Paton[2] stated and examined some of the basic premises and postulates implicit in the accounting thought of that time. For the next fifty years, the American Institute of Certified Public Accountants (AICPA) and American Accounting Association (AAA) have been continuously making attempts to discuss concepts underlying the conventions of accounting, but most of the time they presented and discussed specific rules and recommendations as isolated problems in the context of an implicit structure of postulates and basic principles. The efforts to develop a conceptual framework in the US did not finally materialize until the late 1970s, when (in 1978) the FASB issued its SFAS 1 *Objectives of Financial Reporting by Business Enterprises* and in 1980 its SFAS 2 and SFAS 3 on *Qualitative Characteristics* and *Elements*. In 1982–1984, the work on the idea of a conceptual framework slowed as the FASB had encountered some difficulties in dealing with issues of recognition and measurement. Eventually though, the set of six *Statements of Accounting Concepts* was created.

The mass efforts to develop an international conceptual framework began with a limited study on the objectives of financial statements initiated by IASC back in 1982. Ironically, this occurred simultaneously with the IASC's statement that it was not its intention to prepare an "international conceptual framework." Two years later, when the IASC started revising IAS 1, *Disclosure of Accounting Policies*, initially published in 1974, it decided to merge the objectives project with this revision. The final decision to merge projects covering assets, liabilities, equity, and expenses (originating in 1984–1985) into a framework project was made in 1986, and the initially proposed revision of IAS 1 was deferred. From the onset, the Framework was intended to be separate from the standards to avoid binding with any particular accounting treatment. The Framework was completed and issued in 1989 and had not been revised until the joint IASB-FASB framework project started. The importance of the Framework in the international setting was never underrated even though the joint conceptual framework project is not formally a part of the MoU work plan. After the consultations with the representatives of the European Commission and SEC staff, and consistently with already established priorities and available recourses, IASB and FASB identified the framework project as of highest priority. This was because all other convergence projects would occur in the context of the ongoing work on the conceptual framework as the Framework addresses the issues of measurement attributes (including cost and fair value).

The joint IASB-FASB conceptual framework project from the beginning was divided into eight phases as follows:

1. objectives and qualitative characteristics
2. elements, recognition, and measurement
3. measurement
4. reporting entity
5. presentation and disclosure
6. purpose and status
7. application to not-for-profit entities
8. finalization

As the final product the international Framework represents a body of interconnected objectives (goals and purposes of financial standards) and fundamentals (concepts supporting those objectives) that inspire standard-setting process. Three distinct parts can be identified in the framework as follows: (a) the definitions of the objectives; (b) the explanation of qualitative characteristics of accounting information and definition of the elements; and (c) the rules of recognition and reporting. The Framework is a concise document of thirty-six pages, which does not override any specific standard and is not an IAS or IFRS itself (that is, it is something of a meta-standard, not a true standard in and of itself). In the case of a conflict between the Framework and an IAS/IFRS, the requirements of the latter prevail, but the Framework is quite influential in the preparation of new individual standards. For example, the Framework definitions of assets and liabilities had a great impact on the preparation of IFRS 3, *Business Combinations*; IAS 37, *Provisions, Contingent Liabilities and Contingent Assets*; IAS 38, *Intangible Assets*; and IAS 39, *Financial Instruments: Recognition and Measurement*. Another way of characterizing the Framework is to deem it as exemplifying IAS/IFRS with respect to issues yet to be covered in those standards. For example, the IASB will be guided by the Framework in the development of future IFRSs and in reviewing existing ones, so that the number of conflicting cases between the Framework and the international standards are likely to diminish over time.

The type of structure used to house the international Framework is informal or implicit, arrived at by using a pragmatic (inductive) approach as opposed to a formal approach informed by the axiomatic (deductive) method. In the deductive approach, the structure for logical reasoning should be fairly formal to obtain general agreement, whereas the inductive approach's rules of action can be converted into accounting principles. The accounting standard setters derived the conceptual Framework from the best practices, which in turn have been identified based on assumed objectives of financial reporting. Simultaneously, attention has obviously been paid to conceptual coherence, as the Framework is written in a descriptive style (the word *should* is only used in standards, not in the Framework) even though the Framework is intended to be normative in its nature as it provides guidance to setting and interpreting accounting standards.

As discussed earlier, the Framework does not have a status of a standard, and its purpose is stated as follows (paragraph 1):

- To assist the Board of IASC in the development of future IASs and in its review of existing IASs;
- To assist the Board of IASC in promoting harmonization of regulations, accounting standards and procedures relating to the presentation of financial statements by providing a basis for reducing the number of alternative accounting treatments permitted by IASs;
- To assist national standard-setting bodies in developing national standards;
- To assist preparers of financial statements in applying IASs and in dealing with topics that have yet to form the subject of an IAS;
- To assist auditors in forming an opinion as to whether financial statements conform with IASs;
- To assist users of financial statements in interpreting the information contained in financial statements prepared in conformity with IASs;
- To provide those who are interested in the work of the IASC with information about its approach to the formulation of accounting standards.

The scope of the conceptual framework is summarized in paragraph 5 of the Framework as follows:

- Objectives of financial statements.
- Qualitative characteristics that determine the usefulness of financial statement information.
- Definition, recognition, and measurement of financial statement elements.
- Concepts of capital and capital maintenance.

The Framework is concerned with "general purpose financial statements," including consolidated financial statements, and not including special purpose reports such as prospectuses and tax computations (paragraph 6). The "general purpose financial statements" include a balance sheet, an income statement, a statement of changes in financial position, notes, other statements, and explanatory material that are an integral part of the financial statements. Supplementary schedules and information derived from and expected to be read with financial statements may also be included. For example, segment reporting and information about the effects of changing prices. General purpose financial statements do not include such items as directors' reports, chairman's statements, management reports, and similar material that may be included in a financial or annual report (paragraph 7). The Framework applies to the financial statements of all commercial, industrial, and business reporting entities, in both private and public sectors (paragraph 8), which are prepared and filed at least annually to fulfill the common information needs of a wide range of users. Paragraph 9 of the Framework identifies seven categories of "users" of financial statements as follows: investors, employees, lenders, suppliers and other trade creditors, customers, governments and their agencies, and the public.

Consistently with other conceptual frameworks (the FASB's set of Statements of Financial Accounting Concepts, for instance), the IASB's Framework covers the following topics:

1. *Objective of financial statements.* The Framework argues that (a) because investors are capital providers to the entity, financial statements that meet their needs will also meet "most of the needs of other users that financial statements can satisfy" and (b) there are needs for financial statement information that are common to all users (paragraph 10). Following this line of reasoning, "the objective of financial statements is to provide information about the financial position, performance, and changes in financial position of an entity that is useful to a wide range of users in making economic decisions, including assessment of the stewardship or accountability of management."

The Framework in paragraphs 22 and 23 states that, in order to meet the Framework objectives, two "underlying assumptions" are used to prepare the financial statements—the "accrual basis" and the "going concern" basis. In particular, paragraph 22 presents conventional arguments as to why financial statements are prepared on the accrual basis, rather than on a cash basis (to "provide the type of information about past transactions and other events that is most useful to users in making economic decisions"). If the going concern assumption cannot be applied because "the enterprise has . . . an intention or need . . . to liquidate or curtail materially the scale of its operations, the financial statements may have to be prepared on a different basis and, if so, the basis used is disclosed" (paragraph 23).

2. *Qualitative characteristics of financial statement information.* The Framework names four main "qualitative characteristics: understandability, relevance, reliability, and comparability." Materiality is referred to as an aspect of relevance. "Faithful representation," "substance over form," "neutrality" (freedom from bias), "prudence" (subject to neutrality), and "completeness" (within the bounds of materiality and cost) are quoted as the aspects of reliability. The Framework does not explicitly embrace the concepts of "true and fair view" (TFV) or "fair presentation" (FP), but identifies that "the application of the principal qualitative characteristics and of appropriate accounting standards normally results in financial statements that convey what is generally understood as [a TFV or FP] of such information."

> To satisfy the requirement of reliability—one of the most complex qualitative characteristics—an item should possess a cost or value that can be measured consistently, otherwise it is not appropriate to recognize it. However, in many cases, cost (value) can be only estimated, and in this case the use of reasonable estimates is an essential part of the financial reporting process and should not be undermined by the reliability requirement. In cases where an item satisfies the definition of an element but not the recognition criteria, it will not be recognized on the face of financial statements, but its relevance is likely to require its disclosure in the notes to the financial statements or in other supplementary disclosures. This applies when the item meets the definition of an element, and a probability criterion of the recognition but not the reliability criterion. The key issue here is whether the item is considered to be relevant to the evaluation of financial position, performance, or changes in financial position. An item that does not satisfy the recognition criteria for an asset or a liability at some point of time may do so later, if/when more information relevant to estimating its probability, cost, or value becomes available. (paragraphs 86–88)

3. *Elements of financial statements.* The Framework links the elements of financial statements to the measurements of financial position and performance. Financial position comprises a number of attributes, including

liquidity, solvency, leverage, asset and liabilities structure, reserves available to cover dividends, etc. Whereas the process of measurement of the elements is described in the Framework, it is not fully clear what is meant by "measurement" of financial position.

As the elements of financial position it identifies the balance sheet properties and provides definitions of assets, liabilities, and equity. As elements of performance it identifies the income statement properties and defines income, revenue, gains/losses, and expenses. The Framework does not identify any elements associated uniquely with the changes in the financial position, but states that it is usually associated with the "income statement elements and changes in balance sheet elements" (paragraph 47). Because the Framework considers elements to be "directly related to the measurement of financial position," the section with the definition of assets, liabilities, and equity (paragraphs 48–80) compiles the core of the Framework as a prescriptive basis for standard-setting.[3] In particular: The Framework defines income and expenses in terms of "increases and decreases in economic benefits that are equated with changes in assets and liabilities."

The latter are defined in terms of "resources controlled" and "present obligations" to exclude some items that have been previously recognized as assets or liabilities (accruals and deferrals) in the name of "matching" expenses and revenues.

4. *Principles for recognition of the elements.* The Framework defines *recognition* as the process of recording in the financial statements (subject to materiality) all items that meet the definition of an element and satisfies two recognition criteria: (a) "it is probable that any future economic benefit associated with the item will flow to or from an entity," and (b) "the item has a cost or value that can be measured with reliability." Assessments of the degree of probability of the inflow/outflow of future economic benefits "are made when the financial statements are prepared." There is an overlap between definitions and recognition criteria because satisfying the definition of an element is the principal criterion for the recognition.

The measurement issues are addressed in paragraphs 99–101 of the Framework. *Measurement* is described as "the process of determining the monetary amounts at which the elements of the financial statements are to be recognized and carried in the balance sheet and income statement." The elements considered to be "directly related to the measurement of financial position" are assets, liabilities, and equity, which are defined as follows (paragraph 49):[4]

1. An asset is a resource (a) controlled by the enterprise, (b) as a result of past events, and (c) from which future economic benefits are expected to flow to the enterprise. The recognition of an asset, thus, requires that all three components of the definition, (a), (b), and (c), are satisfied.

2. A liability is (a) a present obligation of the enterprise, (b) arising out of past events, (c) the settlement of which is expected to result in an outflow from the enterprise of resources embodying economic benefits. The recognition of a liability, thus, requires that all three components of the definition, (a), (b), and (c), are satisfied.
3. Equity is defined as the residual interest in the assets of the enterprise after deducting all its liabilities.

It should be noted here that merely satisfying the preceding definitions does not entail the recognition of an asset or a liability because other criteria should also be satisfied. First, the principle of "substance over form" should be fulfilled; and second, the recognition criteria identified in paragraphs 82–98 should be satisfied as well. In paragraphs 82–98 the recognition is described as "the process of incorporating in the balance sheet or [the] income statement an item that meets the definition of an element and satisfies the criteria for recognition set out in paragraph 83."[5] The failure to recognize the items (*in the main financial statements*) that satisfy the relevant definition and recognition criteria is not rectified by disclosure of the accounting policies used or by the use of notes or other explanatory material.

The additional recognition criteria are set out in paragraph 83 as follows:

- It is probable that any future economic benefit associated with the item will flow to or from the entity; and
- The item has a cost or value that can be measured with reliability.

To meet the Framework's recognition criteria, an entity may recognize revenue, if it is earned, and it should be associated with a simultaneous increase in assets or decrease in liabilities. In other words, the recognition of income occurs simultaneously with the recognition of increases in assets or decreases in liabilities (or a combination of the two). It restricts the recognition of income to items that meet the Framework's recognition criteria of *probability* (a sufficient degree of certainty). The concept of probability used in the recognition criteria refers "to the degree of uncertainty [as to whether] the future economic benefits associated with the item will flow to or from the enterprise . . . in keeping with the uncertainty that characterizes the environment in which an enterprise operates." The Framework does not offer much guidance beyond this definition on the interpretation of "probable," and the latter is scattered over several IAS/IFRSs. For instance, IAS 37, *Provisions, Contingent Assets and Contingent Liabilities*, contains an interpretation of "probable" as "more likely than not," which may reasonably be interpreted as a probability in excess of 50 percent. However, the standard itself states that this interpretation is not intended to be applied in other contexts. In the case of receivables, the allowances for probably uncollectible accounts would normally be based on past statistics, i.e., the assessments of uncertainty are made on the basis of the evidence available when the financial statements are prepared (paragraph 85).

To add to the intricacy of the issue, the interrelationships among qualitative characteristics can at times become highly complicated. For instance, recognition is subject to materiality. The Framework states that "information is material if its omission or misstatement could influence the economic decisions of users taken on the basis of the financial statements . . . the size of the item or error [being] judged in the particular circumstances of its omission or misstatement" (paragraph 30). Thus, the key characteristic in defining the materiality is relevance (information that could influence economic decisions), and materiality should be interpreted as a guide to relevance, and at the same time, materiality restricts recognition, as an item's cost (value) should be material to meet a criterion of the recognition.

5. *Bases for measurement of the elements.* This section of the Framework is not prescriptive and mostly cites a number of different measurements (historical cost, revaluation model, etc.) and suggests that measurement bases are being commonly combined with each other.

Four different measurement bases are specifically mentioned and depicted (with no claim to exhaustiveness): historical cost, current cost (of replacement or settlement), realizable or (for liabilities) settlement value, and present value. Historical cost is mentioned as the measurement basis most commonly adopted by entities in preparing their financial statements, usually in combination with other measurement bases. An example of the latter is the carrying of inventories at the lower historical cost and net realizable value. Marketable securities may be carried at market value, and pension liabilities are carried at their present value. Current cost may be used as a means of taking into account the effects of changing prices of nonmonetary assets.

6. *Concepts of capital and capital maintenance.* The Framework identifies two main concepts of capital: the financial and the physical. In either case, capital is identified with the equity (in either nominal or real financial terms); in other words, it is linked to an entity's net assets measured in those terms. The Framework does not explicitly distinguish between nominal and real financial capital, but it defines that the financial concept of capital takes two forms: invested money (nominal financial) or invested purchasing power (real financial) capital. Physical capital is a form of "real" capital concept. It is based on the notion of the productive capacity or operating capability of the entity, as embodied in its net assets. The Framework identifies that the physical capital maintenance concept requires the use of a particular measurement basis, such as current cost, whereas neither form of the financial capital maintenance concept requires any particular mea-

surement basis. Most enterprises adopt a financial concept of capital, in the absence of severe inflation (paragraph 102).

The choice of concept of capital is related to the concept of capital maintenance and is most meaningful given its implications in the realm of profit measurement, and the informational needs of the users of financial statements. The Framework defines the capital maintenance as follows in paragraphs 103–106:

- *Maintenance of nominal financial capital.* Under this concept a profit is earned only if the net assets at the end of the period exceed the net assets at the beginning of the period, after excluding any distributions to, and contributions from, equity owners during the period.
- *Maintenance of real financial capital.* Under this concept a profit is earned only if the net assets at the end of the period exceed the net assets at the beginning of the period, restated in units of the same purchasing power, after excluding distributions to, and contributions from, owners. Normally, the units of purchasing power employed are those of the currency at the end of the period, into which the net assets at the beginning of the period are restated.
- *Maintenance of real physical capital.* Under this concept a profit is earned only if the operating capability embodied in the net assets at the end of the period exceeds the operating capability embodied in the net assets at the beginning of the period, after excluding distributions to, and contributions from, owners. Operating capability embodied in assets may, in principle, be measured by employing the current cost basis of measurement.

The main difference among the three concepts of capital maintenance is the treatment of the effects of changes in the carrying amounts of the entity's assets and liabilities. Under nominal financial capital maintenance, increases in the carrying amounts of assets held over the period (to the extent that they are recognized as gains) are part of profit.

Under real financial capital maintenance, such increases are part of profit only if they are "real" increases, that is, increases that remain after carrying amounts have been restated in units of the same purchasing power. The total amount of the restatement is known as a "capital maintenance adjustment" and is transferred to a capital maintenance reserve, which is part of equity (but not of retained profits). Real financial capital maintenance may be used in conjunction with historical cost as a measurement basis, but would more normally be used in conjunction with current cost, which serves as a more common basis.

Under real physical capital maintenance, changes in the prices (current costs) of assets and liabilities held over the period are considered not to affect the amount of operating capability embodied in those items; therefore, the total amounts of those changes are treated as capital maintenance adjustments and are excluded from profit.

NOTES

1. In 2000 the IASC changed its name to the International Accounting Standards Board (IASB).
2. Paton (1922).
3. The recognition of provisions in IAS 22 and IAS 37 were developed using the definition of a liability; the recognition of intangible items in IAS 22 and IAS 38 were developed using the definition of an asset from the Framework.
4. Accounting interrelationships are significant for the elements recognition because recognition in the financial statements of an item that meets the definition and recognition criteria for a particular element, for example, an asset, entails the recognition of another (counterpart) element, such as income or a liability (paragraph 84).
5. The statement of changes in financial position is not mentioned because its elements consist of those that are also elements of financial position or performance.

REFERENCES

FASB and IASB. *Reaffirm Commitment to Memorandum of Understanding.* www.iasb.org.

Framework for the Preparation and Presentation of Financial Statements. www. iasplus.com.

Paton, W. A. 1922. *Accounting theory.* New York: Ronald Press Co.

2 US Perspectives on Implementation of IFRS

Ervin Black, Greg Burton, and Spencer Paul

1. INTRODUCTION

The world's economic environment is becoming increasingly interconnected. The role and relevance of minor financial markets have grown,
highlighting our cross-border interdependence. Multinational corporations
are becoming more commonplace. Investors depend on financial statements, which when built on solid foundations, facilitate flow of capital. As
the flow of foreign sources of capital has increased, the need for globally
accepted accounting principles has strengthened. International Financial
Reporting Standards (IFRS) are uniquely positioned to fill that role.

In the United States, long the dominant financial market of the developed world, Generally Accepted Accounting Principles (US GAAP) are
used for financial reporting. Over the years, US GAAP has become deeply
integrated into and become a reflection of the US economic landscape. As
IFRS continues to push for global acceptance, some within the US are hesitant to join, whereas others seek to embrace IFRS's widely accepted principles-based standards domestically (US). This chapter seeks to expound
upon those responses.

2. HISTORICAL BACKGROUND

For many years, countries developed their own accounting standards. They
were influenced by a nation's culture, economics, and political influences
(McGee and Bandyopadhyay 2009). US GAAP was created by the Financial
Accounting Standards Board (FASB) in 1973 and has since grown to well
over three thousand pages (Myddelton 2004). US GAAP, like its foreign
counterparts, satisfies the requirements of the unique business and legal
environment of the country it serves. An extensive, rules-based standard
fits appropriately with an economic climate like the US, which has been
described as litigious in nature (Kroeker 2009).

IFRS was created by the International Accounting Standards Board
(IASB) in 2001. The IASB is a private organization with no regulatory

mandate and, therefore, no enforcement mechanism (Ojo 2010). On the other hand, they maintain independence as they are only accountable to the public interest.

IFRS uses assumptions and principles just like US GAAP; however, they are much simpler and more open to interpretation. In 2002, IFRS was validated by passage of a referendum of the European Parliament, requiring public firms of EU member states to present financial statements in accordance with IFRS. The standards, in whole or in part, have since been adopted in more than one hundred countries; a number expected to increase to 150 in 2011 (Barry 2010). Much of this growth stems from the maturation of financial systems in emerging markets, which generated a need for high-quality accounting standards.

In the last decade, US GAAP and IFRS have emerged as preeminent global standards; however, most believe that one set of standards will prevail worldwide for the sake of commonality and comparability. Capital markets are no longer the domain of the US, and many believe IFRS is poised to fulfill the role of the lingua franca for financial accounting. The FASB and IASB recognized this early on and created initiatives for incubating convergence between the two standards many years ago.

In November 2008, the Securities and Exchange Commission (SEC or the 'Commission'), the US regulatory agency over capital markets, issued the *Roadmap for the Potential Use of Financial Statements Prepared in Accordance with International Financial Reporting Standards by US Issuers* (hereafter 'Proposed Roadmap'), which laid out a timeline for the potential adoption of IFRS by public companies within the US. A year earlier, the SEC had agreed to accept foreign corporations' financial statements prepared in accordance with IFRS, without reconciliation to US GAAP. Responses from US stakeholders to the SEC's gradual IFRS harmonization have been mixed.

Prior SEC commissioner Christopher Cox made great strides in forwarding IFRS implementation. The recently elected US presidency and subsequent change in SEC administration have slowed down such development although IFRS does remain a priority of current commissioner Mary Schapiro (McGee and Bandyopadhyay 2009).

3. GOVERNMENT

The SEC was created to serve the interests of US investors and markets. Long before debates about the merits of IFRS, the SEC had believed and continues to believe that US investors would benefit from a single set of high-quality, globally-accepted accounting standards. SEC Chairman Mary L. Schapiro said, "For nearly 30 years, the Commission has promoted a single set of high quality standards, which would advance the dual goals of improving financial reporting within the US and reducing country-by-country disparities in financial reporting" (SEC 2010). The Commission seeks to accomplish these goals through convergence of US GAAP with IFRS.

Convergence was primarily championed by former SEC chairman Christopher Cox, who said, "An international language of disclosure and transparency is a goal worth pursuing on behalf of investors who seek comparable financial information to make well-informed investment decisions" (SEC 2008c). Under Mr. Cox's tenure, a series of IFRS conversion milestones were laid out by the SEC and now are commonly known as the Proposed Roadmap. Such milestones relate to improvements in IFRS accounting standards, improvements in the ability to use interactive data for IFRS reporting, etc. (SEC 2008b).

With Mary Schapiro's appointment, interested stakeholders have wondered if the SEC would push forward with IFRS convergence as diligently as it did under Commissioner Cox. Although comments from Ms. Schapiro have indicated that she is in favor of a single set of global accounting standards, she has also indicated that she will initially deal with issues more pressing than IFRS, such as investor protection (Millman 2009).

Chairman Schapiro has said, "When it comes to international accounting standards, it's critical that these standards are converged in a way that does not kick off a race to the bottom. American investors deserve and expect high standards of financial reporting, transparency, and disclosure—along with a standard setter that is free from political interference and that has the resources to be a strong watchdog. At this time, it is not apparent that the IASB meets those criteria, and I am not prepared to delegate standard-setting or oversight responsibility to the IASB" (Schapiro 2009).

The Proposed Roadmap states that if several areas of weakness are resolved, such as improved standards, the commission will decide in 2011 whether to incorporate IFRS into the financial reporting system. If the Commission decides in 2011 to adopt IFRS, US issuers would be required to prepare financial statements under the new standard no earlier than 2015 (SEC 2010). This four-to-five-year lead time originated from comment letters to the SEC in response to the Proposed Roadmap. Originally, issuers would have been required to begin reporting under IFRS in 2014.

The SEC has delegated responsibility for developing and maintaining US GAAP to the FASB, a private, not-for-profit organization. If the SEC mandates usage of IFRS for US issuers, the role of FASB comes into question. The SEC addresses this in the Proposed Roadmap:

> This release does not address the method the Commission would use to mandate IFRS for US issuers. One of the options would be for the Financial Accounting Standards Board ("FASB") to continue to be the designated standard setter for purposes of establishing the financial reporting standards in issuer filings with the Commission. In this option our presumption would be that the FASB would incorporate all

provisions under IFRS, and all future changes to IFRS, directly into generally accepted accounting principles as used in the United States ("US GAAP"). This type of approach has been adopted by a significant number of other jurisdictions when they adopted IFRS as the basis of financial reporting in their capital markets. (SEC 2008b)

The FASB agrees with the SEC in regards to the benefit of a global accounting standard. FASB Chairman Robert Herz has said, "If you were to look back from the year 2020 to the year 2001 you would say 'What chaos!' and 'What inefficient capital markets!' People will look back and say, 'How did people get along back then?' It will be like we now say, 'How did people get along without cell phones?' When you are in the middle of it, it is always difficult. It is important just to keep on towards that end goal" (KPMG 2006).

US President Barack Obama has also signified his administration's support for a single set of global accounting standards. At the G-20 Leaders' Summit on Financial Markets and the World Economy, held in London, UK, in April 2009, President Obama signed the *Declaration on Strengthening the Financial System*. Among other things, the document sought "to call on the accounting standard setters to work urgently with supervisors and regulators to improve standards on valuation and provisioning and achieve a single set of high-quality global accounting standards" (HM Treasury 2009).

Whereas the SEC and FASB are in general agreement on the merits of IFRS adoption, some are critical of the SEC's Proposed Roadmap. Charles Niemeier, formerly an acting chair of the Public Company Accounting Oversight Board (PCAOB), has expressed such criticism. The PCAOB was created by the Sarbanes-Oxley Act of 2002 to oversee the auditors of public companies. It has five board members who are appointed by the SEC for five-year terms.

Whereas the PCAOB has no official view on IFRS adoption, Mr. Niemeier has been a vocal critic. He states that the stringent regulations of US GAAP have bolstered investor confidence, leading to the lowest cost of capital in the world. A supporter of 'convergence,' Niemeier believes the SEC has abandoned US GAAP and moved away from 'convergence' to 'capitulation.' He also, among many other things, says that improved comparability and better investor protection are 'myths' about IFRS. Niemeier presented his views at a 2008 conference sponsored by the New York State Society of CPAs (Leone 2008).

Responding to Mr. Niemeier's remarks, SEC spokesman John Nester said, "The Commission's proposal comes directly in response to the fact that more US investors are investing in more foreign companies in more international markets than ever before, which suggests the need for an international language of disclosure and transparency to protect investors and facilitate their comparisons of corporate financials" (Leone 2008).

As Mr. Niemeier's views are not official pronouncements of the PCAOB, the US government, including the White House, the SEC, and the FASB, appear united in pursuance of IFRS as the global accounting standard.

4. INDUSTRY

US corporations are mixed in their opinions of IFRS. Whereas comment letters to the SEC generally appear negative, it should be noted that many of the comment letters are written by those with a special interest in the proceedings and may not necessarily be a fair representation of prevailing views.

For example, a nonscientific survey performed by 'Big Four' accounting firm Deloitte reported 70 percent of respondents believe the SEC should approve its Proposed Roadmap or a modified version of it (Deloitte 2009). Two surveys conducted by rival firm KPMG report similar findings (KPMG 2009). Grant Thornton, a multinational firm focused on small to midsize businesses, showed fifty-fifty support (Grant Thornton 2009).

Comment letters to the SEC that called the Proposed Roadmap into question primarily cited cost concerns. Two aspects of this argument were prevalent (McGee and Bandyopadhyay 2009). Many corporations, such as ExxonMobil and Citigroup, believe the costs of IFRS adoption are too high, potentially higher than any benefit received from the conversion. Other companies, such as Walmart, think that implementing changes to financial accounting during a depressed economic climate does not seem wise. The US Chamber of Commerce, the world's largest nonprofit lobbying group, subscribes to this second view and believes that businesses would be better off spending their money on rebuilding and getting the economy back into order (SEC 2008a).

Irrespective of whether a company believes in the merits of IFRS, a large proportion of corporations have exhibited a certain level of frustration with the SEC for 'pushing off' the issue until a later date, 2011. In a view echoed by academics and accounting professionals, businesses need the SEC to provide a definitive date for IFRS conversion, if conversion is going to occur. It becomes costly for affected firms to continually be on notice should the SEC suddenly initiate a mandate for adopting IFRS, although the SEC assures US issuers that a generous four-to-five-year phased-in approach will be utilized should a decision to adopt be made. US issuers are justifiably concerned considering conversion costs for issuers in the European Union (EU) were much higher when an issuer got a late start. Concerns have been voiced that the SEC's planning uncertainty may lead to timing problems for US firms (SEC 2008a).

Some comment letters also opined that the US has a very unique business history that the IFRS standards do not match. Implementing IFRS in the US might be more challenging than in other countries due to country-specific environments. Other letters noted concerns about specific IFRS policies. For instance, Hot Topic, a niche clothing and accessory retail operation, wrote about their distaste for the retail method of accounting under IFRS (SEC 2008a). Specific concerns were also raised about provisions of IAS 41—agriculture, guidance for regulated industries, and the need for completion of the joint IASB/FASB project on accounting for insurance contracts (American Institute of Certified Public Accountants [AICPA] 2009).

It has also been observed that the prohibition of the last-in first-out inventory accounting method (LIFO) under IFRS may create an immediate tax burden for some businesses (SEC 2008a). The Internal Revenue Service (IRS), the US tax-collecting governmental entity, requires inventory be accounted for under the same method for tax and financial accounting purposes. Thus a tax expense may be created from the acceleration of income when corporations are forced to switch to the first-in first-out inventory accounting method (FIFO) for tax purposes due to a change required for financial accounting purposes (AICPA 2009).

On the other hand, some businesses observed positive consequences for domestic (US) adoption of IFRS, most markedly for multinational firms. In a similar vein to benefits noted by the SEC, businesses would have decreased costs over the long term for preparing and interpreting financial statements. This is due to the dissolution of compliance with unique national standards and the modest streamlining of consolidation procedures. Adoption of IFRS may also lower the cost of capital, support reception of foreign investment, facilitate cross-border acquisitions, assist in integrating global IT systems, and aid in better understanding the financial statements of overseas partners (PricewaterhouseCoopers [PwC] 2010). Whereas adoption of a global standard will give rise to a variety of benefits for multinational corporations, companies with primarily domestic (US) operations will not recognize such benefits to the same degree (AICPA 2009).

Of those that supported the SEC's Proposed Roadmap, businesses were divided into two groups of opinion (McGee and Bandyopadhyay 2009). One group preferred continuing convergence between US GAAP and IFRS as opposed to a certain time for adoption. If converged standards were published one by one over time, it would allow US issuers to transition to IFRS in a natural progression. The other group believed that outright adoption is superior because IFRS could slowly lose its character if US GAAP pulled too hard on the convergence process. However, both groups believed in IFRS as the future global standard, merely differing in the process to get there (SEC 2008a).

In an interview, Grant Thornton CEO Edward E. Nusbaum explained how an IFRS mandate on large public corporations could create market pressures on small and/or private corporations to take up IFRS as well (Reilly 2009). If a small and/or private company decided to stick with US GAAP, citing concerns with conversion costs, it could create a wedge in their access to capital markets. Investment bankers could even seek conformance to IFRS before granting them access to equity or loan capital (Sunder 2009).

Overall, whereas many businesses have a variety of concerns, a majority believe the ultimate goal should be a single set of globally accepted accounting standards (Gannon 2010).

5. PROFESSIONALS

The accounting firms state their continuing belief that the US will transition to IFRS in the near future and that great benefits will be realized upon completion. In agreement with other stakeholder groups, accounting professionals believe in the importance of achieving a globally-accepted accounting language. The Big Four accounting firms also hold that the existing body of IFRS has proven to be high quality; a worthy standard for US capital markets (SEC 2008a).

Accounting firms, it should be noted, stand to inherit large sums of revenue should the SEC mandate adoption of IFRS, thus their responses are possibly motivated by self-interest and probably expansive due to their vast resources and ability to organize (Sunder 2009). Although not directly mentioned by the accounting firms, a global accounting standard such as IFRS would permit easier movement of auditors and accountants across borders as well as facilitate standardized global education and training for the firms (Austin and Tschakert 2009).

PwC, a global accounting firm, writes in their comment letter that the interconnected nature of capital markets around the world, as shown by the recent financial crisis, plainly demonstrates the need for a global standard. Deloitte, another Big Four firm, has gone even further and states that fundamental changes should be made now because of the depressed economic state, not in spite of it (SEC 2008a).

The firms believe that convergence should be partially accomplished by a mandatory change to IFRS (SEC 2008a). In other words, whereas step-by-step agreements between US GAAP and IFRS help businesses transition, mandatory adoption must be required at some point. PwC explains that a long-term, convergence-only process risks derailing the goal of achieving global standards. If the process is too drawn out, IFRS stakeholders outside the US are likely to become less willing to cooperate and may disengage from the convergence process if the US does not demonstrate clear commitment to IFRS (PwC 2009).

In a comment letter to the SEC, Deloitte agreed with US issuers in observing that the significant uncertainty of the SEC's decision about IFRS has been and will continue to be problematic for preparers, users, auditors, and academia because they will be hesitant to commit resources to transition to IFRS before the commission makes a final decision (SEC 2008a).

In the SEC's Proposed Roadmap, the SEC states that for IFRS adoption to be mandated, the accountability and funding of the International Accounting Standards Committee (IASC) Foundation (the 'Foundation'), the overseer of the IASB, must be reviewed. The Foundation is a stand-alone, not-for-profit organization incorporated in Delaware. The accounting firms agree with the SEC's stance. Standard setters have traditionally been accountable to a securities regulator, and the Commission, along with the firms, believes the IASC should be accountable to what has been termed a 'Monitoring Group,' a consortium of national securities authorities. The Monitoring Group would approve IASC Foundation trustees and review funding arrangements (SEC 2008b).

The US audit market for large public companies is very concentrated. The Government Accountability Office (GAO), an investigative arm of US Congress, surveyed large public companies in 2008 and found that 82 percent see their auditor choice as limited to the Big Four because small and midsize audit firms lack the capacity (e.g., international outreach), if not also the technical know-how and reputation, to adequately service their needs. Additionally, 60 percent of those companies view competition in the audit sector as inadequate (Bloom and Schirm 2008). IFRS adoption has the potential to exacerbate this lack of competitive forces. If IFRS were mandated, the Big Four may link their international aura to IFRS and imply custody of greater expertise than their smaller competitors, resulting in a further increase in market concentration for audit services (Sunder 2009). KPMG's Global Head of Audit, Michael Hughes, said, "IFRS brings more discipline and more rigor. Companies say that if IFRS continue to base themselves on economic realities then they look at their own businesses differently and it helps them manage themselves better. Companies need to feel the figures are equally relevant for decision-making" (KPMG 2006).

The multinational accounting firms collectively support the SEC's Proposed Roadmap. IFRS, from their experience, is robust and high quality, capable of bringing comparability and consistency to the US capital market. Smaller firms, such as Mayer Hoffman McCann PC, although supportive of convergence and global accounting standards, expressed concerns over further concentration of the audit market. They also noted the possibility that if US issuers used IFRS, the international audit firms would outsource certain accounting and auditing functions to emerging markets; negatively affecting future accounting graduates as well as smaller firms, who may not have such outsourcing arrangements available to them (SEC 2008a).

6. ACADEMIA

In the world of academia, we will look at two perspectives. First, the opinion of academics regarding the validity and appropriateness of the Proposed Roadmap. Second, the potential effects of IFRS adoption on accounting education.

6.1 Opinion

In general, academics' opinion of the SEC's Proposed Roadmap is favorable. In a nonscientific survey, professors from Salem State College found that 59 percent of accounting department chairs/deans believed that US GAAP/IFRS convergence would provide easier access to world markets for global companies. Seventy percent believe there should be a single set of globally-accepted accounting principles, but many had significant doubt about the likelihood of arriving at one set of standards. Those who doubted expect that certain adjustments would be negotiated by different nations due to cultural and economic differences even if one standard were to be adopted in principle (McGee and Bandyopadhyay 2009).

Continuing with the aforementioned survey, 65 percent of chairs/deans believed that accounting graduates should be as familiar with IFRS as they are with US GAAP; however, an equal distribution was noted among those who disagreed, were neutral, or agreed that students' job opportunities would increase from any specialty acquired in IFRS. This demonstrates that accounting faculty are still unsure of any benefit from teaching US GAAP/IFRS convergence to students (McGee and Bandyopadhyay 2009).

IFRS has received a fair amount of criticism in comments from a small number of academics. For example, some accounting professors cite a lack of evidence in response to many of the SEC's claims regarding the global standard. Even McDonald's, the worldwide fast-food restaurateur, wrote that there exists no evidence to support the claim that IFRS will enable better reporting than US GAAP (SEC 2008a).

Shyam Sunder, professor of accounting at Yale University and former president of the American Accounting Association (AAA), has been most critical of IFRS implementation. Among his many criticisms, he holds that there is no evidence that one global standard is better than two competing standards (Jamal and Sunder 2007), suggesting that the global monopoly would stifle innovation as well as fail to bring greater comparability due to wide-ranging differences in market structures. He also questions the SEC's description of IFRS as 'high quality,' explaining that such a term is difficult to quantify and lacks meaning. He challenges the SEC to identify an accounting standard that would not be considered 'high quality' (Joyce, Libby, and Sunder 1982).

Some were also concerned that a principles-based standard would yield a wider variety of results. As a result, the situation would force IFRS to become more rules-based over time (AICPA 2009). Shyam Sunder commented on this, pointing out that the IFRS rule book is thinner than US GAAP merely because they have not been in business as long. He continues by saying that two bodies (the FASB and IASB) with similar structures and financing will write standards with similar characteristics and detail (Sunder 2009).

Academics also note that the US will need to change in several areas (legal, regulation, corporate governance) prior to IFRS adoption. Financial accounting standards have wider-ranging effects than simply a change in the preparation and presentation of financial statements for publicly traded companies (SEC 2008a).

6.2 Curriculum

Many questions arise when considering the impact of IFRS on accounting education in the US. One notable question stems from the observation that following an SEC mandate on IFRS usage by US issuers, US GAAP would continue to be used by private companies. Would students need to learn both IFRS and US GAAP? Some in the academic community have raised this issue of information overload for accounting students (AICPA 2009).

Professor Paul F. McGee (McGee and Bandyopadhyay 2009) has ascertained several challenges for integrating IFRS into curriculum: faculty shortage, outside pressures in covering other relevant topics such as ethical cases and forensic accounting, and inadequate support from educational institutions and textbook publishers. In surveys Professor McGee performed, he concludes that academics have high expectations from textbook publishers that they'll meet their training and course coverage needs should adoption of IFRS occur (McGee and Bandyopadhyay 2009).

In response to the perceived problem of information overload for students, some have suggested following the path of law schools. Teach general principles and high-level, nonroutine skills that are largely independent of the specifics of the standards, thus graduates would develop the ability to read, apply, and use any given set of standards they come across (Sunder 2009).

7. CONCLUSION

There certainly is support for the Proposed Roadmap from the US government. The White House, the SEC, and the FASB have all publicly declared their support. Others who are particularly supportive include the largest US accounting firms and large multinational corporations (AICPA 2009).

Although in the minority, some US registrants supported the Proposed Roadmap and mandatory adoption in the near term. Other US issuers and some smaller CPA firms opposed IFRS all together, citing a myriad of concerns. Academics were generally positive although a few who are critical of IFRS presented very thorough comment letters stating their opposition due to lack of research supporting SEC conclusions.

It seems the only thing all stakeholders agree on is that they are keenly interested to observe the SEC's next steps and where US GAAP/IFRS convergence leads.

REFERENCES

American Institute of Certified Public Accountants. 2009. *Where will the SEC take the IFRS roadmap? An AICPA analysis of comment letters on the SEC's proposal.* http://www.ifrs.com/updates/aicpa/IFRS_SEC.html (accessed March 31, 2010).

Austin, S. G., and N. Tschakert. 2009. *Major differences in US GAAP & IFRS and latest developments.* http://www.swensonadvisors.com/assets/MajorDifferencesBetweenUSGAAPandIFRS.pdf (accessed March 31, 2010).

Barry, J. 2010. *Current situation and next steps.* http://www.PwC.com/us/en/issues/ifrs-reporting/transition-to-ifrs-status.jhtml (accessed March 31, 2010).

Bloom, R., and D. Schirm. 2008. *An analysis of the GAO study on audit market concentration.* http://www.nysscpa.org/cpajournal/2008/408/perspectives/p6.htm (accessed March 31, 2010).

Deloitte. 2009. IFRS *Survey results 2009: Current issues.* September. http://www.deloitte.com/assets/Dcom-UnitedStates/Local%2520Assets/Documents/AERS/us_aers_IFRS%2520SurveyCurrent%2520Issues_1009.pdf (accessed March 31, 2010).

Gannon, D. J. 2010. *The IFRS convergence quandary.* http://businessfinancemag.com/article/convergence-quandary-0512 (accessed March 31, 2010).

Grant Thornton. 2009. *CFOs split over IFRS use.* http://www.grantthornton.com/portal/site/gtcom/menuitem.550794734a67d883a5f2ba40633841ca/?vgnextoid=327bad8dba3f0210VgnVCM1000003a8314acRCRD&vgnextchannel=d321d90df58cf110VgnVCM1000003a8314acRCRD (accessed March 31, 2010).

HM Treasury. 2009. *Declaration on strengthening the financial system—London, April 2, 2009.* http://www.g20.org/Documents/Fin_Deps_Fin_Reg_Annex_020409_-_1615_final.pdf (accessed March 31, 2010).

Jamal, K., and S. Sunder. 2007. *Monopoly or competition: Standard setting in the private and public sector.* http://ssrn.com/abstract=1075705 (accessed March 31, 2010).

Joyce, E. J., R. Libby, and S. Sunder. 1982. FASB's qualitative characteristics of accounting information: A study of definitions and validity. *Journal of Accounting Research* 20 (2): 654–75.

Kroeker, J. 2009. *What's beeded for IFRS: A perspective from SEC chief accountant James Kroeker.* October. http://www.journalofaccountancy.com/Multimedia/Kroeker.htm (accessed March 31, 2010).

KPMG. 2006. *International Financial Reporting Standards: Views on a financial reporting revolution.* http://us.kpmg.com/microsite/FSLibraryDotCom/docs/IFRS_financial_reporting_revolution.pdf (accessed March 31, 2010).

———. 2009. *KPMG's executive report of findings on the Proposed IFRS Roadmap.* March. http://www.kpmginstitutes.com/ifrs-institute/insights/2009/pdf/kpmgs-executive-report-of-findings-on-the-proposed-ifrs-roa.pdf (accessed March 31, 2010).

Leone, M. 2008. *Regulator rips into global accounting plan.* http://www.cfo.com/article.cfm/12202211 (accessed March 31, 2010).

McGee, P. F., and J. Bandyopadhyay. 2009. A contribution to practice: Exploring the curriculum impact of IFRS—US GAAP convergence. *Competition Forum* 7 (2) 496–504.

Millman, G. 2009. Execs hail Mary Schapiro for folding IFRS Roadmap. *IFRS Reporter* (January) http://ifrsreporter.com/index.php?option=com_content&view=article&id=52:execs-hail-mary-schapiro-for-folding-ifrs-roadmap&catid=36:sec&itemid=53 (accessed January 7, 2011).

Myddelton, D. R. 2004. *Unshackling accountants.* London: The Institute of Economic Affairs. http://www.iea.org.uk/files/upld-book241pdf?.pdf (accessed March 31, 2010).

Ojo, M. 2010. The role of the IASB and auditing standards in the aftermath of the 2008/2009 financial crisis. MPRA Paper 20330, University Library of Munich, Germany. http://ideas.repec.org/p/pra/mprapa/20330.html (accessed March 31, 2010).

PricewaterhouseCoopers. 2009. *IFRS Perspectives: An executive survey.* http://www.PwC.com/en_US/us/issues/ifrs-reporting/assets/ifrs-perspective-executive-survey.pdf (accessed March 31, 2010).

———. 2010. *Benefits of changing to IFRS.* http://www.PwC.com/gr/en/ifrs-services/ifrs-benefits.jhtml (accessed March 31, 2010).

Reilly, D. 2009. Interview: Grant Thornton CEO Edward E. Nusbaum. *CPA Journal* (July): 79, 7, 34.

Schapiro, M. 2009. *Questions from Senator Carl Levin for Mary Schapiro, nominee to be chair of the Securities and Exchange Commission.* http://levin.senate.gov/newsroom/supporting/2009/PSI.SchapiroResponses.012209.pdf (accessed March 31, 2010).

Securities and Exchange Commission. 2008a. *Comments on roadmap for the potential use of financial statements prepared in accordance with International Financial Reporting Standards by US issuers.* October. http://www.sec.gov/comments/s7-27-08/s72708.shtml (accessed March 31, 2010).

———. 2008b. Proposed SEC rule: Roadmap for the potential use of financial statements prepared in accordance with International Financial Reporting Standards by US issuers. November, SEC Release No. 33-8982; SEC File No. s7-27-08. http://www.sec.gov/rules/proposed/2008/33-8982.pdf (accessed March 31, 2010).

———. 2008c. SEC proposes roadmap toward Global Accounting Standards to help investors compare financial information more easily. Securities and Exchange Commission Press Release, August. http://www.sec.gov/news/press/2008/2008-184.htm (accessed March 31, 2010).

———. 2010. SEC approves statement on Global Accounting Standards. Securities and Exchange Commission Press Release, February. http://www.sec.gov/news/press/2010/2010-27.htm (accessed March 31, 2010).

Sunder, S. 2009. IFRS and the accounting consensus. *Accounting Horizons* 23 (1): 101-11.

Part II

Recent Developments in Accounting, Corporate Governance, and Auditing in Europe

3 New Corporate Governance Rules and Practices

Victoria Krivogorsky and Wolfgang Dick

1. INTRODUCTION

Corporate governance (CG), laws, and regulations are important constituents of an institutional framework for thriving market economies. Although CG is defined differently in the variety of national economies, in general it involves (a) the mechanisms by which business is organized, directed, and controlled in a limited liability corporate form, and (b) the mechanisms by which corporate managers are held accountable for corporate conduct and performance. Over the past two decades, an interest in the role of CG has intensified in the academic community and among practitioners all over the world due to the competitive pressure of globalization as manifested in the creation of common economic zones, European Union (EU) in particular. In an attempt to develop a single capital market, the EU adopted common currency and freed the flow of capital, goods, services, and people across EU borders. The EU creation was accompanied by the growth and diffusion of shareholdings and increased merger activity among the largest corporations and stock exchanges, which made countries—members of the EU (EUM)—a perfect candidate for mandatory adoption of the International Financial Reporting Standards (IFRS) in 2005. In this respect, an analysis of the commonalities and differences among national CG laws and practices will be instrumental in eliminating any related barriers to the development of a single capital market by streamlining all CG regulations and practices within the EU economic zone.

Recent developments in the area of harmonization show that IFRS is becoming a common financial reporting system around the world. In this respect, leading questions in CG include (a) whether CG codes (CGC) follow the financial reporting on the road of convergence, and (b) whether any particular given CGC (or its component) enjoys relative competitive advantage worthy to be adopted by others. If only the most robust practices can survive globalization, theoretically it is plausible to predict that given a long window, national CGC will loosen their systematic differences without political and/or administrative intervention and converge to similar optimum practices due to concerns about local firms' performance in international markets. There is no consensus on this issue so far while, Goergen, Martynova, and Renneboog (2005) seem to confirm the convergence of CG practices in about thirty European countries, other authors (Khanna and Palepu 2004) find no evidence of similarity in CG practices among countries despite the latest trends in convergence of CG laws.

Overall, an extensive body of research addresses differences and similarities in CG issues, identifying and evaluating national variations in CG regulations and practices (LaPorta, Lopes-de-Salines, and Shleifer 1999; LaPorta et al. 1998, 2000; Bushman and Smith 2001; Gugler, Mueller, and Yurtoglu 2003; Leuz, Nanch, and Woysocki 2003; Gilson 2005; Aoki and Jackson 2007; Krivogorsky, Grudnitski, and Dick 2011). Unfortunately, even as this stream of literature has become broader and more reliable, answers to the upshot questions regarding competitive advantage and the likelihood of evolutionary convergence have also become more elusive. Working hypotheses have been changing rapidly, more in response to external events than to developments in the discourse. Unsurprisingly, in this respect the comparative governance literature offers alternative theoretical frameworks that support conflicting hypotheses. The theoretical approach that commands widest acceptance scrutinizes present national CG regimes and posits suboptimal performance caused by the operation of political forces over time. It thereby dismisses the possibility of evolutionary efficiency in its account of the *status quo* (Roe 1994, 1996). That said, it does not dismiss mandatory convergence (which obviously requires well-developed enforcement mechanisms) and presents a brighter future of constructive cross-reference between the two dominating types of market systems: (a) "market-centered" systems found mainly in English-speaking countries and characterized by widely dispersed shareholding and thick liquid trading markets; and (b) "blockholder" or "relational investor" systems, found in varied form in most capitalist economies and characterized by control by insider coalitions or wealthy families, lack of liquidity, and thin trading of noncontrolling stakes.

Meanwhile, the differences continue to exist and this comparative study offers the analysis of the CG regulations and practices among EUM from both systems through an examination of CGC,[1] and, to a limited extent, relevant elements of the underlying legal framework. The choice to analyze codes is due to their distinct nature. Comprised of the methodology and criteria of CG ratings, the practices and recommendations, CGC themselves are neither legally nor contractually binding; as opposed to the laws and standards that serve as the base for best practices described in the codes, which are legal and contractual documents.

Here it is perhaps important to note that many EUM have more than one operational CGC, which makes CGC complicated and sometimes inconsistent. For example, the UK had eleven codes, in addition to two international and two pan-European codes relevant to all EUM companies, which affects UK companies as well. The CGC are issued by a broad array of groups such as governmental or quasi-governmental entities; committees (or commissions) organized by stock exchanges; business, industry, academic, and directors' associations; and investor-related groups. As one might therefore expect, compliance mechanisms and the "official" status of the codes vary widely. Some codes advocate listing requirements and mandate disclosure by listed companies together with an explanation of any areas of noncompliance garnered through connection to stock exchanges. "Comply-or-explain" requirements exert some coercive pressure in creating incentives to comply.[2] Note that even though the CGC are voluntary in nature given the investment community's significant economic power, these codes have considerable influence on CG practices and, thus, need to be simplified in order to streamline CG practices and increase efficiency in the process as a whole.

2. CONSOLIDATING/MERGING CGC

Analysis of CGC suggests that only two countries, Belgium and the UK, show efforts to consolidate CGC. In Belgium, the codes issued by the Belgian Banking and Finance Commission and the codes issued by the Brussels Stock Exchange (Cardon Report) were consolidated in December 1998 into a single document entitled *Corporate Governance for Belgian Listed Companies* (referred to in the following as the "Dual Code").

In the UK, the Combined Code, which was issued in July 1998, has integrated some of the recommendations from the Cadbury Report with those of the Greenbury and Hampel Commissions. The Combined Code is now linked to the London Stock Exchange listing rules for disclosure purposes. In addition, national CGC have been updated from time to time, with the latest editions replacing the old ones. Updated codes include the Hellebuyck Commission Recommendations (issued in June 1998 and updated in October 2001), the PIRC UK Shareholder Voting Guidelines (issued in April 1994 and periodically updated, most recently in 2010), the Hermes Statement (issued in March 1997, updated 2001 and 2002), the Combined Code (updated 2006 and 2008), and the German Corporate Governance Code (updated 2003, 2005, 2006, 2007, 2008, and 2009).[3]

3. COMPARATIVE ANALYSIS

3.1 The Role of Culture, Property Rights Relations, and Law

EUM exhibit a rich diversity in CG practices, structures, and participants, reflecting differences in culture, traditional financing options, corporate ownership concentration patterns, and legal origins. This rich diversity complicates CG comparisons among nations. The latest changes in CGC and practices reveal that with increased reliance on equity financing and broader shareholdings, a new role of CG in modern European corporations is emerging. First, growing academic literature focuses on the qualitatively distinct environmental impact on CGC (LaPorta et al. 1998, 2000; LaPorta, Lopes-de-Salines, and Shleifer 1999; Boot and Macey, 1998), which manifests itself in inconsistencies among EUM in emphasizing different CG characteristics. For instance, on one side of the continuum, Germany emphasizes cooperative relationships and consensus (codetermination, works councils) and, on the other side, the UK emphasizes competition and market processes in their CGC. Second, the importance of equity markets for corporate finance is also vary significantly throughout EUM, although equity financing appears to be gaining in importance throughout Europe. Traditionally, bank lending in most continental European countries has been a far more important source of financing than the stock markets (Krivogorsky, Grudnitski, and Dick 2011). With less reliance on equity financing, shareholdings have been concentrated and stable over time (Krivogorsky, Grudnitski, and Burton 2009). Concentrated shareholdings,[4] low liquidity, and relatively weak secondary markets (a) initiated a distinct market culture with long-term strategy, reliance on direct debt, strong relationships with banks, network oriented, and heavily influenced by the controlling shareholder (Krivogorsky, Grudnitski, and Burton 2009), and (b) created a predisposition for different CG laws and practices. In particular, when ownership rights are not dispersed, control rights are not fully separated from ownership, and the majority of capital comes from banks and/or internal equity and personal wealth, the concerns shift to ensuring the fair treatment of minority shareholders (Appendix 3.1, Panel 3); as opposed to economic systems with widely dispersed ownership where the "collective action" problem becomes central. In this respect, in "market-centered" economies, boards are seen as guards against "agency" and "moral hazard" problems, and thus, CGC in those countries tend to emphasize disclosure and distinct boards practices, trying to ensure that boards are independent entities, capable of expressing and implementing their viewpoints with no influence from management (Appendix 3.1, Panels 2, 4).

3.2 Is CGC Cross-Penetration Advantageous?

The question whether any particular given CGC (or its component) enjoys relative competitive advantage worthy to be adopted by others has been on a radar of academics and practitioners for a long period of time (Udayasankar and Das 2007; Chahine and Filatotchev 2008). We think that the answer to this question is contingent on the identifying and measuring the outcome of this advantage. Because CG is seen as an integral part of the companies economic success, we tend to support the common belief that each company's economic performance is heavily affected by corporate governance regulations and practices. There is no consensus, however, on the direction of corporate governance mechanisms' impact on companies' performance in a variety of national economies; that is, the same CG mechanisms can serve as a catalyst or impediment of economic success in different national settings. While advancing, the CG practices are becoming an organic part of each particular business environment, as they become interconnected with a company's operation strategies and management practices on a micro level, and with property rights relations, markets strategies, and culture on a macro level. For instance, the CG institutions in Anglo-Saxon countries have been developed under the strong pressure of an agency conflict and therefore they stress the mechanisms necessary to address this problem by developing more advanced shareholder protection and disclosure practices, and they show higher micro-performance properties. Whether it suggests that Continental European countries, after possessing Anglo-Saxon institutions, will show better micro-economic performance remains to be determined.

3.3 Selected Points of Divergence

3.3.1 Definition of Corporate Governance

The definition of the term "corporate governance" varies from country to country (Appendix 3.1,[5] Panel 1). We believe that CG definitions reflect cultural differences as well as variations in the relationships between countries' legal origins and their business environments.

For example, the German definition emphasizes "legal and factual regulatory framework for managing and supervising a company"; the Italian definition shows more concern about "norms, traditions and patterns of behavior developed by each economic and legal system"; and the Dutch definition emphasizes the importance of "sound management and proper supervision . . . [and] division of duties and responsibilities and powers effecting the satisfactory balance of influence of all the stakeholders."

The term "corporate governance" is susceptible to both broad and narrow definitions—and many of the codes do not even attempt to articulate what is included in those definitions. Overall, the majority of the definitions articulate CG relevance to a company "control," corporate management, or company/managerial conduct. Perhaps the simplest and most common definition was initially provided by the Cadbury Report (UK), and later included in the combined code, which is frequently quoted or paraphrased as: "Corporate governance is the system by which businesses are directed and controlled." Another common theme in CG definitions concerns the "supervision" of a company or management. Numerous definitions, mostly from countries of German legal origin,

Table 3.1   Corporate Governance Definitions

EU Member States
"Corporate governance is the system by which companies are directed and controlled." Cadbury Report, ¶ 2.5 (UK)
"'Corporate governance' refers to the set of rules applicable to the direction and control of a company." Cardon Report, ¶ 2 (Belgium)
"[Corporate governance is] the organization of the administration and management of companies." Recommendations of the Federation of Belgian Companies, Foreword
"[Corporate governance is] [t]he goals, according to which a company is managed, and the major principles and frameworks which regulate the interaction between the company's managerial bodies, the owners, as well as other parties who are directly influenced by the company's dispositions and business (in this context jointly referred to as the company's stakeholders). Stakeholders including employees, creditors, suppliers, customers and the local community." Nørby Report, Introduction (Denmark)
"Corporate governance describes the legal and factual regulatory framework for managing and supervising a company." Berlin Initiative Code, Preamble (Germany)
"Corporate Governance, in the sense of the set of rules according to which firms are managed and controlled, is the result of norms, traditions and patterns of behaviour developed by each economic and legal system." Preda Code, § 2 (Italy)
"[T]he concept of Corporate Governance has been understood to mean a code of conduct for those associated with the company . . . consisting of a set of rules for sound management and proper supervision and for a division of duties and responsibilities and powers effecting the satisfactory balance of influence of all the stakeholders." Peters Report, § 1.2 (Netherlands)
"Corporate Governance is used to describe the system of rules and procedures employed in the conduct and control of listed companies." Comissão do Mercado de Valores Mobiliáros, Introduction (Portugal)
Pan-European & International
"[C]orporate governance . . . involves a set of relationships between a company's management, its board, its shareholders and other stakeholders. Corporate governance also provides the structure through which the objectives of the company are set, and the means of attaining those objectives and monitoring performance are determined." OECD, Preamble
"Corporate governance comprehends that structure of relationships and corresponding responsibilities among a core group consisting of shareholders, [supervisory] board members and managers designed to best foster the competitive performance required to achieve the corporation's primary objective." Millstein Report, p. 13

relate CG to legal rules and procedures and private sector conduct. Finally, the common thread in the definitions of the international and pan-European codes encompasses relationships between shareholders, (supervisory) boards, and managers.

3.3.2 Board Structure

Major CG differences among EUM embedded in law relate to board structure, which can be (a) unitary or two-tier, (b) with separate supervisory or management leadership required or not, and (c) with distinct employees role in supervisory body (Appendix 3.1, Panels 2, 4, and 5).

In Austria, Germany, the Netherlands, and arguably Denmark, the two-tier structure is predominant for certain types and sizes of the corporations, with a supervisory board and a distinct executive board of management.[6] Other distinctive board characteristics include a separate board of directors and a general manager or managing director (Sweden) and a unitary board of directors with a separate board of auditors.

The central feature of a two-tiered board lies in the organizational and personal division of management and control by a two-tier structure (mandatory for all public corporations in Germany). The management board responsibilities in Germany are defined by corporate law, and they are comprised of actions related to running the business; the role of supervisory boards is not delineated.[7] Most of the codes reiterate directly or contemplate the legal proposition that the supervisory body assumes responsibility for monitoring the performance of the corporation, whereas the management body has authority over the day-to-day operations of the businesses. In particular, the supervisory board is viewed as the management board's

Table 3.2   Predominant Board and Leadership Structure

State	Board Structure	Employee Role in Supervisory Body	Separate Supervisory and Management Leadership
Austria	Two-tier	Yes	Yes
Belgium	Unitary*	No	Not Required
Denmark	Two-tier	Yes	Yes
France	Unitary*	Company-specific articles may provide the details	Not Required
Germany	Two-tier	Yes	Yes
Italy	Unitary**	No	Not Required
Netherlands	Two-tier	Company-specific articles may provide the details	Yes
Portugal	Unitary* **	No	Not Required
Spain	Unitary	No	Not Required
Sweden	Unitary	Yes	Yes
United Kingdom	Unitary	No	Not Required

* Other structure also available. ** Board of auditors also required.

overseer, with other roles boiled down to networking, ensuring compliance with law and business strategies, and managing the external auditor. The supervisory board controls and elects the management by supervision and removes management board members. It cannot directly become involved in managing the company, but if articles so provide or the supervisory board so decides, specific types of transactions may become subject to its approval. Thus, the supervisory board has the ultimate ability to affect company policies by affecting managers' decisions. This capability is not challenged because CG rules are lenient in regard to independence rules[8] and required disclosures. For instance, there is nothing in German codes that addresses the conflict of interest. A portion of the supervisory board comprised of employees is not necessarily versed in accounting or corporate management, and thus is less adept at noticing or addressing glaring accounting or auditing issues stemming from a management board's misconduct. To further complicate the CG landscape, the role of banks is very robust. Banks' representatives often sit on supervisory councils and/or the management board, interlocking directorates, providing capital, and overall creating a very strong long-term relationship.Notwithstanding formal structural differences between two-tier and unitary board systems, the similarities in actual board practices exist (Appendix 3.1, Panel 4). Generally, both the unitary board of directors and the supervisory board (in the two-tier structure) are elected by shareholders. Both boards have a supervisory function and a managerial function, although this distinction is more formalized in the two-tier structure. The two-tier boards are larger in size, which, according to common belief, correlates with less efficiency (Appendix 3.1, Panel 5). The unitary board and the supervisory board similarly appoint the members of the managerial body (the management board in the two-tier system, or a group of managers to whom the unitary board delegates authority). In addition, both bodies usually have the responsibility to ensure that financial reporting and control systems are functioning appropriately and for ensuring that the corporation is in compliance with the law (Appendix 3.1, Panels 8, 9).

It is believed that each system has its unique benefits. The one-tier system may result in closer relations and better information flow between the supervisory and managerial bodies; the two-tier system encompasses a clearer, formal separation between the supervisory body and those being "supervised," making independent supervisory board decisions possible (Appendix 3.1, Panel 9). Lately, however, the distinct perceived benefits traditionally attributed to each system appear to be lessening as newly developed practices converge and the codes express some consensus on issues relating to board structure, function, roles, and responsibilities.[9] The codes differ in the level of specificity with which they describe the distinct roles of the supervisory and managerial bodies, and some of the specific ways in which the duties are allocated. This most likely reflects variations in the degree to which company law or listing standards already specify supervisory and managerial body responsibilities, rather than any significant substantive differences. For example, the Dual Code (Belgium) provides that: "The board of directors is responsible for all strategic decisions, for ensuring that the necessary resources are available to achieve the objectives, for appointing and supervising the executive management and, lastly, for reporting to the shareholders on the performance of its duties" (§ I.A.2). Other governance guidelines and codes are far less specific (Appendix 3.1, Panel 4).

Also, there are distinctions in how codes place emphasis on the roles of management and supervisory boards, which may be due in part to the more formal division in two-tier board structures between the supervisory and the managerial bodies.[10]

3.3.3 The Role of Labor (Codetermination)

Labor has always played an important role in European CGC. The role of employees' participation in CGC varies across countries with the highest level recorded in Germany and lowest in the UK; all other Western European countries are situated in between. Germany retains the unique legal structure of its codetermined two-tiered board, where the *Vorstand* management board has sole responsibility for the management of the company, and the *Aufsichtsrat*, or supervisory board, oversees and elects the management board.[11]

To address the advantageous and disadvantageous properties of labor codetermination, some scholars analyze board codetermination effects on company's reported outcomes with mixed results. Dinh (1999) provides an analysis of the contrary nature between the German and US CGC with a focus on board codetermination, in which he asserts that board codetermination leads to a greater degree of domestic production and job retention than is seen in the US. On the other hand, a study by FitzRoy and Kraft (1993) found that although labor costs did not increase as a result of the 1976 Codetermination Act, a loss of productivity in firms led to reduced profits. Additionally, Gorton and Schmid (2002) found that German firms that carry one-half employee representation in supervisory boards have a market to book ratio lower as compared to firms with one-third representation.

Later studies suggest that whereas having employees on boards has measurable negative impact on productivity, it may be a consequence of the inefficiencies resulting from larger board size. Such inefficiency is cited as one of the reasons for Allianz's move from a German corporation to a Societas Europaea (SE), as the latter allows only twelve supervisory board members compared to the previous twenty (Allianz 2006; Wiesmann 2006).

Works councils as another form of law-mandated codetermination imposed on most German firms were reviewed by the European Foundation for the Improvement of Living and Working Conditions (EuroFound 2005). Additional surveys of the repercussions of the 2001 reform of the

1972 Works Constitution Act were conducted by FitzRoy and Kraft (2004), Addison, Bellmann, and Kölling (2004), and by Hübler and Jirjahn (2003) and have yielded mixed outcomes. For example, studies by Addison, Schnabel, and Wagner (1997) and FitzRoy and Kraft (2004) indicate a negative relationship between productivity and works councils. Contrary to these results, Addison et al. (2004), using interview data from the German Federal Labour Service, demonstrate a positive relationship between works council presence and plant closings. The results of the Hübler and Jirjahn (2003) study provide evidence indicating positive effects of works councils on productivity when collective bargaining agreements are in place and negative effects otherwise. In a similar regard, the utility of works councils is perceived as being more beneficial to employees than to unions as studied by Hobson and Dworkin (1986). They believe that this perception is due to the power structure of works councils and unions in the firm: unions have strong national power but do not have the right to represent a firm or an employee, whereas works councils do (Weiss 2006).

Therefore, CG mechanisms such as labor representation and works councils yield measurable effects on companies' reported outcomes, and therefore as such should be scrutinized along with financial reports in order to obtain a complete picture of the economic consequences of variations in companies' CG practices.

3.4 Selected Points of Convergence

3.4.1 Disclosure

To enhance the chance of creating a common capital market and stay competitive in times of globalization, the EUM embarked on numerous undertakings to harmonize disclosure rules. The main focus, however, has so far been paid to financial disclosure, which is highly regulated under the securities laws of the EUM.

De jure disclosure requirements were consolidated under the Transparency Directive (2004).[12] [13] However, disclosure practices continue to differ among EUM and the variation in information available to investors likely poses some impediment to a single European equity market (Appendix 3.1, Panel 11). Nonetheless, across EUM disclosure is becoming more similar, due to the use of IFRS requiring that financial data must be disclosed on an annual basis in all instances, and often on a semiannual or quarterly basis.

Many codes advocate voluntary disclosure above and beyond what is mandated by IAS/IFRS and corporate law, including disclosure of corporate activities and performance as a means of ensuring accountability to shareholders and other stakeholders (Appendix 3.1, Panels 6, 7, 8). According to the Cardon Report (Belgium), "[t]ransparency is the basis on which trust between the company and its stakeholders is built" (Dual Code of the Brussels Stock Exchange/CBF, § I.A.7).

The disclosure of executive compensation across the EUM has drawn considerable attention lately (Appendix 3.1, Panel 7). This disclosure has been mandated in the UK by listing requirements, and most shareholder groups are in favor of such disclosure. Following the UK's example, listing rules and/or legislation have passed or been proposed to require greater transparency in France, the Netherlands, and Belgium.[14] Until fairly recently, however, resistance to such disclosure has been significant among executives. Nevertheless, in the past three years, new listing rules were passed requiring greater remuneration transparency in Ireland and France, and legislative reforms have been proposed in the Netherlands and Belgium (Appendix 3.1, Panels 10, 12). Many codes recommend that the entire body of policies upon which supervisory and managerial body members are compensated be disclosed (European Shareholders Group 2000, Euroshareholders Guidelines, Guideline V; European Association of Securities Dealers [EASD] 2000, Principles & Recommendations, Principle VI; Recommendations of the Federation of Belgian Companies 1998, § 1.7; Dual Code of the Brussels Stock Exchange/CBF, §§ I.B.2.1, I.B.3.1, and II.B.2; Danish Shareholders Association Guidelines, § II.; Ministry of Trade and Industry [Finland] 2000, Guidelines, § 2.2.2). That said, resistance from senior executives considerably slows the process and the future of this legislature remains unclear.

Another area that seems to be very slow to improve and converge is board composition disclosure. Even though the CGC tend to encourage greater voluntary transparency related to the executives and directors' information, share ownership, and CG practices, as a means of ensuring accountability to shareholders, the actual level of CG disclosure remains low.

The amount of disclosure in annual reports and stock exchange filings related to shareholder protection varies among EUM. In various countries (Germany, Denmark, Spain) the accuracy of disclosed information regarding supervisory and managerial bodies is subject to legal requirements; CGC duplicate them by advocating accurate and full disclosure prior to the annual general meeting of shareholders (Appendix 3.1, Panel 14).[15] For example, the EASD *Principles and Recommendations* (2000) advocate for disclosure of information on: (a) company objectives, (b) company accounts, (c) significant shareholders, (d) supervisory and key managerial body members, (e) material foreseeable risk factors, (f) related party transactions, (g) arrangements giving certain shareholders disproportionate control, (h) governance structures and policies, and (i) internal controls (Recommendations VIII.1). The Organisation for Economic Co-operation and Development (OECD) principles[16] add to this list (a) the financial and operating results of the company; (b) voting rights; (c) remuneration of supervisory board and key managerial board members; and (d) material issues regarding employees and other stakeholders (OECD 1999, Principle IV.A). These principles, along with guiding corporate strategy, tend to assign the board its responsibilities for monitoring managerial performance and achieving an adequate return for shareholders, while preventing conflicts of interest and balancing competing demands. From the legal perspective the OECD principles promote boards' responsibilities in ensuring that the corporations comply with all laws, including tax, competition, labor, environmental, equal opportunity, health, and safety laws as well as environmental and social standards (OECD 1999, Principle V, Annotation 40). Unfortunately, OECD principles are silent on the merits of consolidation and convergence of all related laws and regulations.

The area of disclosure is slowest to converge concerns with treatment of stakeholders and social issues. For example, the Millstein Report, which was a precursor to the OECD principles, recommended that corporations "disclose the extent to which they pursue projects and policies that diverge from the primary objective of generating long-term economic profit so as to enhance shareholder value in the long term" (Millstein Report 1998, Perspective 21). The EASD (2000) *Principles and Recommendations* advocate disclosure and explanation of instances in which concerns other than overall shareholder return or shareholder interests guide corporate decision making (Preamble).

Finally, several codes contemplate disclosure of information relevant to the interests of stakeholders related to environmental and social issues (Ministry of Trade and Industry Guidelines [Finland] 2000, § 2.1.2; Association of Unit Trusts and Investment Funds [AUTIF] Code [UK] 2001, Key Principle 9; Hermes Pensions Management Limited 2002, *The Hermes Principles* [UK], Principle 9; Pensions Investment Research Consultants Ltd. [PIRC] 2010, Guidelines [UK], Part 7; Environmental Reporting—see Appendix 3.1, Panel 4).

3.4.2 Independent Directors and Committees

Two areas of significant convergence belong to the development of the institutions of independent directors and auditing independency. In May 2003 the European Commission proposed to the European Parliament a modernization of the Eighth Directive to provide a comprehensive legal basis for statutory audits conducted within the EU. This modernized Eighth Directive was voted in May 2006, with a deadline for EUM of transposition into respective national law by June 2008[17] (see the details in Chapter 5 of this volume). In accordance with new developments publicly traded corporations should have independent directors on their boards and establish a variety of committees to oversee different corporations' activities, such as directors' compensation schemes and accuracy of disclosed information. The institution of independency is developed to provide the appropriate structures and procedures to ensure that the board can function independently of management and be instrumental in solving agency problem by monitoring managers' actions. In this regard CGC (IFSA Report 1999;[18]

OECD recommendations;[19] not covered in Viénot I Report 1995; Viénot II Report 1999; Berlin Initiative Group 2000; Preda Code 1999; Millstein Report 1998) encourage "the independent directors meet periodically as a body to review the performance of management and of the members of the board" as well as advocate for the independent directors executive session meetings with the chairman and the chief executive officer to discuss the matters of immediate significance.

Big importance is assigned to the audit committee, which is expected to confidentially meet with the internal and external auditors (including statutory auditors) annually to discuss the accuracy of disclosed information and compliance with financial reporting rules. The exclusion of the executive directors from those meetings is supposed to ensure free discussion and information flow in both directions. In most cases the remuneration committee is also required; in case of its absence, however, it is the board of directors' responsibility to come up with the executives' compensation scheme.

In two-tier boards, the supervisory board (which contains independent directors) is encouraged to meet without the management board to promote open discussion on the important issues, including its own performance and relationship with the management board (the composition, performance, and the compensation of the management board). Also different committees' members are supported in communicating with stockholders and employee representatives to build up the meeting's agenda, but they never take action without the meeting's decisions (OECD 1999; not covered in Peters Report 1997; Comissão do Mercado de Valores Mobiliáros [CMVM] 1999; Olivencia Report 1998; Committee on the Financial Aspects of Corporate Governance 1995; Hampel Report, UK; The Combined Code 2000).

4. EVIDENCE OF COMPLIANCE

CGC tend to express the best-case scenarios, thus the translation into actual practice can be slow, especially if the best practices are significantly different from the common ones. So, an analysis of CGC and regulations efficiency would not be complete without information on companies' compliance with CGC and regulations. Until market mechanisms create strong incentives for companies to comply, adherence may not be absolute; compliance, therefore, should be closely monitored. The importance of compliance is not underestimated by EUM; therefore, governmental and quasi-governmental agencies analyze this issue from time to time and issue special reports on the status of compliance.[20] Not surprisingly, the UK was the first country among EUM that started to emphasize CG disclosure, and numerous English agencies oversee the companies' compliance with disclosure requirements.

According to the *Report of the Committee on the Financial Aspects of Corporate Governance (Cadbury Committee), Compliance with the Code of Best Practice*, issued in 2005, the majority of listed companies have split the roles of chairman and chief executive officer; and there are more independent directors on boards of companies where the roles remained combined, as is recommended by the Code of Best Practices. The majority of nonexecutive directors were already independent in the UK back in 1995, and companies were disclosing required information regarding formal terms of appointment for nonexecutive directors as well as their relation to the company. The report also identifies a significant increase in the disclosure of Audit, Nomination, and Remuneration Committees since the publication of the Combined Code.

Another agency, the Financial Services Authority (FSA), which is charged with ensuring listing rule compliance, regularly reviews the extent to which listed companies make required disclosures in line with the Combined Code using randomly selected samples from the London Stock Exchange. This agency assesses the quality of disclosed information and issues sanctions against companies that fail to comply with mandatory disclosures, such as public censure or fine. In its recent report from 2007 the FSA admitted that even though the quality and quantity of disclosed information vary from company to company, overall they tend to improve over time.

Another recent report comes from the National Association of Pension Funds (NAPF), which has a voting issues service (available to subscribers) that tracks compliance with the Combined Code by the 350 largest listed UK companies. According to it, compliance with the disclosure requirement is high and compliance with substantive provisions of the Combined Code has been improving over a long period of time. Nevertheless, as the report states, listed companies remain free to deviate from the Combined Code's substantive recommendations if they so decide.

The Stock Exchange in Italy has recently announced that it will be disclosing information about companies that failed to comply with the Preda Report's mandatory disclosure requirements on the Internet, making it publicly available information, and therefore hopefully enforcing the rules.

According to the Peters Report (the Netherlands) issued in 1997, companies are requested to disclose financial and CG information in their annual reports. However, the Netherlands does not have an enforcement mechanism to ensure compliance with this disclosure request. According to an official monitoring survey, "Monitoring Corporate Governance in Nederland," published by the *Tilburg Economic* a year following the Peters Report, only 55 percent of Dutch companies fully disclosed requested information. Another 36 percent selectively provided the information. The Tilburg survey indicated that companies generally complied more readily with provisions relating to supervisory board processes than with provisions relating to shareholder rights.

The Belgian Banking and Finance Commission has also conducted surveys of compliance with its recommendations. Its 1998 survey (Etudes et Documents No. 5, October 1998) concluded that CG disclosure has been improved with approximately 55 percent of companies introduced in their 1997 annual report, a special section on CG. Disclosure about CG was noticeably more prevalent among the BEL-20, as 80 percent of these companies included such a section in their 1997 annual reports. Note, however, that only 6 percent of companies provided more than twenty specific items of CG information out of a possible thirty, and 36 percent provided information on fewer than six elements. Further improvement was observed during 1999 (Etudes et Documents No. 10, November 1999) and 2003 and 2007 follow-up surveys. The results of the surveys suggest that 87 percent of all companies included a section on CG, with as many as 95 percent of BEL-20 companies including such a section. The quantity of information disclosed expanded as well, and 27.5 percent of listed companies provided more than twenty specific items of CG information.

A report issued by CMVM, Portugal, in 2001 suggests that 70 percent of the companies listed on the market with official quotations voluntarily disclosed financial information, although only 23.2 percent of those stated compliance with CMVM recommendations as far as CG structure and practices disclosure. Furthermore, there remains no consistency in the content of disclosed information from year to year.

In Spain, the regulatory authority (Comisión Nacional del Mercado de Valores 2007) also reviews this issue and the survey from 2007 suggests that compliance with the Olivencia Report is significant given that the recommendations are wholly voluntary (*Análisis de los Resultados del Cuestionario sobre el Código de Buen Gobierno Relativo al Ejercicio*). Note that in Spain, many listed companies issue their own CG guidelines, and often include them in their annual report.

In France, the Commission des Opérations de Bourse has issued several reports about CG compliance, including Bulletin COB n° 352 (December 2000) and Bulletin COB n° 338 (September 1999).

In addition to the official surveys of compliance, in some EUM various entities (on their own initiative) have conducted unofficial surveys to track compliance in reference to a code. For example, in Germany, a survey of the DAX 100 carried out at the end of 2000 found that, although CG is the subject of intense interest, large German listed companies were not yet implementing CG reforms on a wide scale (Pellens, Hillebrandt, and Ulmer 2001).

The analyses of the companies' compliance with CGC suggest that EUM companies appear to be responding to codes' recommendations with various degrees of acquiescence. Until full compliance with codes is achieved, the CGC may help communicate the need for reform and the benefits that may be associated with it.

5. CONCLUSIONS

The growing interest in CGC among EUM may reflect an understanding that equity investors, whether foreign or domestic, are considering the quality of CG along with financial performance and other factors when deciding whether to invest in a company.

The CGC analyzed here originate from nations with diverse cultures, financing traditions, ownership structures, and legal origins. Given their distinct origins, the codes are remarkable in their similarities, especially in terms of the attitudes they express about the key roles and responsibilities of the board of directors, incentive mechanisms, and the recommendations they make concerning composition and practices. Whereas some EUM may embed more governance requirements in law (German legal origin) than others, it has at this point been recognized by all parties that good governance practices are beneficial to listed companies everywhere and capital markets give rewards for good governance. As equity financing gains importance, companies will have stronger incentives to implement the best governance practices and fully disclose this information. In the meantime, however, while market enforcement mechanisms are not strong enough, the most efficient way to ensure compliance with what is viewed as the best governance practices is by using governmental structures as enforcement devices.

NOTES

1. CGC are generally defined as nonbinding sets of principles, standards, or best practices issued by a collective body that relate to the internal governance of corporations.
2. This leads some commentators to express concerns that comply-or-explain disclosure requirements may lead to an overly mechanical and uniform approach to a company's decisions about ordering its corporate governance—a mere "box-ticking" exercise.
3. Note that in France, the first code issued by the committee chaired by Marc Viénot, now known as Viénot I, was neither superseded by nor consolidated into the code issued by the second Viénot committee, known as Viénot II. However, both Viénot codes as well as the so-called Bouton code (2002) have been merged into the Corporate Governance Code of Listed Companies by AFEP-MEDEF in 2003.
4. For instance, in Austria, Belgium, Germany, and Italy more than half of listed industrial companies have a large holder of stock who accounts for 50 percent or more of the company's ownership. Such large controlling shareholders are far less common in the United Kingdom.
5. Appendix 3.1 is comprised from the latest edition of national CGC mostly revised between 2005 and 2009.
6. Dual board structure, however, can be observed in other EUM.
7. Both stock corporations and nonstock corporations with over five hundred employees must have a supervisory board. Those companies with five hundred to two thousand German employees must also have a supervisory board

where one-third of its members are elected by employees. Companies with over two thousand must have 50 percent employee representation. The absolute number of employee-members depends on the total number of supervisory board seats, with a maximum set at twenty for companies with over twenty thousand employees.

8. For example, there is no strict definition of the concept of independence, as opposed to what's provided by the NYSE.

9. Many newly developed practices are designed to enhance the distinction between the roles of the supervisory and managerial bodies, including supervisory body independence, separation of the chairman and CEO roles, and reliance on board committees. The majority of EUM laws do not encompass employees' role in the supervisory body (although Finish, Dutch, and French company articles may provide that right).

10. For instance, in discussing the apportionment of responsibilities in the German two-tier structure, the Berlin Initiative Code explains: "The supervisory board plays an important role with its selection and supervision of the management board. It does not, however, have any managerial function" (Thesis 6). It serves as "supervisory authority which controls and advises the management board in the sense of 'checks and balances.' Thus, it is not on an equal footing next to, or even above, the management board." Rather it serves as a "counterweight" (Commentary on Thesis 6). According to the Berlin Initiative Code, it is the management board that "forms the company's clear focus of decision-making" (§ I.6). In France a one-tier "board of directors . . . determines the company's strategy, appoints the corporate officers charged with implementing that strategy, supervises management, and ensures that proper information is made available to shareholders and markets concerning the company's financial position and performance, as well as any major transactions to which it is a party" (Viénot I Report 1995, 2).

11. German publicly traded stock companies must utilize a two-tiered board. Whereas this system is not unique in Europe, it is a foreign concept for US investors. The approach is summarized in Figure 1 (Federal Ministry of Economics and Technology of Germany 2002, 2006). The supervisory board is elected by shareholders and, in the case of larger companies, employees. The proportion of shareholder-elected to employee-elected representatives is mandated by the German Codetermination Act, and is summarized in Table 5, Appendix A. Still, even for large companies where employee-representatives make up half of the supervisory board, shareholder interests may dominate as the shareholder-elected chairperson receives a tie-breaking vote.

12. On a still more international level, transparency requirements had been consolidated by the *International Disclosure Standards for Cross-Border Offerings and Initial Listings by Foreign Issuers* of the International Organization of Securities Commissions (1998).

13. Directive 2004/109/EC of the European Parliament and of the Council of December 15, 2004. This directive has been completed with implementing measures by Commission Directive 2007/14/EC of March 8, 2007.

14. Effective in 2001, the Dublin Stock Exchange became the second stock market in Europe (after the London Stock Exchange) to require disclosure of individual executive remuneration.

   In France in 2000, MEDEF, the French employer association, issued a strong recommendation to companies to voluntarily publish such information. Under new regulation, listed companies are now required to disclose specific information on remuneration of two to four of a company's top executives.

   Recently the Dutch Ministries of Justice, Economic Affairs, and Social Welfare and Employment submitted a joint bill to Parliament that would require listed companies to disclose in annual reports individual salary and option grant information for all supervisory and management board members. In Belgium, similar legislation was announced that would require listed companies to disclose the remuneration of individual board members and senior executives.

15. The Danish Shareholders Association Guidelines advocate the disclosure of directors and managers transactions related to company stock (§ V) even though it is required by law or listing requirements to some degree. The Spanish Olivencia Report (1998) implied: "The board of directors, beyond current regulatory requirements should be in charge of furnishing markets with quick, accurate and reliable information, particularly in connection with the shareholder structure, substantial changes in governance rule, and especially relevant transactions" (§ III.19).

16. *Principles of Corporate Governance* (OECD 1999); *Business Sector Advisory Group on Corporate Governance: Corporate Governance: Improving Competitiveness and Access to Capital in Global Markets* (Millstein Report 1998).

17. Directive 2006/43/EC of the European Parliament and of the Council, May 17, 2006.

18. The IFSA Report (as revised in 1999) is reflected in the International Comparison of Corporate Governance Guidelines and Codes of Best Practice—Investor Viewpoints. NY1:\6851\11\5@B11!.DOC \99990.0899 2.

19. Excerpts from Business Sector Advisory Group on Corporate Governance Report to the OECD NY1:\6851\11\5@B11!.DOC\99990.0899 154.

20. For example, the UK's Committee on the Financial Aspects of Corporate Governance (1995) issued a detailed report entitled *Compliance with the Code of Best Practice*. The Committee reviewed the top five hundred listed companies, plus a random sample of other listed companies, and found that every company report contained the required information. The committee also admitted that full compliance with disclosure requirements is most likely to be made by top five hundred companies, whereas midsize and small firms limit themselves only to the information mandated by corporate law, living out the information required by CGC.

REFERENCES

Addison, J. T., L. Bellmann, and A. Kölling. 2004. Works councils and plant closings in Germany. *British Journal of Industrial Relations* 42 (1): 125–48.

Addison, J. T., L. Bellmann, C. Schnabel, and J. Wagner. 2004. The reform of the German Works Constitution Act: A critical assessment. *Industrial Relations* 43 (2): 392–420.

Addison, J. T., C. Schnabel, and J. Wagner. 1997. On the determinants of mandatory works councils in Germany. *Industrial Relations* 36 (4): 419–44.

Allianz. 2006a. *Allianz Completes Conversion into SE*. http://www.allianz.com/azcom/dp/cda/0,,1266136–44,00.html (accessed October 19, 2006).

———. 2006b. *2005 SEC 20–F Report*. LexisNexis Academic database (accessed July 30, 2006).

Aoki, M., and G. Jackson. 2007. *Understanding an emergent diversity of corporate governance and organizational architecture: An essentiality-based approach*. www.ssrn.com.

Association Francaise des Enterprises Privees and Mouvement des Entreprises de France. 2003. *Association Francaise des Enterprises Privees (AFEP) & Mouvement des Entreprises de France (MEDEF): The corporate governance of listed corporations*.

Association of Unit Trusts and Investment Funds. 2001. *Code of good practice—institutional investors and corporate governance (AUTIF Code)*.

Belgian Banking and Finance Commission. 1998. Etudes et Documents No. 5, October.

———. 1999. Etudes et Documents No. 10, November.

Berlin Initiative Group. 2000. *German code on corporate governance*. www.gccg.de.

Boot, A. W. A., and J. R. Macey. 1998. Objectivity, control and adaptability in corporate governance. *Columbia Law School, Corporate Governance Today* 213: 222–24.

Brussels Stock Exchange. *Dual code of the Brussels Stock Exchange/CBF*.

Bushman, R.M., and A.J. Smith. 2001. Financial accounting information and corporate governance. *Journal of Accounting and Economics* 32:237–333.

Chahine, S., and I. Filatotchev. 2008. The effects of information disclosure and board independence on IPO discount. *Journal of Small Business Management* 46 (2): 219–41.

Combined Code. 2000. *Committee on corporate governance: The Combined Code—principles of good governance and code of best practice*.

Comisión Nacional del Mercado de Valores. 2007. *Análisis de los resultados del cuestionario sobre el Código de Buen Gobierno Relativo al Ejercicio*.

Comissão do Mercado de Valores Mobiliáros. 1999. *Recommendations on corporate governance (Portugal)*.

Commission des Opérations de Bourse. 2000. Bulletin COB n° 352, December.

———. 1999. Bulletin COB n° 338, September.

Committee on the Financial Aspects of Corporate Governance. 1995. *Report of the Committee on the Financial Aspects of Corporate Governance (Cadbury Committee), compliance with the Code of Best Practice (Cadbury Report)*.

Dinh, V. D. 1999. Codetermination and corporate governance in a multinational business enterprise. *Journal of Corporation Law* 24 (4): 975–99.

European Association of Securities Dealers. 2000. *Corporate governance—principles and recommendations*.

European Foundation for the Improvement of Living and Working Conditions. 2005a. *Germany Betriebsrat (works council)*. October 4. http://www.eurofound.eu.int/emire/GERMANY/WORKSCOUNCIL-DE.html (accessed April 1, 2006).

———. 2005b. *Germany Betriebsverfassung (works constitution)*. October 4. http://www.eurofound.eu.int/emire/GERMANY/WORKSCONSTITUTION-DE.html (accessed April 1, 2006).

———. 2005c. *Germany Koalition (collective industrial organization)*. October 4. http://www.eurofound.eu.int/emire/GERMANY/COLLECTIVEINDUSTRI-ALORGANIZATION-DE.html (accessed May 1, 2006).

———. 2005d. *Germany Koalitionsfreiheit (freedom to association)*. October 4. http://www.eurofound.eu.int/emire/GERMANY/FREEDOMOFASSOCIA-TIONRIGHTTOORGANIZE-DE.html (accessed May 1, 2006).

———. 2005e. *Germany Mitbestimmungsrechte Des Betriebsrats (codetermination rights of the works council)*. October 4. http://www.eurofound.eu.int/emire/GERMANY/CODETERMINATIONRIGHTSOFTHEWORKSCOUN-CIL-DE.html (accessed April 1, 2006).

European Shareholders Group. 2000. *Euroshareholders corporate governance guidelines 2000*. www.cg.org.cn/theory/zlyz/Europeinterest.pdf.

Federation of Belgian Companies. 1998. *Corporate governance—recommendations*. www.vbo-feb.de.

FitzRoy, F. R., and K. Kraft. 1993. Economic effects of codetermination. *Scandinavian Journal of Economics* 95 (3): 365–75.

———. 2004. Co-determination, efficiency, and productivity. The Institute for the Study of Labor (IZA) Discussion Papers, 1442.

———. 2005. Controlling shareholders and corporate governance: Complicating the comparative taxonomy. Columbia University Center for Law and Economic Research Paper Series Research Paper no. 281.

Goergen, M., M. Martynova, and L. Renneboog. 2005. Corporate governance convergence: Evidence from takeover regulation reforms in Europe. *Oxford Review of Economic Policy* 21:243–68.

Gorton, G., and F. Schmid. 2002. Class struggle inside the firm: A study of German code-termination. Federal Reserve Bank of St. Louis, Working Paper Series 2000–025B. http://research.stlouisfed.org/wp/2000/2000–025.pdf (accessed September 1, 2006).

Government Commission on the German Corporate Governance Code. 2009. *German Corporate Governance Code as amended on June 18, 2009 (first issued in 2002).* http://www.corporate-governance-code.de/index-e.html.

Gugler, K., D. C. Mueller, and B. B. Yurtoglu. 2003. Corporate governance and return on investment. ECGI Finance Working Paper no. 06. www.ecgi.org/wp.

Hellebuyck, J.-P. 1998. *Chairman of the AFG-ASFFI Commission on Corporate Governance. Recommendations on corporate governance. (Hellebuyck I Report).*

———. 2001. *Chairman of the AFG-ASFFI Commission on Corporate Governance. Recommendations on corporate governance. (Hellebuyck II Report).*

Hermes Pensions Management Limited. 1997. *Hermes statement 1997.*

———. 2001. *Hermes statement 2001.*

———. 2002. The Hermes Principles—what shareholders expect of public companies—and what companies should expect of their investors. www.ecgi.org/codes/documents/hermes_principles.pdf.

Hobson, C. J., and J. B. Dworkin. 1986. West German labor unrest: Are unions losing ground to worker councils? *Monthly Labor Review* 109 (2): 46–48.

Hübler, O., and U. Jirjahn. 2003. Works councils and collective bargaining in Germany: The impact on productivity and wages. *Scottish Journal of Political Economy* 50 (4): 471–91.

IFSA Report. 1999. IFSA: Corporate governance: A guide for investment managers and corporations. IFSA Guidance Note No. 2.00.

Khanna, T., and K. G. Palepu. 2004. Globalization and convergence in corporate governance: Evidence from Infosys and the Indian software industry. *Journal of International Business Studies* 35 (6): 484–507.

Krivogorsky, V., G. Grudnitski, and G. Burton. 2009. Dominant owners and financial performance of Continental European firms. www.ssrn.com.

Krivogorsky, V., G. Grudnitski, and W. Dick. 2011. Bank debt and performance of Continental European firms. *International Journal of Economics and Business Research.*

LaPorta, R., F. Lopes-de-Salines, and A. Shleifer. 1999. Corporate ownership around the world. *Journal of Finance* 54:471–517.

LaPorta, R., F. Lopes-de-Salines, A. Shleifer, and R. Vishny. 1998. Law and finance. *Journal of Political Economy* 106:1113–56.

———. 2000. Investor protection and corporate governance. *Journal of Financial Economics* 58:3–27.

Leuz, C., D. Nanda, and P. D. Woysocki. 2003. Investor protection and earnings management: An international comparison. *Journal of Financial Economics* 69:505–27.

Millstein Report. 1998. *Business sector advisory group on corporate governance: Corporate governance: Improving competitiveness and access to capital in global markets.*

Ministry of Trade and Industry (Finland). 2000. *Guidelines for handling corporate governance issues in state-owned companies and associated companies.*

Nørby Report. 2001. *The Nørby Committee's report on corporate governance in Denmark.*

Olivencia Report. 1998. *Special commission to consider a code of ethics for companies' boards of directors: The governance of listed companies.*

Organisation for Economic Co-operation and Development. 1999. *Principles of corporate governance.*

Pellens B., F. Hillebrandt, and B. Ulmer. 2001. Umsetzung von Corporate-Governance-Richtlinien in der Praxis. *Betriebs-Berater* 56:1243–50.

Pensions Investment Research Consultants Ltd. 2010. *UK shareholder voting guidelines.*

Peters Report. 1997. *Committee on corporate governance: Recommendations on corporate governance in the Netherlands.*

Preda Code. 1999. *Committee for the corporate governance of listed companies, Borsa Italiana: Report & code of conduct (The Preda Code).* http://www.borsaitaliana.it/homepage/homepage.htm.

Roe, M. J. 1994. *Strong managers, weak owners: The political roots of American corporate finance.*

———. 1996. Chaos and evolution in law and economics, 109. *Harvard Law Review* 641: 643–62.

Tilburg Economic. 1998. Monitoring corporate governance in Nederland.

Udayasankar, K., and S. S. Das. 2007. Corporate governance and firm performance: The effects of regulation and competitiveness. *Corporate Governance: An International Review* 15 (2): 262–71.

Viénot I Report. 1995. *Conseil National du Patronat Francais (CNPF) & Association Francaise des Entreprises Privees (AFEP): The board of directors of listed companies in France.*

Viénot II Report. 1999. *Mouvement des Entreprises de France (MEDEF) & Association Francaise des Enterprises Privees (AFEP): Recommendations of the committee on corporate governance chaired by Mr. Marc Viénot.*

Weiss, M. 2006. The effectiveness of labour law: Reflections based on the German experience. *Managerial Law* 48 (3): 275–87.

Wiesmann, G. 2006. Germans eye UK listings as a way out of worker law. *Financial Times*, May 24, 28.

APPENDIX 3.1

The appendix was prepared by W. Dick, ESSEC, France.
Information in these panels is based on CG codes as available in June 2008:

- Belgium: The Belgian Code on CG (December 2004)
- Denmark: Recommendations for CG of August 15, 2005, section VI revised by February 6, 2008
- France: The CG of Listed Corporations (2003)
- Germany: German CG Code (June 2007)
- Italy: CG Code (March 2006)
- Netherlands: The Dutch CG Code (December 2003)
- Portugal: CG Code and Legal Framework Consolidation (April 2007)
- Spain: Unified Code on Good CG (January 2006)
- Sweden: Swedish Code of CG (September 2007)
- United Kingdom: The Combined Code on CG (June 2006)

Summary

	Panel 1 Definition	Panel 2 Mission of Board of Directors	Panel 3 Role of stakeholders	Panel 4 Board job description	Panel 5 Board size	Panel 6 Evaluating Board performance	Panel 7 Board Compensation review	Panel 8 Board Meetings and Agenda	Panel 9 Board Information Flow....	Panel 10 Executive Compensation	Panel 11 Content and Character of Disclosure	Panel 12 Disclosure Regarding Compensation...	Panel 13 Disclosure Regarding CG	Panel 14 Accuracy of Disclosure, Internal Control systems...	Total Covered (max. 14)
Belgium	Yes	NCD	NCD	Yes	Yes	Yes	Yes	Yes	Yes	Yes	Yes	Yes	Yes	Yes	12
Denmark	Yes	Yes	NCD	Yes	Yes	Yes	Yes	Yes	Yes	Yes	Yes	Yes	Yes	Yes	13
France	NC	Yes	NC	Yes	NC	Yes	Yes	Yes	Yes	Yes	Yes	Yes	Yes	Yes	11
Germany	NCD	Yes	NC	Yes	Yes	Yes	Yes	Yes	Yes	NC	Yes	Yes	Yes	Yes	11
Italy	Yes	Yes	NCD	Yes	Yes	Yes	Yes	Yes	Yes	Yes	Yes	NC	Yes	Yes	11
Netherlands	Yes	NCD	Yes	NCD	NC	NCD	Yes	NC	NC	NC	NC	Yes	Yes	NC	5
Portugal	NC	Yes		Yes	NC	NCD	Yes	NC	Yes	Yes	Yes	Yes	Yes	Yes	9
Spain	NCD	Yes		Yes	Yes	Yes	Yes	Yes	Yes	NC	Yes	Yes	Yes	Yes	11
Sweden	Yes	Yes	Yes	Yes	Yes	Yes	Yes	Yes	Yes	NC	Yes	Yes	Yes	Yes	13
United Kingdom		Yes	NCD	Yes	Yes	NCD	Yes	Yes	Yes	Yes	Yes	Yes	Yes	Yes	11
Total covered (max. 10)	4	8	2	9	7	7	10	8	9	6	9	9	10	9	

NC – not covered, NCD – not covered directly

Panel 1: Definition

Belgium	CG is a set of rules and behaviors according to which companies are managed and controlled. A good CG model will achieve its goal by setting a proper balance between entrepreneurship and control, as well as between performance and conformance.
	For entrepreneurship, CG rules should not only facilitate performance-driven direction, but should also provide mechanisms for direction and leadership while ensuring integrity and transparency in the decision-making process.
	Good CG should help determine a company's objectives, the means through which these objectives are attained and how performance is to be evaluated. In this sense, CG should provide incentives for the board and management to pursue objectives that are in the interest of the company, its shareholders, and other stakeholders.
	Control means effective evaluation of performance, careful management of potential risks, and proper supervision of conformity with agreed procedures and processes. Here, the emphasis is on monitoring whether robust control systems are effectively in operation, whether potential conflicts of interest are managed, and whether sufficient checks are in place to prevent abuse of power leading to private benefits prevailing over corporate benefits.
Denmark	The concept of CG can be defined as:
	The goals, according to which a company is managed, and the major principles and frameworks that regulate the interaction between the company's managerial bodies, the owners as well as other parties, who are directly influenced by the company's dispositions and business (in this context jointly referred to as the company's stakeholders). The debate regarding good CG has more recently moved from primarily being driven by a wish to stimulate "owner activism" and increase the supervision of the management, to having a broader view of the company and its relationship with its other stakeholders. In line with this, the Danish debate about the relationship between the board and management has also changed its focus from a narrow control and supervision perspective to a broader and more forward-looking strategic perspective.
France	Not Covered.
Germany	Not covered directly, but see § I. This German CG code presents essential statutory regulations for the management and supervision of German exchange-listed companies and includes internationally and nationally recognized standards for good and responsible CG.
Italy	Not Covered.
Netherlands	CG relates to the management and control of companies, to responsibility and participation, and to accountability and supervision. Integrity and transparency play a major role.
	The principle applied in the Netherlands is that a company is a long-term form of collaboration between the various parties involved. The stakeholders are the groups and individuals who directly or indirectly influence (or are influenced by) the achievement of the aims of the company: employees, shareholders and other providers of capital, suppliers and customers, but also government and civil society. The executive board and supervisory board should take account of the interests of the different stakeholders.
Portugal	Not Covered.
Spain	Not Covered Directly.
Sweden	CG deals with the management of companies with a view to meeting the owners' required return on invested capital and thus it contributes to economic growth and efficiency.
United Kingdom	Corporate governance is a system by which businesses are directed and controlled.

Panel 2: Mission of Board of Directors

Belgium	Not Covered Directly.

Denmark   The supervisory board is responsible for safeguarding the interests of the shareholders with care and due consideration of the other stakeholders. As concerns the managerial division of tasks between the supervisory board and the executive board, the supervisory board is assigned with, and responsible for, undertaking the overall management of the company as well as establishing guidelines for and supervising the executive board's work. One important management task is to develop and establish appropriate strategies for the company. It is essential that the supervisory board ensure ongoing development of and follow-up on the necessary strategies in collaboration with the executive board.

France   1.1. Regardless of its membership or how it is organized, the board of directors is and must remain a collegial body representing all shareholders collectively. It is required to act at all times in the interests of the company.
1.2. In exercising its statutory prerogatives, the board of directors is carrying out a fourfold mission: it defines the corporation's strategy, appoints the corporate officers in charge of managing the corporation in line with that strategy, selects the form of organization (separation of the offices of chairman and chief executive officer or combination of such offices), and monitors the management and secures the quality of information provided to shareholders and to the market, through the accounts or in connection with major transactions.
1.3. It is not desirable, with regard to the great diversity of listed corporations, to impose formal and identical ways of organization and operation for all boards of directors. The organization of the board's work, and likewise its membership, must be suited to the shareholder makeup, to the size and nature of each firm's business, and to the particular circumstances facing it. Each board is the best judge of this, and its foremost responsibility is to adopt the ways of organization and operation enabling it to carry out its mission in the best possible manner.

Germany   Supervisory Board
The task of the supervisory board is to advise regularly and supervise the management board in the management of the enterprise. It must be involved in decisions of fundamental importance to the enterprise.
The supervisory board appoints and dismisses the members of the management board. Together with the management board it shall ensure that there is a long-term succession planning. The supervisory board can delegate preparations for the appointment of members of the management board to a committee, which also determines the conditions of the employment contracts including compensation.
Management Board
The management board is responsible for independently managing the enterprise. In doing so, it is obliged to act in the enterprise's best interests and undertakes to increase the sustainable value of the enterprise.

(continued)

The management board develops the enterprise's strategy, coordinates it with the supervisory board, and ensures its implementation.

The management board ensures that all provisions of law and the enterprise's internal policies are abided by and works to achieve their compliance by group companies (compliance).

The management board ensures appropriate risk management and risk controlling in the enterprise.

Italy   Listed companies are governed by a board of directors that meets at regular intervals, and that adopts an organization and a modus operandi that enable it to perform its functions in an effective, efficient manner.

The directors act and pass resolutions with full knowledge of the facts and autonomously pursue the priority of creating value for the shareholders. Consistent with this goal, they shall also take into account the directives and policies defined for the group of which the issuer is a member, as well as the benefits deriving from being a member of a group.

Netherlands Not Covered Directly.

Portugal   The board of directors is responsible for the decision making on any matters related to the management of the company (II.2.2). The company's articles of association may stipulate authorization for the board of directors to delegate one or more executive directors or an executive committee to be responsible for the day-to-day management of the company. However, the following are not within the delegation duties' scope: (i) appointment of the chairperson (if not the general meeting); (ii) co-opting managing directors; (iii) request for convening general meetings; (iv) annual reports and accounts; (v) providing personal and real guarantees for the company; (vi) changes in head-office and capital increase, under the terms provided for in the articles of association; (vii) plans for mergers, spin-offs, and company conversion (80. II.2.3). The board of directors' resolution shall set the limits for delegating powers and in the event of the creation of an executive committee, it shall establish its composition as well and how it is run (II.2.4). Delegating powers does not exclude the board of directors from adopting resolutions on the same subject matters; other directors are responsible, under the law, for the overall supervision on how the executive director or chief executive officers or, further yet, the executive committee, as well as for damages caused through acts or omissions, when it is aware of such acts or omissions or their intent to carry out such actions and do not alert the board to take the appropriate measures.

Spain   The board of directors shall perform its duties with unity of purpose and independence from management, according all shareholders the same treatment. It shall be guided at all times by the company's best interest, to be understood as maximizing the company's value over time.

It will ensure that the company abides by the laws and regulations in its relations with stakeholders; fulfills its obligations and contracts in good faith; respects the customs and good practices of the sectors and territories where it does business; and upholds any additional social responsibility principles it has subscribed to voluntarily.

(continued)

Panel 2 (*continued*)

Sweden	The principal task of the board of directors is to manage the company's affairs in such a way as to satisfy the owners that their interests in a good long-term return on capital are being met in the best possible way (3.1.1). To meet its obligations to the company's owners, the board of directors is to pay particular attention to: establishing the overall goals for the company and deciding the company's strategy for achieving these goals; evaluating the company's operative management on an ongoing basis and, if necessary, appointing or dismissing the managing director; ensuring that there is an effective system for follow-up and control of the company's operations and financial position vis-à-vis the established goals; ensuring that the company's external communications are open, objective, and appropriate for the target audience; ensuring that there is a satisfactory process for monitoring the company's compliance with laws and other regulations that apply to the company's operations; and ensuring that the necessary guidelines governing the company's ethical conduct are established (3.1.2). The board is to ensure that there is an annual evaluation of its work and that this evaluation employs a systematic and structured process.
United Kingdom	Every company should be headed by an effective board that is collectively responsible for the success of the company. The board's role is to provide entrepreneurial leadership of the company within a framework of prudent and effective controls, which enables risk to be assessed and managed. The board should set the company's strategic aims and ensure that the necessary financial and human resources are in place for the company to meet its objectives and review management performance. The board should set the company's values and standards and ensure that its obligations to its shareholders and others are understood and met. All directors must take decisions objectively in the interests of the company. As part of their role as members of a unitary board, nonexecutive directors should constructively challenge and help develop proposals on strategy. Nonexecutive directors should scrutinize the performance of management in meeting agreed goals and objectives and monitor the reporting of performance. They should satisfy themselves on the integrity of financial information and that financial controls and systems of risk management are robust and defensible. They are responsible for determining appropriate levels of remuneration of executive directors and have a prime role in appointing, and where necessary removing, executive directors, and in succession planning.

Panel 3: Role of Stakeholders

Belgium	Not Covered Directly.
Denmark	Not Covered Directly.

It is essential for a company's prosperity and future possibilities that the company have a good relationship with its stakeholders. Stakeholders are everyone directly affected by the company's decisions and business. Thus, it is desirable that the company's management run and develop the company with due consideration of its stakeholders, and that the management provide an incentive for dialogue with these stakeholders. Successful interaction between the company and its stakeholders implies openness and mutual respect.

The committee recommends that the supervisory board adopt a policy on the company's relationship with its stakeholders. Such a policy could, for example, include the company's business concept and its basic values and objectives, and one element could be guidelines for the company's publication of information about environmental and social issues.

The committee recommends that the supervisory board ensure that the interests and roles of the stakeholders are respected in accordance with the company's policy on such issues. As part of this purpose, it is natural that the supervisory board ensures that the executive board and the company's stakeholders are in active dialogue in order to develop and strengthen the company.

To a varying extent, it is necessary to provide shareholders, including potential shareholders, and other stakeholders with information about the company. Understanding and relating to the company depend on the amount of information and the quality of information published or provided by the company. Openness and transparency are essential conditions for ensuring that the company's shareholders and other stakeholders are able to regularly evaluate and relate to the company and its prospects and so to contribute to constructive interaction with the company.

France	Not Covered.
Germany	Not Covered.
Italy	Not Covered Directly.
Netherlands	CG relates to the management and control of companies, to responsibility and participation, and to accountability and supervision. Integrity and transparency play a major role.

The principle applied in the Netherlands is that a company is a long-term form of collaboration between the various parties involved. The stakeholders are the groups and individuals who directly or indirectly influence (or are influenced by) the achievement of the aims of the company: employees, shareholders, and other providers of capital; suppliers and customers; but also government and civil society. The executive board and supervisory board should take account of the interests of the different stakeholders.

Portugal

Spain

Sweden   Shareholders' influence in the company is exercised at the shareholders' meeting, which is the company's highest decision-making body. To create the best possible conditions for the active exercise of the ownership role, the shareholders' meeting should be conducted in such a manner that as high a percentage as possible of the total number of shares and votes can be represented at the meeting and that active participation on the part of current shareholders in the discussions and decision making is facilitated.

United   Not Covered Directly.
  Kingdom

Panel 4: Board Job Description

Belgium	The board's composition should ensure that decisions are made in the corporate interest. It should be determined on the basis of the necessary diversity and complementary skills, experience, and knowledge. A list of the members of the board should be disclosed in the CG chapter of the annual report. No individual or group of directors should dominate the board's decision making. No one individual should have unfettered powers of decision making. At least half the board should comprise nonexecutive directors and at least three of them should be independent. To be considered independent, a director should be free from any business, close family, or other relationship with the company, its controlling shareholders or the management of either that creates a conflict of interest such as to affect that director's independent judgment.
Denmark	The board discusses and establishes its most important tasks related to the overall strategic management as well as the financial and managerial supervision of the company and regularly evaluates the executive board's work. The board's most important tasks normally include: • establishing the overall goals and strategies and being responsible for follow-up in this respect • ensuring clear guidelines for responsibility, distribution of responsibilities, planning and follow-up as well as risk management • appointing a qualified executive board, establishing conditions of employment for the members of the board, including preparing guidelines for its appointment and composition, as well as ensuring that the remuneration of the members of the board reflects their performance • ensuring that relations with the company's stakeholders are good and constructive
France	The board of directors should consider and decide upon transactions with a genuinely strategic importance, after review by an ad hoc committee if appropriate. The internal rules of the board of directors should specify: • the cases in which prior approval by the board of directors is required, setting out the related principles, which may differ as a function of which division of the group is concerned • the principle that any material transaction outside the scope of the firm's stated strategy is subject to prior approval by the board of directors • the rules according to which the board of directors is informed of the corporation's financial situation, cash position, and commitments All these rules relate not only to external acquisitions or divestments, but also to major investments in organic growth or internal restructuring action. The board of directors should be informed in a timely fashion of the corporation's cash position, and where appropriate take decisions relating to its funding and indebtedness.

(continued)

Germany   The management board and supervisory board work closely together for the benefit of the enterprise.

Supervisory Board

For transactions of fundamental importance, the Articles of Association or the supervisory board specify approval provisions reserved to the supervisory board. They include decisions or measures that fundamentally change the asset, financial, or profit situations of the enterprise.

The task of the supervisory board is to advise regularly and supervise the management board in the management of the enterprise. It must be involved in decisions of fundamental importance to the enterprise.

The supervisory board appoints and dismisses the members of the management board.

The supervisory board shall issue Terms of Reference.

Management Board

The shareholders' general meeting is to be convened by the management board.

The management board ensures that all provisions of law are abided by and works towards their compliance by group companies.

The management board ensures appropriate risk management and risk controlling in the enterprise.

The management board shall establish principles and guidelines for the enterprise.

Terms of Reference shall regulate the allocation of business in the management board.

Italy   Listed companies are governed by a board of directors that meets at regular intervals, and that adopts an organization and a modus operandi that enable it to perform its functions in an effective, efficient manner.

The directors act and pass resolutions with full knowledge of the facts and autonomously and pursue the priority of creating value for the shareholders. Consistent with this goal, they shall also take into account the directives and policies defined for the group of which the issuer is a member, as well as the benefits deriving from being a member of a group.

The board of directors shall:

- Examine and approve the company's strategic, operational, and financial plans and the corporate structure of the group it heads, if any.
- Evaluate the adequacy of the organizational, administrative, and accounting structure of the issuer and its subsidiaries having strategic relevance, as established by the managing directors, in particular with regard to the internal control system and the management of conflicts of interest.
- Delegate powers to the managing directors and to the executive committee and revoke them; it shall specify the limits on these delegated powers, the manner of exercising them, and the frequency, as a rule no less than once every three months, with which the bodies in question must report to the board on the activities performed in the exercise of the powers delegated to them.

(continued)

Panel 4 (*continued*)

- Determine, after examining the proposal of the special committee and consulting the board of auditors, the remuneration of the managing directors and of those directors who are appointed to particular positions within the company and, if the shareholders' meeting has not already done so, determine the total amount to which the members of the board and of the executive committee are entitled.
- Evaluate the general performance of the company, paying particular attention to the information received from the executive committee (when established) and the managing directors, and periodically comparing the results achieved with those planned.
- Examine and approve in advance transactions carried out by the issuer and its subsidiaries having a significant impact on the company's profitability, assets, and liabilities or financial position, paying particular attention to transactions in which one or more directors hold an interest on their own behalf or on behalf of third parties and, in more general terms, to transactions involving related parties; to this end, the board shall establish general criteria for identifying the transactions that might have a significant impact.
- Evaluate, at least once a year, the size, composition, and performance of the board of directors and its committees, eventually characterizing new professional figures whose presence on the board would be considered appropriate.
- Provide information, in the report on CG, on the application of the present Article 1 and, in particular, on the number of meetings of the board and of the executive committee, if any, held during the fiscal year, plus the related percentage of attendance of each director.

Netherlands　Not Covered Directly.

Portugal　The companies' directors shall display due care towards the company, by exhibiting willingness, technical capability, and an understanding of the company's business that is appropriate to their roles, and shall execute their duties with the diligence of a careful and organized director. The companies' directors shall act with loyalty on behalf of the company's interests and take the shareholders' long-term interests into account, as well as other relevant parties, such as employees, clients, and creditors by way of ensuring the company's sustainability. Members of the corporate bodies with supervisory duties shall carry out their duties in the interests of the company, executing proper care and employing high standards of professional diligence and loyalty.

Spain　The board of directors shall perform its duties with unity of purpose and independence from management, according all shareholders the same treatment. It shall be guided at all times by the company's best interest, to be understood as maximizing the company's value over time.

(*continued*)

It will ensure that the company abides by the laws and regulations in its relations with stakeholders; fulfills its obligations and contracts in good faith; respects the customs and good practices of the sectors and territories where it does business; and upholds any additional social responsibility principles it has subscribed to voluntarily.

The core components of the board's mission shall be to approve the company's strategy, authorize the organizational resources to carry it forward, and ensure that management meets the objectives set while pursuing the company's interests and corporate purpose.

Sweden   The principal task of the board of directors is to manage the company's affairs in such a way as to satisfy the owners that their interests in a good long-term return on capital are being met in the best possible way. To meet its obligations to the company's owners, the board of directors is to pay particular attention to:
- establishing the overall goals for the company and deciding the company's strategy for achieving these goals
- evaluating the company's operative management on an ongoing basis and, if necessary, appointing or dismissing the managing director
- ensuring that there is an effective system for follow-up and control of the company's operations and financial position vis-à-vis the established goals
- ensuing that the company's external communications are open, objective, and appropriate for the target audience
- ensuring that there is a satisfactory process for monitoring the company's compliance with laws and other regulations that apply to the company's operations
- ensuring that the necessary guidelines governing the company's ethical conduct are established

The board is to ensure that there is an annual evaluation of its work and that this evaluation employs a systematic and structured process.

United   The board's role is to provide entrepreneurial leadership of the
Kingdom   company within a framework of prudent and effective controls that enable risk to be assessed and managed. The board should set the company's strategic aims, ensure that the necessary financial and human resources are in place for the company to meet its objectives, and review management performance. The board should set the company's values and standards and ensure that its obligations to its shareholders and others are understood and met.

All directors must take decisions objectively in the interests of the company.

As part of their role as members of a unitary board, nonexecutive directors should constructively challenge and help develop proposals on strategy. Nonexecutive directors should scrutinize the performance of management in meeting agreed goals and objectives and monitor the reporting of performance. They should satisfy themselves on the integrity of financial information and that financial controls and systems of risk management are robust and defensible. They are responsible for determining appropriate levels of remuneration of executive directors and have a prime role in appointing, and where necessary removing, executive directors, and in succession planning.

Panel 5: Board Size

Belgium	The board should be small enough for efficient decision making. It should be large enough for its members to contribute experience and knowledge from different fields and for changes to the board's composition to be managed without undue disruption.
Denmark	The Commission *recommends* that the supervisory board have only so many members as to allow a constructive debate and an effective decision-making process that enables all the members of the supervisory board to play an active role and so that the size of the supervisory board allows the competence and experience of the supervisory board members to match the requirements of the company. The Commission *recommends* that at regular intervals, the supervisory board considers whether the number of supervisory board members is appropriate in relation to the requirements of the company.
France	Not Covered.
Germany	**Supervisory Board** Not Covered. **Management Board** The management board shall be comprised of several persons and have a chairman or spokesman. Bylaws shall govern the work of the management board, in particular the allocation of duties among individual management board members, matters reserved for the management board as a whole, and the required majority for management board resolutions (unanimity or resolution by majority vote).
Italy	The board of directors shall evaluate, at least once a year, the size, composition, and performance of the board and its committees, eventually characterizing new professional figures whose presence on the board would be considered appropriate.
Netherlands	Not Covered.
Portugal	Not Covered.
Spain	In the interests of the effectiveness and participatory nature of its functioning, the board of directors should comprise between seven and fifteen members. The board of directors should have an adequate diversity of knowledge, gender, and experience to perform its tasks efficiently, objectively, and in an independent manner.
Sweden	The board should have a size and composition that enable it to embrace the various qualifications and experience needed and to meet the independence criteria required to manage the company's affairs effectively and independently. The renewal of the board should be paced with due consideration for the development of the company's operations as well as for the need for continuity in the work of the board.
United Kingdom	The board should not be so large as to be unwieldy. The board should be of sufficient size that the balance of skills and experience is appropriate for the requirements of the business and that changes to the board's composition can be managed without undue disruption.

Panel 6: Evaluating Board Performance

Belgium	1. Under the lead of its chairman, the board should regularly (e.g., at least every two to three years) assess its size, composition, operation, and interaction with executive management. Regular evaluation by the board of its own effectiveness should promote continuous improvement in the governance of the company.
	2. The nonexecutive directors should regularly (preferably once a year) assess their interaction with executive management. In this respect, nonexecutive directors should meet at least once a year in absence of the CEO and the other executive directors.
	3. There should be a periodic evaluation of the contribution of each director aimed at adapting the composition of the board to take account of changing circumstances. When dealing with reelection, the director's commitment and effectiveness should be evaluated in accordance with a preestablished and transparent procedure. Special attention should be given to the evaluation of the chairman of the board and the chairmen of the committees.
	4. The board should act on the results of the performance evaluation by recognizing its strengths and addressing its weaknesses. Where appropriate, this will involve proposing new members for appointment, proposing not to reelect existing members, or taking any measure deemed appropriate for the effective operation of the board.
Denmark	The committee recommends that the supervisory board *establish* an assessment procedure that regularly and systematically evaluates the work, results, and composition of the supervisory board as well as the work and results of the individual members, including the chairman, for the purpose of improving the supervisory board's work and that the criteria of assessment are clearly defined.
	The committee recommends that such assessment be made *once* a year, that the chairman of the supervisory board be in charge of this process, drawing on external support, if necessary, that the outcome be discussed by the entire supervisory board, and that the supervisory board provide details of its procedures of self-assessment in the company's annual report.
	The committee *recommends* that the supervisory board assess the executive board's work and results once a year according to previously established explicit criteria.
	The committee *recommends* that the executive board and the supervisory board establish a procedure to assess the collaboration between the two boards at an annual meeting between the CEO and the chairman of the supervisory board and that the outcome of such assessment be presented to the entire supervisory board.
	Comment: Assessing the supervisory board as a whole implies a clear need to evaluate the extent to which previously established strategic goals and plans have been met.
France	1. For good CG, the board of directors should evaluate its ability to meet the expectations of the shareholders having entrusted authority to it to direct the corporation and by reviewing from time to time its membership, organization, and operation (which implies a corresponding review of the board's committees).

(*continued*)

Panel 6 (*continued*)

Accordingly, each board should think about the desirable balance in its membership and that of the committees created from among its members, and consider from time to time the adequacy of its organization and operation for the performance of its tasks.

2. The evaluation should have three objectives:
- Assess the way in which the board operates.
- Check that the important issues are suitably prepared and discussed.
- Measure the actual contribution of each director to the board's work through his or her competence and involvement in discussions.

3. The evaluation, which it would be desirable to see becoming annual, should be performed in the following manner:
- Once a year, the board should dedicate one of the points on its agenda to a debate concerning its operation.
- There should be a formal evaluation at least once every three years. It could be implemented, possibly under the leadership of an independent director, with help from an external consultant.
- The shareholders should be informed each year in the annual report of the evaluations carried out and, if applicable, of any steps taken as a result.
- It is recommended that the directors that are external to the company (i.e., are neither corporate officers nor employees) meet periodically without the "in-house" directors. The internal rules of operation of the board of directors could provide for such a meeting once a year, at which time the evaluation of the chairman and chief executive officer's respective performance would be carried out and the participants could reflect on the future of the company's executive management.

Germany	**Supervisory Board** The supervisory board shall examine the efficiency of its activities on a regular basis. **Management Board** Not Covered Directly. (Compensation of the members of the management board is determined by the supervisory board on the basis of a performance assessment.)
Italy	The board of directors shall evaluate, at least once a year, the size, composition, and performance of the board of directors and its committees, eventually characterizing new professional figures whose presence on the board would be considered appropriate.
Netherlands	Not Covered Directly.
Portugal	Not Covered Directly. (The CG report includes the following matters pertaining to the general meeting: information of the intervention by the general meeting on matters concerning the remuneration policy of the company and the performance assessment of the members of the board of directors.)

(*continued*)

Spain	The board will evaluate the following points on a yearly basis, starting from the report furnished by the Nomination Committee: • the quality and efficiency of the board's stewardship • how well the chairman and chief executive have carried out their duties This power will be exercised directly by the board, and may not be delegated to the executive committee. The board will also evaluate the performance of its committees on the basis of the reports furnished by the same.
Sweden	The chair of the board of directors sees that the work of the board is evaluated annually and that the nomination committee is informed of the result of the evaluation.
United Kingdom	Not Covered Directly. (When evaluating companies' governance arrangements, particularly those relating to board structure and composition, institutional investors should give due weight to all relevant factors drawn to their attention.)

Panel 7: Board Compensation Review

Belgium	7.1. Levels of remuneration should be sufficient to attract, retain, and motivate directors and executive managers who have the profile determined by the board. 7.2. The company should disclose its remuneration policy in its CG charter. **Nonexecutive Directors' Remuneration** 7.3. The remuneration of nonexecutive directors should take into account their responsibilities and time commitment. 7.4. Nonexecutive directors should not be entitled to performance-related remuneration such as bonuses, stock related long-term incentive schemes, fringe benefits, or pension benefits. Under Belgian law, any director's mandate may be terminated "ad nutum" (at any time) without any form of compensation. 7.5. In the CG chapter of the annual report, the company should disclose on an individual basis the amount of the remuneration and other benefits granted directly or indirectly to nonexecutive directors, by the company or any other undertaking belonging to the same group. **Executive Directors' Remuneration** 7.6. Provisions on the remuneration of nonexecutive directors apply to the remuneration of executive directors in their capacity as board members. 7.7. Provisions on the remuneration of executive managers apply to the remuneration of executive directors in their executive capacity. **Executive Managers' Remuneration** 7.8. The board should determine formal and transparent procedures on the remuneration of executive managers. No individual should be involved in deciding his or her own remuneration. 7.9. The board determines the remuneration policy for executive managers. The level and structure of the remuneration of executive managers should be such that qualified and expert professionals can be recruited, retained, and motivated, taking into account the nature and scope of their individual responsibilities.

(continued)

Panel 7 (*continued*)

7.10. If an executive manager is also an executive director, the remuneration should be determined taking into account the compensation received in that person's capacity as a board member.

7.11. An appropriate proportion of an executive manager's remuneration package should be structured so as to link rewards to corporate and individual performance, thereby aligning the executive managers' interest with the interest of the company and its shareholders.

7.12. Where executive managers are eligible for incentives, their grant should be subject to relevant and objective performance conditions designed to enhance corporate value. Evaluation and review procedures for executive managers' performance should be established.

7.13. Schemes under which executive managers are remunerated in shares, share options, or any other right to acquire shares should be subject to prior shareholder approval by way of a resolution at the annual general meeting. The approval should relate to the scheme itself and not to the grant to individuals of share-based benefits under the scheme. As a rule, shares should not vest and options should not be exercisable within less than three years.

7.14. At least once a year, the remuneration committee should discuss with the CEO both the operation and performance of executive management. The CEO should not be present at the discussion of his or her own evaluation. The evaluation criteria should be clearly specified.

7.15. In the CG chapter of the annual report, the company should disclose, on an individual basis, the amount of the remuneration and other benefits granted directly or indirectly to the CEO, by the company or any other undertaking belonging to the same group. This information should be disclosed with a split between:

- basic remuneration
- variable remuneration: any incentive relating to the financial reported year
- other components of the remuneration, such as cost of pension, insurance coverage, and monetary value of other fringe benefits, with an explanation and, if appropriate, the amounts of the main components

7.16. In the CG chapter of the annual report, the company should disclose, on a global basis, the amount of the remuneration and other benefits granted directly or indirectly to the other members of executive management, by the company or any other undertaking belonging to the same group. This information should be disclosed with a split between:

- basic remuneration
- variable remuneration: any incentive relating to the financial reported year
- other components of the remuneration, such as cost of pension, insurance coverage, and monetary value of other fringe benefits, with an explanation and, if appropriate, the amounts of the main components

7.17. For the CEO and the other executive managers, the CG chapter of the annual report should disclose, on an individual basis, the number and key features of shares, share options, or any other right to acquire shares, granted during the year.

(*continued*)

7.18. The company should disclose in the CG chapter of the annual report the main contractual terms of hiring and termination arrangements with executive managers. Compensation commitments in the event of early termination should be carefully considered. The aim should be to avoid rewarding poor performance.

Denmark

Competitive remuneration is a prerequisite for attracting and retaining competent members of the supervisory board and the executive board. The remuneration of the members of the supervisory and executive boards should be reasonable in relation to the tasks assigned and the responsibilities involved in performing these tasks.

Performance-related pay may result in convergence of interests between the shareholders and the management of the company and may cause the management to focus on increasing the company's value creation.

It is essential that there be openness about all important issues regarding the principles and amounts of the total remuneration offered to the members of the supervisory board and the executive board.

France

The law provides that the board of directors has sole authority to determine the compensation of the chairman, chief executive officer, and chief operating officers. It also provides a duty for corporations to specify in their annual reports the total compensation and benefits of all kinds paid, during the financial year, to each corporate officer, and the amount of compensation and benefits of all kinds received during the financial year by each such officer from group affiliates.

Germany

Supervisory Board

Compensation of the members of the supervisory board is specified by resolution of the general meeting or in the Articles of Association.

It takes into account the responsibilities and scope of tasks of the members of the supervisory board as well as the economic situation and performance of the enterprise. Members of the supervisory board shall receive a fixed salary as well as performance-related compensation. Performance-related compensation should also contain components based on long-term performance of the enterprise.

Management Board

Compensation of the members of the management board is determined by the supervisory board under consideration of group payments, if any, at an appropriate sum and on the basis of a performance assessment. Criteria for determining the appropriateness of compensation are, in particular, the tasks of the member of the management board, performance, the economic situation, [and] the performance and outlook of the enterprise.

Compensation of the members of the management board shall be comprised of a fixed salary and variable components. Variable compensation should include one-time and annually payable components linked to the performance of the enterprise as well as long-term incentives. In particular, stock options or comparable instruments (e.g., phantom stocks) serve as variable compensation components with long-term incentive effect.

(*continued*)

Panel 7 (*continued*)

Italy	7.P.1. The remuneration of directors shall be established in a sufficient amount to attract, maintain, and motivate directors endowed with the professional skills necessary for managing the issuer successfully. 7.P.2. The remuneration of executive directors shall be articulated in such a way as to align their interests with pursuing the priority objective of creating value for the shareholders in a medium- to long-term time frame. 7.P.3. The board of directors shall establish among its members a remuneration committee, made up of nonexecutive directors, the majority of which are independent.
Netherlands	1. The overall remuneration package must be tested for reasonableness and effectiveness. With regard to the level of remuneration, the supervisory board must form an independent judgment and not only assess it on the basis of market comparisons or historical precedents. 2. The link between the remuneration policy and the company's long-term strategic objectives must be explicitly defined and must be testable. A substantial part of the overall remuneration package must be linked directly to predetermined performance objectives; the executive remuneration must also be largely of a long-term nature. 3. The remuneration system must take account of the prevailing social standards and values. This will prevent outcomes that could be seen as excessive. A good remuneration system provides the right incentives but does not unintentionally encourage behavior that conflicts with the interests of the company or leads to the reporting rules or other legal provisions being applied in a way that runs counter to their material purpose.
Portugal	1. The remuneration may be set or may consist partially of a percentage of the profits for the financial year; however, the maximum value of that percentage shall be authorized in the articles of association. 2. The remuneration of the members of the general and supervisory board, the audit board, and the audit committee shall consist exclusively of a fixed amount.
Spain	The company's remuneration policy, as approved by its board of directors, will specify at least the following points: a) the amount of the fixed components, itemized where necessary, of board and board committee attendance fees, with an estimate of the fixed annual payment they give rise to b) performance-related components, in particular: i) the types of directors they apply to, with an explanation of the relative weight of variable to fixed remuneration items ii) performance evaluation criteria used to calculate entitlement to the award of shares or stock options or any performance-related remuneration iii) the main parameters and justification for any system of annual bonuses or other, noncash benefits c) main characteristics of pension systems (for example, supplementary pensions, life insurance, and similar arrangements) In the case of performance-related awards, the remuneration policy statement will be accompanied by an estimate of the total remuneration resulting as a function of degree of compliance with the applicable benchmarks.

(*continued*)

Remuneration policy will also specify the conditions to apply to the contracts of executive directors exercising senior management functions. Among them:
a) the term of their contracts
b) notice periods
c) any other clauses covering hiring bonuses, as well as indemnities or 'golden parachutes' in the event of early termination of the contractual relation between company and executive director

Sweden   The board is responsible for seeing that the company has a formal process, which is transparent for all board members, for establishing the company's policy for remuneration and other terms of employment for senior management and for deciding the managing director's remuneration and other terms of employment.

United   Levels of remuneration should be sufficient to attract, retain, and
Kingdom   motivate directors of the quality required to run the company successfully, but a company should avoid paying more than is necessary for this purpose. A significant proportion of executive directors' remuneration should be structured so as to link rewards to corporate and individual performance.

Supporting Principle

The remuneration committee should judge where to position their company relative to other companies. But they should use such comparisons with caution, in view of the risk of an upward ratchet of remuneration levels with no corresponding improvement in performance. They should also be sensitive to pay and employment conditions elsewhere in the group, especially when determining annual salary increases.

Panel 8: Board Meetings and Agenda

Belgium   The chairman sets the agenda of the board meetings, after consultation with the CEO, and ensures that procedures relating to preparatory work, deliberations, passing of resolutions, and implementation of decisions are properly followed. The minutes of the meeting should sum up the discussions, specify any decisions taken, and state any reservations voiced by directors.
The agenda should list the topics to be discussed and specify whether they are for information, for deliberation, or for decision-making purposes.
The chairman is responsible for ensuring that the directors receive accurate, timely, and clear information before the meetings and, where necessary, between meetings. All directors should receive the same board information.
The number of board and board committee meetings and the individual attendance record of directors should be disclosed in the CG chapter of the annual report.
The board should meet sufficiently regularly to discharge its duties effectively.

(*continued*)

Panel 8 (*continued*)

Denmark	The committee recommends that the general meeting be called with sufficient notice to enable the shareholders to prepare for the meeting and consider the business to be transacted at the general meeting that the notice of meeting, including the agenda, be drawn up in such a way as to give the shareholders a satisfactory picture of the business covered by the items on the agenda and that proxies given to a company's supervisory board, as far as possible, include the position of the shareholders regarding each item on the agenda. The chairman aims to ensure that the supervisory board's meeting frequency is planned in such a way as to allow it to act as a sounding board for the members of the executive board and to respond quickly and effectively at any time. The committee recommends that the supervisory board meet at regular intervals according to a predetermined meeting and work schedule or when meetings are deemed necessary or appropriate as required by the company, and that the annual meeting frequency be published in the annual report.
France	10.1. The number of meetings of the board of directors and of the committees held during the past financial year should be mentioned in the annual report, which must also provide the shareholders with any relevant information relating to the directors' attendance at such meetings. 10.2. The frequency and duration of meetings of the board of directors should be such that they allow in-depth review and discussion of the matters subject to the board's authority. The same applies for meetings of the board's committees (audit, compensation, options, appointments, etc.). 10.3. Proceedings should be unambiguous. The minutes of the meeting should summarize the discussion and specify the decisions made. They are of particular importance because they provide, if necessary, a record of what the board has done in order to carry out its duties. Without being unnecessarily detailed, they should mention briefly questions raised or reservations stated.
Germany	**Supervisory Board** The chairman of the supervisory board coordinates the work of the supervisory board (§ I). In supervisory boards with codetermination, representatives of the shareholders and employees should prepare the supervisory board meetings, each separately, possibly with members of the management board. The chairman of the supervisory board coordinates work within the supervisory board and chairs its meetings. The chairman of the supervisory board shall prepare the supervisory board meetings. **Management Board** The chairman of the management board coordinates the work of the management board's members.
Italy	The chairman shall call the meetings of the board. The chairman shall coordinate the activities of the board of directors and moderate its meetings.

(*continued*)

Netherlands	Not Covered.
Portugal	Not Covered.
Spain	The chairman shall be responsible for the proper operation of the board of directors. He or she will ensure that directors are supplied with sufficient information in advance of board meetings, and will work to ensure a good level of debate. He or she will organize and coordinate regular evaluations of the board and, when different from the chairman of the board, the company's chief executive, along with the chairmen of the relevant committees.
Sweden	The chair of the board of directors, after consulting with the managing director, draw up proposals for the board meeting's agenda.
United Kingdom	The board should meet regularly. The board should have a formal schedule of matters specifically reserved to it for decision making.

Panel 9: Board Information Flow, Materials, and Presentations

Belgium	The chairman is responsible for ensuring that the directors receive accurate, timely, and clear information before the meetings and, where necessary, between meetings. All directors should receive the same board information. The chairman should ensure that all directors can make a knowledgeable and informed contribution to board discussions and that there is sufficient time for consideration and discussion before decision making.
Denmark	The committee recommends that the supervisory board establish procedures for how the executive board reports to the supervisory board and for any other communication between the supervisory board and the executive board with a view to ensuring that such information about the company's business as required by the supervisory board is regularly provided to the supervisory board. *Comment:* In all circumstances, the executive board must ensure that the supervisory board is provided with essential information, whether the supervisory board has requested such information or not. The directors are solely responsible for actively obtaining knowledge and continuously keeping themselves posted about the conditions of the company and the industry in question.
France	Corporations are bound to provide to their directors the information required for effective participation in proceedings of the board, prior, if appropriate, to meetings of the board, in order to enable them to perform their duties in an appropriate manner. The same is true throughout the life of the corporation between meetings of the board, if the importance or urgency of the information so require. That permanent disclosure should also include any relevant information, including criticism, relating to the corporation, such as articles in the press and financial analysts' reports.

(continued)

Panel 9 (*continued*)

	Conversely, the directors are bound to request the appropriate information that they consider as necessary to perform their duties. Accordingly, if a director considers that he or she has not been enabled to take part in the proceedings with appropriate information, he or she is bound to say so to the board and to demand the necessary information. The director is under a duty to obtain information. To that end, he or she should demand of the chairman in due time the information required for useful meeting participation with respect to the matters on the board's agenda.
Germany	Providing adequate information to the supervisory board is the joint responsibility of the management board and supervisory board. The management board informs the supervisory board regularly, without delay and comprehensively, of all issues important to the enterprise with regard to planning, business development, risk situation, and risk management. The management board brings up deviations in planning from previously formulated objectives and indicates the reasons. The supervisory board shall specify the management board's information and reporting duties. The management board's reports to the supervisory board are, as a rule, to be submitted in written form. Documents required for decisions, in particular, the annual financial statements, the consolidated financial statements, and the auditors' report, are to be sent to the members of the supervisory board, if possible, in due time before the meeting. Good CG requires an open discussion between the management board and supervisory board as well as among the members within the management board and the supervisory board. The comprehensive observance of confidentiality is of decisive importance for this. All board members ensure that the staff members they employ observe the confidentiality obligation in the same manner.
Italy	The chairman of the board of directors shall use his/her best efforts in order to ensure that the material information and documents for enabling the board to make its decisions are made available to its members according to adequate procedures and timing. The board of directors may request of the managing directors that executives of the issuer or the group participate in the meetings of the board, in order to supply the appropriate supplemental information on the items on the agenda. In particular, the lead independent director shall collaborate with the chairman for the purpose of ensuring that the directors are addressees of complete timely flows of information. The managing directors shall ensure the correct handling of corporate information; to this end they shall propose to the board of directors the adoption of a procedure for the internal handling and disclosure to third parties of documents and information concerning the issuer, having special regard to price sensitive information.
Netherlands	Not Covered.

(*continued*)

Portugal	When directors that carry out executive duties are requested by other board members to supply information, the former shall do so in a timely manner and the information supplied shall adequately suffice the request made.
Spain	The chairman shall be responsible for the proper operation of the board of directors. He or she will ensure that directors are supplied with sufficient information in advance of board meetings, and will work to ensure a good level of debate. Board members will be provided with sufficient information far enough in advance to properly fulfill their duties of care under the Public Limited Companies Law.
Sweden	In order to be able to fulfill their responsibilities, the members of the board should have access to correct, relevant, and current information.
United Kingdom	The board should be supplied in a timely manner with information in a form and of a quality appropriate to enable it to discharge its duties. All directors should receive induction on joining the board and should regularly update and refresh their skills and knowledge. The chairman is responsible for ensuring that the directors receive accurate, timely, and clear information. Management has an obligation to provide such information but directors should seek clarification or amplification where necessary. The chairman should ensure that the directors continually update their skills and the knowledge and familiarity with the company required to fulfill their roles both on the board and on board committees. The company should provide the necessary resources for developing and updating its directors' knowledge and capabilities.

Panel 10: Executive Compensation

Belgium	1. Levels of remuneration should be sufficient to attract, retain, and motivate directors and executive managers who have the profile determined by the board. 2. The company should disclose its remuneration policy in its CG charter. The board should determine formal and transparent procedures on the remuneration of executive managers. No individual should be involved in deciding his or her own remuneration. 3. The board determines the remuneration policy for executive managers. The level and structure of the remuneration of executive managers should be such that qualified and expert professionals can be recruited, retained, and motivated, taking into account the nature and scope of their individual responsibilities. 4. If an executive manager is also an executive director, the remuneration should be determined taking into account the compensation received in that person's capacity as a board member. 5. An appropriate proportion of an executive manager's remuneration package should be structured so as to link rewards to corporate and individual performance, thereby aligning the executive managers' interest with the interest of the company and its shareholders.

(*continued*)

Panel 10 (*continued*)

Denmark	Competitive remuneration is a prerequisite for attracting and retaining competent members of the supervisory board and the executive board. The remuneration of the members of the supervisory and executive boards should be reasonable in relation to the tasks assigned and the responsibilities involved in performing these tasks. Performance-related pay may result in convergence of interests between the shareholders and the management of the company and may cause the management to focus on increasing the company's value creation. It is essential that there be openness about all important issues regarding the principles and amounts of the total remuneration offered to the members of the supervisory board and the executive board.
France	The law provides that the board of directors has sole authority to determine the compensation of the chairman, chief executive officer, and chief operating officers. It also provides a duty for corporations to specify in their annual reports the total compensation and benefits of all kinds paid, during the financial year, to each corporate officer, and the amount of compensation and benefits of all kinds received during the financial year by each such officer from group affiliates.
Germany	Not Covered.
Italy	1. The remuneration of directors shall be established in a sufficient amount to attract, maintain, and motivate directors endowed with the professional skills necessary for managing the issuer successfully. 2. The remuneration of executive directors shall be articulated in such a way as to align their interests with pursuing the priority objective of creating value for the shareholders in a medium-to long-term time frame. 3. The board of directors shall establish among its members a remuneration committee, made up of nonexecutive directors, the majority of which are independent.
Netherlands	Not Covered.
Portugal	The general meeting of shareholders or a remuneration committee appointed by the general meeting shall be responsible for setting the remuneration of each of the members of the board of directors, including the members of the audit committee, audit board, and the general and supervisory board.
Spain	Not Covered.
Sweden	Not Covered.
United Kingdom	There should be a formal and transparent procedure for developing policy on executive remuneration and for fixing the remuneration packages of individual directors. No director should be involved in deciding his or her own remuneration. The remuneration committee should consult the chairman and/or chief executive about their proposals relating to the remuneration of other executive directors. The remuneration committee should also be responsible for appointing any consultants in respect of executive director remuneration. Where executive directors or senior management are involved in advising or supporting the remuneration committee, care should be taken to recognize and avoid conflicts of interest. The chairman of the board should ensure that the company maintains contact as required with its principal shareholders about remuneration in the same way as for other matters.

Panel 11: Content and Character of Disclosure

Belgium	9.1. The company should establish a CG charter describing all the main aspects of its CG policy, including at least the elements listed in the provisions of Appendix F.
	9.2. The company should state in its CG charter that it follows the CG principles laid down in this code.
	9.3. The CG charter should be updated as often as needed to reflect the company's CG at any time. It should be available on the company's website specifying the date of the most recent update.
	9.4. The company should establish a CG chapter in its annual report describing all relevant CG events that took place during the year under review. That document should include at least the elements listed in the provisions of Appendix F. If the company does not fully comply with one or more provisions of this code, it should explain why in the CG chapter of its annual report.
	9.5. Whenever price-sensitive information or information relating to changes in the shareholders' rights occur in relation to CG, the company should disclose it immediately.
	Price-sensitive information or information relating to changes in the shareholders' rights must be understood within the meaning of Article 6, § 1 of the Royal Decree of March 31, 2003, on the obligations of issuers of financial instruments admitted to trading on a Belgian regulated market.
Denmark	To a varying extent, it is necessary to provide shareholders, including potential shareholders, and other stakeholders with information about the company. Understanding and relating to the company depend on the amount of information and the quality of information published or provided by the company. Openness and transparency are essential conditions for ensuring that the company's shareholders and other stakeholders are able to regularly evaluate and relate to the company and its prospects and so to contribute to constructive interaction with the company.
	Furthermore, the committee recommends that the company draw up procedures to ensure immediate publication of all essential information of importance for how the shareholders and the financial markets evaluate the company and its activities as well as its business goals, strategies, and results in a reliable and sufficient manner unless publication can be omitted according to stock exchange legal rules.
	The committee recommends that information be published in both Danish and English, and, if necessary, in any other relevant languages; this also applies to the company's website, which must display identical information in these languages.
France	Each corporation should have a very rigorous policy for communications with analysts and the market. Certain practices of "selective disclosure," intended to assist analysts with their forecasts of results, should be dropped. The normal method for communication is a press release, which makes the same information available to all at the same time.
	Listed corporations should take all appropriate action to comply with the following schedule:

(*continued*)

Panel 11 (*continued*)

	• Final consolidated half-yearly accounts should be published no later than two and a half months after the end of the first half if estimated or provisional accounts have not been published earlier. • If the corporation publishes estimated or provisional consolidated annual accounts, they should be published no later than one month after the close of the financial year and followed by final accounts no later than three months after that time. Otherwise, the final accounts should be published within two months after the close of the financial year.
Germany	The management board submits to the general meeting the established annual financial statements and the consolidated financial statements. The management board shall not only provide the reports and documents, including the annual report, required by law for the general meeting, and send them to shareholders upon request, but shall also publish them on the company's Internet site together with the agenda. The company shall inform all domestic and foreign financial services providers, shareholders, and shareholders' associations, who, in the preceding twelve months, have requested such notification, of the convening of the general meeting together with the convention documents, upon request, also using electronic channels. The management board will disclose any new facts that have arisen within the enterprise's field of activity that are not known publicly without delay, if such facts could, owing to their impact on the asset and financial situations or general business development, substantially influence the stock price of the company's registered securities. The company's treatment of all shareholders in respect of information shall be equal. It shall make all new facts that have been made known to the financial analysts and similar addressees available to the shareholders without delay. The consolidated financial statements shall be publicly accessible within ninety days of the end of the financial year; interim reports shall be publicly accessible within forty-five days of the end of the reporting period.
Italy	Directors and members of the board of auditors shall keep confidential the documents and information acquired in the performance of their duties and shall comply with the procedure adopted by the issuer for the internal handling and disclosure to third parties of such documents and information. The managing directors shall ensure the correct handling of corporate information; to this end they shall propose to the board of directors the adoption of a procedure for the internal handling and disclosure to third parties of documents and information concerning the issuer, having special regard to price sensitive information.
Netherlands	Not Covered.
Portugal	All information on securities and its issuers that might influence the investors' decisions or is supplied to supervisory entities as well as to the market, settlement systems, and centralized securities systems management entities, shall be complete, true, current, clear, objective, and lawful.

(*continued*)

The companies issuing securities admitted to trading on a regulated market situated or functioning in Portugal are obliged to ensure the disclosure of a set of information on the CG structure and practices either as a chapter in the annual management report specially drawn up for the purpose or as an annex to same.

Spain

The financial information that listed companies must periodically disclose. The committee shall ensure that intermediate statements are drawn up under the same accounting principles as the annual statements and, to this end, may ask the external auditor to conduct a limited review.

Sweden

The CG report is to present information on the manner in which the board ensures the quality of the financial reports and communicates with the company's auditors.

The CG report is also to provide the following information, if it is not included in the annual report:

- a statement explaining the procedures leading to the appointment of the board of directors and auditors
- the composition of the company's nomination committee and where appropriate, a separate nomination committee appointed to propose auditors (if a member of such a committee has represented a particular owner, that owner's name is to be stated)
- for auditors, the information to be provided
- the division of work among directors and a statement on how the work of the board was conducted during the most recent financial year, including the number of board meetings and each member's attendance at board meetings
- the composition, tasks, and decision-making authority of board committees, if any, and each member's attendance at committee meetings
- for the managing director:
  - age and principal education and work experience
  - significant professional commitments outside the company
  - his or her own holdings of shares and other financial instruments in the company or those holdings by related natural or legal persons
  - material shareholdings and part ownership in enterprises with which the company has business ties

United Kingdom

The board should present a balanced and understandable assessment of the company's position and prospects (Principle D.1).

The directors should explain their responsibility for preparing the accounts, and there should be a statement by the auditors about their reporting responsibilities (Code § 1, D.1.1).

The board's responsibility to present a balanced and understandable assessment extends to interim and other price-sensitive public reports and reports to regulators as well as to information required to be presented by statutory requirements (Code § 1, D.1.2).

The directors should, at least annually, conduct a review of the effectiveness of the group's system of internal control and should report to shareholders that they have done so. The review should cover all controls, including financial, operational, and compliance controls and risk management (Code § 1, D.2.1).

The board should establish formal and transparent arrangements for considering how they should apply the financial reporting and internal control principles and for maintaining an appropriate relationship with the company's auditors (Principle D.3).

Panel 12: Disclosure Regarding Compensation and Director Assessment

Belgium	In the CG chapter of the annual report, the company should disclose on an individual basis the amount of the remuneration and other benefits granted directly or indirectly to nonexecutive directors, by the company or any other undertaking belonging to the same group.
Denmark	The committee recommends that the annual report include information about the amounts of total remuneration of the individual members of the supervisory board and the executive board provided by the company or other companies within the same group.
	The annual report should contain all clear and comprehensible information about the remuneration of the individual members of the management body that is easy to understand by the individual shareholder and that enables the shareholder to follow up on the compliance with the remuneration policy and the general guidelines adopted for incentive pay.
France	It seems reasonable that more complete information should be provided to the shareholders and that they should be made aware clearly not only of the individual compensation paid to corporate officers, but also of the overall cost of their group's general management and the policy applied for the determination of their compensation.
	Listed corporations' annual reports should include a chapter, drafted with assistance from the compensation committee, dedicated to information to the shareholders relating to the compensation received by managers, containing the following three parts:
	• *The first part* should set out in detail the policy for the determination of corporate officers' compensation: principles for allocation of fixed and variable portions, criteria determining the grounds used for the variable parts, rules for awards of bonuses.
	• *The second part* should specify in detail the individual compensation of each corporate officer and the total amount of compensation collected by the corporate officers during the elapsed financial year, compared with the previous financial year, and broken down between fixed and variable parts in aggregate.
	• *The third part* should specify the aggregate and individual amount of attendance fees paid to the directors and the rules for allocation among them, and the rules for collection of attendance fees paid to members of the general-management team in connection with corporate offices held in group affiliates.
	The compensation committee should define the rules for determination of this variable portion, ensuring that they are consistent with the annual evaluation of the corporate officers' performance and the corporation's medium-term strategy; it should then review the annual application of those rules. It should also evaluate the total compensation and benefits collected by such managers, if any, from other group affiliates, including pension benefits and other benefits of all kinds.
	The committee should be informed of the policy for compensation of the main managers who are not corporate officers. For this, the committee shall act in conjunction with the corporate officers.
Germany	**Supervisory Board**
	The total compensation of the members of the supervisory board shall be reported in the notes of the consolidated financial statements, subdivided according to components. Also payments made by the enterprise to the members of the supervisory board or advantages extended for services provided individually, in particular advisory or agency services, shall be listed separately in the notes to the consolidated financial statements.

(continued)

Management Board

The concrete details of a stock option plan or comparable compensation system shall be disclosed in a suitable form.

Compensation of the members of the management board shall be reported in the notes of the consolidated financial statements subdivided according to fixed, performance-related, and long-term incentive components. The figures should be individualized.

The consolidated financial statements shall contain information on stock option programs and similar securities-based incentive systems.

Italy	Not Covered.
Netherlands	All aspects of executive remuneration, including the policy, objectives, and results, must be reported on transparently, fully, and consistently in the annual report.
Portugal	Information should be disclosed on the actual remuneration of each member of the board of directors and executive management of the company.
Spain	Remuneration comprising the delivery of shares in the company or other companies in the group, stock options or other share-based incentives, or incentive payments linked to the company's performance or membership of pension schemes shall be confined to executive directors. The delivery of shares is excluded from this limitation, when such delivery is contingent on directors retaining the shares till the end of their tenure. Director remuneration shall sufficiently compensate them for the commitment, qualifications, and responsibility that the post entails, but should not be so high as to jeopardize their independence. In the case of remuneration linked to company earnings, deductions should be computed for any qualifications stated in the external auditor's report. In the case of performance-related awards, remuneration policies should include technical safeguards to ensure they reflect the professional performance of the beneficiaries and not simply the general progress of the markets or the company's sector, atypical or exceptional transactions, or circumstances of this kind.
Sweden	The CG report is also to provide the following information, if it is not included in the annual report the policy on remuneration and other terms of employment for senior management approved at the most recent shareholders' meeting and, in the event of significant differences from the preceding year's terms, a statement of what these differences are and the procedures followed by the board in preparing matters of remuneration for senior management.
United Kingdom	Companies should establish a formal and transparent procedure for developing policy on executive remuneration and for fixing the remuneration packages of individual executive directors. No director should be involved in deciding his or her own remuneration. The company's annual report should contain a statement of remuneration policy and details of the remuneration of each director. The board should report to the shareholders each year on remuneration. The report should form part of, or be annexed to, the company's annual report and accounts. It should be the main vehicle through which the company reports to shareholders on directors' remuneration. The report should set out the company's policy on executive directors' remuneration. It should draw attention to factors specific to the company. In preparing the remuneration report, the board should follow the provisions in Schedule B to this code. Shareholders should be invited specifically to approve all new long term incentive schemes (as defined in the Listing Rules) save in the circumstances permitted.

Panel 13: Disclosure Regarding CG

Belgium	9.1. The company should establish a CG charter describing all the main aspects of its CG policy, including at least the elements listed in the provisions of Appendix F. 9.2. The company should state in its CG charter that it follows the CG principles laid down in this code. 9.3. The CG charter should be updated as often as needed to reflect the company's CG at any time. It should be available on the company's website specifying the date of the most recent update. 9.4. The company should establish a CG chapter in its annual report describing all relevant CG events that took place during the year under review. That document should include at least the elements listed in the provisions of Appendix F. If the company does not fully comply with one or more provisions of this code, it should explain why in the CG chapter of its annual report. 9.5. Whenever price-sensitive information or information relating to changes in the shareholders' rights occur in relation to CG, the company should disclose it immediately. Price-sensitive information or information relating to changes in the shareholders' rights must be understood within the meaning of Article 6, § 1 of the Royal Decree of March 31, 2003, on the obligations of issuers of financial instruments admitted to trading on a Belgian regulated market.
Denmark	The committee recommends that the annual report contain the following information about supervisory board members: • occupation of the individual supervisory board member • other managerial positions or directorships held by the supervisory board member in Danish and foreign companies as well as demanding organizational tasks performed by that individual • number of shares, options, and warrants held by the supervisory board member in the company and group enterprises as well as changes in the member's portfolio of the mentioned securities having taken place during the financial year The committee recommends that the individual company consider the need to explain the system of staff-elected supervisory board members in the company's annual report or on its website. The committee recommends that information about the most important aspects of severance programs be disclosed in the company's annual report.
France	The French position seems unique in that no other country offers the option between a unitary system (board of directors) and a dual system (supervisory board and board of management) in all corporations, including listed corporations. It is essential that the shareholders and third parties be fully informed of the options and of the allocation of powers selected by the board. The annual report is the location for the information due to the shareholders, to which the reasons for, and justification of, the options made by the board should be reported. It ought to be possible to append the rules of operation, having become the basic collection of rules for internal operation, to the bylaws, or at least to disclose them to third parties.

(continued)

Information to the latter relating to the nature of the election made could also be provided by measures such as an entry in the Registry of Commerce and Companies or a mention in the corporate documents.

The annual report should specify the number of meetings of the board of directors and board committees held during the elapsed financial year, and provide the shareholders with information as to the directors' actual attendance at the meetings.

The annual report should specify precisely the dates of the initiation and expiry of each director's term, so as to highlight the staggering of directors' terms.

It should also mention for each director his or her age, major position, and directorships in other listed corporations (other than group affiliates), and specify the names of all the members of each board committee.

Germany	The management board and supervisory board shall report on the enterprise's CG in the annual report. This also includes explanation of possible deviations from this code.
	If a member of the supervisory board did not personally take part in more than half of the meetings of the supervisory board in a financial year, this shall be noted in the report of the supervisory board.
	In its report, the supervisory board shall inform the general meeting of any conflicts of interest that have occurred together with their treatment.
Italy	Among the matters reserved to the competence of the board, this article mentions the evaluation of the adequacy of the organizational, administrative, and accounting structure of the issuer and of its subsidiaries having strategic relevance; it is pointed out that such relevance should be evaluated with reference to criteria that do not concern only the size, to be mentioned in the report on CG.
Netherlands	Companies should state which recommendations of the CG Commission they are not adopting and why.
	A company should only accept a so-called "structure regime" by choice if this decision has been put to (annual) approval of shareholders at the annual meeting.
	The annual report must state whether each supervisory board member is independent from management and any majority shareholders.
	Profiles of the supervisory board and its rules and regulations should be made available to shareholders. The management structure must be transparent.
	The company must clearly disclose its strategy and the decision-making process within the company.
Portugal	Companies shall set up internal control systems in order to efficiently detect any risk to the company's activity by protecting its assets and keeping its CG transparent.
	The company is obliged to disclose in its CG report the identity of its nonexecutive members of the board of directors as well as the members of other established committees that fully comply with the incompatibility rules provided for in II.1.3.1., except for item (ii) and the independence criterion mentioned in II.1.3.6.

(*continued*)

Panel 13 (*continued*)

	The CG report shall include the main elements on the business deals and operations carried out in the company and among the members of the management and supervisory bodies, holders of qualifying holdings, or companies that find themselves in a control or group relation, provided they are significant in economic terms for any of the parties involved, except for businesses or operations that are carried out collectively, under normal market conditions for similar operations and are part of the day-to-day activity of the company.
Spain	The board of directors should include in its public annual report some information concerning its governance rules, providing an explanation in connection with any rules deviating from the recommendations of this committee.

Sweden	In the CG report, the company is to state that it is applying the code and give a brief description of how this has been done in the most recent financial year. The company is to indicate where it has departed from the rules in the code. The reasons for each departure are to be clearly explained.
	5.1.3. The CG report is to present information on the manner in which the board ensures the quality of the financial reports and communicates with the company's auditors in accordance with 3.8.1.
	5.1.4. The CG report is also to provide the following information, if it is not included in the annual report:
	• a statement explaining the procedures leading to the appointment of the board of directors and auditors
	• the composition of the company's nomination committee and where appropriate, a separate nomination committee appointed to propose auditors (if a member of such a committee has represented a particular owner, that owner's name is to be stated)
	• for each member of the board, the information to be provided in accordance with the points listed in 2.2.3
	• for auditors, the information to be provided in accordance with the first and second sentences of 2.3.3
	• the division of work among directors and a statement on how the work of the board was conducted during the most recent financial year, including the number of board meetings and each member's attendance at board meetings
	• the composition, tasks, and decision-making authority of board committees, if any, and each member's attendance at committee meetings
	• for the managing director:
	  – age and principal education and work experience
	  – significant professional commitments outside the company
	  – his or her own holdings of shares and other financial instruments in the company or those holdings by related natural or legal persons
	  – material shareholdings and part ownership in enterprises with which the company has business ties

(*continued*)

- the policy on remuneration and other terms of employment
for senior management approved at the most recent shareholders' meeting and, in the event of significant differences
from the preceding year's terms, a statement of what these
differences are and the procedures followed by the board in
preparing matters of remuneration for senior management
- outstanding share and share-price incentive schemes for the
board and senior management

United Kingdom	The board should establish formal and transparent arrangements for considering how they should apply the financial reporting and internal control principles and for maintaining an appropriate relationship with the company's auditors.

The chairman, chief executive officer, and senior independent director should be identified in the annual report.

Nonexecutive directors considered by the board to be independent
should be identified in the annual report.

The chairman and members of the nomination committee should be
identified in the annual report. The members of the remuneration
committee should be listed each year in the board's remuneration
report to shareholders.

The members of the [audit] committee, a majority of whom should
be independent nonexecutive directors, should be named in the
report and accounts.

Panel 14: Accuracy of Disclosure, Internal Control Systems, Liability

Belgium	It is the board's responsibility to see to the accuracy and complete-ness of the CG charter and CG chapter of the annual report.
Denmark	Efficient risk management is a prerequisite for the board being able to perform the tasks for which it is responsible in the best possible way. Thus it is important that the board ensures that there are appropriate systems for risk management in place and, moreover, ensures that such systems meet the requirements of the company at any time (VII).

The purpose of risk management is:
- to develop and maintain an understanding within the organization of the company's strategic and operational goals, including
identification of the critical success factors
- to analyze these possibilities and challenges that are connected
with the realization of the aforementioned goals and to analyze
the risk of these goals not being met
- to analyze the most important activities of the company in
order to identify the risks attached hereto

The risk management system must define the risk and describe how
this risk is eliminated, controlled, or hedged on a continuous basis.

France	[If French law were amended to allow for the separation of chair-man and CEO roles in a unitary board system, and if] the chair-man of the board of directors is [thus] devoid of management prerogatives, he or she should be subject to either civil or criminal liability only in respect of misconduct in the performance or in connection with performance of his or her personal duties, exclu-sive of mismanagement (p. 8).

(continued)

Panel 14 (*continued*)

The election among various [accounting] standards may be momentous for corporations' earnings, according, for instance, to the duration selected for amortization of goodwill, or the duty to amortize intangible assets or not.

The financial managers and statutory auditors of corporations are naturally in charge of the technical reviews of this matter (p. 18).

The statutory rules with respect to civil and criminal liability will need to be amended so as to provide for the situation where the board of directors elects to separate the positions of chairman and chief executive officer [in a unitary board system], so that the chairman of the board of directors, devoid of management prerogatives, could be held liable only as regards misconduct connected with his personal duties.

Germany

The management board and supervisory board comply with the rules of proper corporate management.

If they violate the due care and diligence of a prudent and conscientious managing director or supervisory board member, they are liable to the company for damages.

If the company takes out directors and officers' liability insurance for the management board and supervisory board, a suitable deductible shall be agreed.

The management board ensures that all provisions of law are abided by and works towards their compliance by group companies.

The management board ensures appropriate risk management and risk controlling in the enterprise. The management board shall establish principles and guidelines for the enterprise.

The consolidated financial statements and interim reports shall be prepared under observance of internationally recognized accounting principles. For corporate law purposes, annual financial statements will be prepared according to national regulations (German commercial code). The consolidated financial statements will be prepared by the management board and examined by the auditor and supervisory board.

Italy

8.P.1. The internal control system is the set of rules, procedures, and organizational structures aimed at making possible a sound and correct management of the company consistent with the established goals, through adequate identification, measurement, management, and monitoring of the main risks.

8.P.2. An effective internal control system contributes to safeguard the company's assets, the efficiency and effectiveness of business transactions, the reliability of financial information, the compliance with laws and regulations.

8.P.3. The board of directors shall evaluate the adequacy of the internal control system with respect to the characteristics of the company.

8.P.4. The board of directors shall ensure that its evaluations and decisions relating to the internal control system, the approval of the balance sheets and the half-yearly reports, and the relationships between the issuer and the external auditor are supported by an adequate preliminary activity. To such purpose the board of directors shall establish an internal control committee, made up of non-executive directors, the majority of which are independent. If the issuer is controlled by another listed company, the internal control committee shall be made up exclusively of independent directors.

(*continued*)

At least one member of the committee must have an adequate experience in accounting and finance, to be evaluated by the board of directors at the time of his/her appointment.

Netherlands	Not Covered.
Portugal	Companies shall set up internal control systems in order to efficiently detect any risk to the company's activity by protecting its assets and keeping its CG transparent.
Spain	The Audit Committee's role will be: 1. With respect to internal control and reporting systems: a) Monitor the preparation and the integrity of the financial information prepared on the company and, where appropriate, the group, check for compliance with legal provisions and the correct application of accounting principles. b) Review internal control and risk management systems on a regular basis, so main risks are properly identified, managed, and disclosed.
Sweden	The board is responsible for the company's internal control, which has the general aim of protecting the shareholders' investment and the company's assets. The board is to ensure that the company has a sound system of internal controls and keeps itself informed of and assesses how well it functions. The board is to submit an annual report on how that part of internal control dealing with financial reporting is organized and how well it has functioned during the most recent financial year. The report is to be reviewed by the company's auditors. The board in companies that do not have a special internal audit function is annually to evaluate the need of such a function and explain the position that it has taken in its report on internal control.
United Kingdom	The board should maintain a sound system of internal control to safeguard shareholders' investment and the company's assets. **Code Provision** The board should, at least annually, conduct a review of the effectiveness of the group's system of internal controls and should report to shareholders that they have done so. The review should cover all material controls, including financial, operational, and compliance controls and risk management systems.

4 International Standards on Auditing
Global Developments, Acting Institutions, and Status of Worldwide Adoption

Holger Erchinger

1. INTRODUCTION

This chapter describes the following organizations involved in setting international auditing standards and discusses the global developments related to International Standards on Auditing (ISAs):

- International Organization of Securities Commissions (IOSCO)
- International Federation of Accountants (IFAC)
- Monitoring Group
- Public Interest Oversight Board (PIOB)
- The Forum of Firms (FOF)
- International Auditing and Assurance Standards Board (IAASB)

2. GLOBAL INSTITUTIONS

2.1 International Organization of Securities Commissions

IOSCO is an association of securities regulators who work together to protect investors and enhance the integrity and orderly operation of the global capital markets. IOSCO is recognized as the leading international policy forum for securities regulators and its members regulate more than 90 percent of the world's securities markets in over one hundred jurisdictions.

IOSCO goals are to:

- Cooperate to promote high regulatory standards to maintain efficient and sound markets.
- Exchange information on respective members' experiences to promote the development of domestic markets.
- Unite efforts to monitor international securities transactions.
- Promote market integrity by effective enforcement against offenses.

IOSCO has encouraged efforts to develop a single set of international auditing standards through the work of the IAASB. It sends an observer to IAASB meetings and has a representative on the IAASB's Consultative Advisory Group (CAG).[1] IOSCO also has responded to exposure drafts issued by the IAASB for its Clarity Project.[2]

The organization believes that a single set of international auditing standards will contribute to uniform global financial reporting that supports investor confidence and decision making. Because many securities regulators accept audits performed using ISAs, they facilitate cross-border securities offerings and listings. IOSCO has actively encouraged their acceptance.

IOSCO recognizes that an independent audit of financial statements is one of the most important items that investors evaluate. The standards by which those audits are conducted are a key contributor to audit quality and the public interest. ISAs, either by themselves or as a touchstone for determining national auditing standards, provide a common auditing language that investors, auditors, audit oversight bodies, and securities regulators can use to carry out their respective roles in the global capital markets

2.2 The International Federation of Accountants

IFAC is the worldwide organization for the accounting profession. Founded in 1977, the organization is comprised of 164 members and associates from 125 countries representing more than 2.5 million accountants employed in public practice, industry, commerce, government, and academe.

IFAC's mission is to serve the public by strengthening the worldwide accountancy profession and contributing to the development of a strong international economy by establishing and promoting adherence to high-quality professional standards, furthering international convergence of standards, and publicly speaking about these issues.

To carry out this mission, IFAC works closely with its members and regional accountancy organizations and obtains input from regulators, standard setters, governments, and others who share IFAC's commitment to a sound global financial system.

IFAC has recognized that a fundamental way to protect the public interest is to develop, promote, and enforce internationally recognized standards to ensure the credibility of information that investors and other stakeholders use.

The IFAC boards set the following standards:

- International Standards on Auditing, Assurance Engagements, and Related Services
- International Standards on Quality Control
- International Code of Ethics
- International Education Standards
- International Public Sector Accounting Standards

IFAC also develops benchmark guidance and promotes sharing resources to serve professional accountants in business. IFAC has also established groups to address issues pertaining to small and medium practices, businesses, and developing nations, which play a critical role in the global economy. International firms that perform audits of financial statements that may be used across national borders are represented in IFAC through the FOF.

Governance of IFAC rests with the IFAC council, which comprises one representative from each member, and the IFAC board. The IFAC board sets policies and oversees operations including implementing programs and the work of IFAC boards and committees.

There are four IFAC standard-setting boards:

- International Accounting Education Standards Board (IAESB)
- International Auditing and Assurance Standards Board (IAASB)
- International Ethics Standards Board for Accountants (IESBA)
- International Public Sector Accounting Standards Board (IPSAB)

Each board follows a due process that supports the development of high-quality standards in a transparent, efficient, and effective manner and has final authority to issue standards. IFAC's constitution and bylaws detail the responsibilities of its council, board, and committees. The PIOB[3] oversees the work of IFAC's Member Body Compliance Program (Program), the IAASB, IAESB, and IESBA.

The Compliance Advisory Panel (CAP) oversees the implementation and operation of the Program. The CAP is also responsible for recommending new members and changes to the application process. IFAC members are required to participate in the Program to demonstrate their good standing and that they are meeting the IFAC membership requirements. The CAP reports annually on its work program, activities, and progress made in achieving its objectives, which is included as part of the IFAC annual report.

IFAC's board is comprised of members who, as representatives of the worldwide accountancy profession, have taken an oath of office to act with integrity and independence in the public interest. The IFAC board's objective, scope of activities, and membership requirements are set out in the Terms of Reference. The board is comprised of the president and twenty-one individuals from eighteen countries who are elected for up to three years and are responsible for setting policy and overseeing IFAC operations, implementing programs, and performing the work of IFAC boards and committees.

The IFAC board is supported by three committees:

- Audit Committee
- Nominating Committee
- Planning and Finance Committee

IFAC has supported the Group of 20 (G-20) leaders' goals that include the adoption of a single set of high-quality global accounting standards. One of the issues at the top of IFAC's agenda, which was reflected in its submission to the G-20 finance ministers in July 2009, is to move forward on implementing common global standards for auditing and auditor independence in additional to accounting standards.

IFAC has steadfastly advocated the adoption of International Financial Reporting Standards (IFRS) and ISAs and believes that global standards will create a level playing field in the interpretation and exchange of financial information and contribute to economic and financial stability. Similarly, the adoption of global standards on auditor independence will help sustain trust in capital markets.

2.2.1 IFAC Strategic Plan 2009–2012

IFAC's Strategic Plan identifies the organization's strategic direction during 2009 to 2012. The following themes and objectives reflect that plan:

- Be recognized as the international standard setter in the areas of auditing and assurance, education, ethics, and governmental financial reporting.
- Actively support the adoption of, and assist in the implementation of, international standards.
- Continually enhance the relevance of the profession.
- Be an influential voice for the global accountancy profession.

2.3 Monitoring Group

The Monitoring Group comprises the regulatory and international organizations responsible for monitoring implementation of the IFAC reforms and acts as an advisor for the IFAC organization. The Monitoring Group also nominates the members of the PIOB, sets its budget, and receives its operating and financial reports.

The Monitoring Group members are:

- Basel Committee on Banking Supervision
- European Commission
- Financial Stability Board
- International Association of Insurance Supervisors
- International Organization of Securities Regulators
- World Bank

The International Forum of Independent Audit Regulators (IFIAR) participates as an observer during the meetings of the Monitoring Group. IFIAR was established in September 2006 as an international organization of public accounting firm oversight organizations.

In July 2009, the Monitoring Group launched its review of the effectiveness of the reforms to the governance of the IFAC, which were agreed on in 2003. This assessment, which was foreseen as part of those reforms, included public consultations and the Final Report was published in November 2010.

The objective of the IFAC reforms was to increase confidence that its activities are responsive to the public interest and will lead to the establishment of high-quality standards and practices in auditing and assurance. The focus of the reforms was the areas that have the greatest impact on the public interest, primarily IFAC standard-setting activities, and include the activities of the IAASB, the body responsible for developing and issuing ISAs.

The IFAC reforms were designed to achieve:

- an externally validated process for monitoring IFAC's standard-setting and compliance regimes
- increased transparency of IFAC governance and its international standard-setting activities
- broad-based external participation in IFAC standard-setting activities
- a more collaborative and comprehensive international process for determining how accountants and auditors can best contribute to the integrity of the international financial system

2.4 Public Interest Oversight Board

The PIOB was established in 2005 from a collaborative effort by the international financial regulatory community and related organizations, including IOSCO, the Basel Committee on Banking Supervision, the World Bank, and the Financial Stability Board. The Nominating Committee of the Monitoring Group nominates PIOB members.

The PIOB's objective is to increase investor and other stakeholder confidence that IFAC's public-interest activities, including standard setting by IFAC's independent Boards, are responsive to the public interest.

PIOB oversees the public-interest activities of these IFAC's Public Interest Activity Committees (PIAC):

- IAESB
- IAASB
- IESBA
- CAP

The PIOB also:

- oversees the respective CAGs of the IAASB, IAESB, and IESBA
- reviews and approves the Terms of Reference for these entities
- evaluates the board's due-process procedures

- oversees the work of the IFAC's Nominating Committee
- suggests projects to be added to the board's work program

2.5 The Forum of Firms

The FOF was established in 2002 as an international association of accounting firms that perform audits of financial statements used across national borders. The FOF has twenty-one full members (as of January 2011) who voluntarily agree to meet the requirements detailed in the FOF Constitution. This commitment contributes to raising the standards of the international practice of auditing.

The FOF's objective is to promote consistent and high-quality standards of financial reporting and auditing practices worldwide. The FOF brings together firms that perform transnational audits and involves them more closely with the IFAC activities.

The FOF conducts its business primarily through the Transnational Auditors Committee (TAC) whose members have been nominated by FOF members. The TAC is the executive arm of the FOF and the official linkage between the FOF and the IFAC. The FOF and IFAC work together to set standards, coordinate efforts with the regulatory community, and promote convergence of international standards.

Membership in the FOF is open to professional networks and firms that:

- Have transnational audit appointments or are interested in accepting such appointments.
- Promote the consistent application of high-quality audit practices worldwide, including the use of ISAs.
- Support convergence of national audit standards with ISAs.
- Agree to meet the FOF's membership obligations.

The FOF's membership obligations require that members:

- Maintain appropriate quality control standards based on International Standards on Quality Control issued by the IAASB in addition to relevant national quality control standards.
- Have policies and methodologies for transnational audits that are based, to the extent practicable, on ISAs.
- Have policies and methodologies that conform to the IFAC *Code of Ethics for Professional Accountants* and national codes of ethics.
- Agree to submit to the secretary of the FOF an annual report.

The work of the FOF, which is primarily conducted by the TAC, includes:

- identifying audit practice issues and communicating those to the appropriate IFAC standard-setting board for review

- providing a forum to discuss good practices in areas including quality control, auditing practices, independence, training, and development
- participating in the IFAC Regulatory Liaison Group and identifying qualified candidates to serve on IFAC standard-setting boards
- acting as a formal conduit for interaction among transnational firms and international regulators and financial institutions related to audit quality, systems of quality control, and transparency of international networks

3. THE INTERNATIONAL AUDITING AND ASSURANCE STANDARDS BOARD

3.1 Composition, Objectives, and Scope of Activities

The IAASB is a standard-setting body designated by and operating under the auspices of the IFAC. It is subject to the oversight of the PIOB.

The IAASB serves the public interest by setting independently and under its own authority high-quality auditing, assurance, quality control, and related services standards, and by facilitating the convergence of national and international standards to enhance the quality and uniform practice globally and strengthen public confidence in the global auditing and assurance profession.

The IAASB consists of a full-time chairman and seventeen volunteer members comprising accountants in public practice with significant experience in the field of auditing and other assurance services, and individuals who are non-practitioners. The IAASB meets approximately four times a year at different locations. Its meetings are open to the public.

The IAASB pronouncements govern audit, assurance, and related service engagements conducted using international standards. Through an extensive consultation process, the IAASB strives to ensure that these standards are responsive to the public interest, reflective of business reality, and can be applied by auditors worldwide. Recognizing that the auditor's ability to carry out his or her responsibilities effectively is empowered by the public's trust, the IAASB continually reviews and updates its standards to accommodate changes in the global business and regulatory environments.

3.2 Due Process

The IAASB believes that if the public is to have confidence in audited financial statements, it also must have confidence in the standards that govern auditors' work. The IAASB follows a rigorous process to develop its standards and guidance, which includes soliciting substantial public input. The

IAASB identifies new projects based on a review of national and international developments and on suggestions from those who are interested in the development of its international pronouncements. If a wide range of views is required, the IAASB may hold a public forum or roundtable.

Generally the due process, which has been approved by the PIOB, is comprised of the following steps:

- Research and consultation: a project task force is established and given the responsibility to develop a draft standard. The task force develops its position based on appropriate research and consultation. The task force may include non-IAASB members who have an interest or expertise in the subject.
- Transparent debate: a proposed standard is presented as an agenda paper for discussion and debate at an IAASB meeting, which is open to the public.
- Exposure for public comment: exposure drafts are placed on the IAASB's website and are widely distributed for public comment. The exposure period is usually at least 120 days.
- Consideration of comments received on exposure: the comments and suggestions received are considered at an IAASB meeting and the exposure draft is revised as appropriate. If the changes made after exposure are viewed by the IAASB to be substantive and require reexposure, the revised document will be reissued for further comment.
- Affirmative approval: approval of exposure drafts, reexposure drafts, international standards, and practice statements is made by the affirmative vote of at least two-thirds of the members of the IAASB.

The IAASB makes it a priority to regularly reach out to its stakeholders so it can understand their needs and the public's expectations.

The IAASB receives advice on its work program and on technical matters from its independently chaired CAG, which is comprised of representatives of businesses, investors, and other standard users. The IAASB also works with national auditing standard setters on convergence, collaboration on projects, and shares resources.

3.3 Strategy

During 2008, the IAASB analyzed the results of public consultations and developed and approved the final IAASB *Strategy and Work Program 2009–2011*. The PIOB confirmed that the IAASB followed a due process in developing and finalizing the strategy and work program and approved its completeness from a public-interest perspective.

The strategy builds on the strong base of standards developed by the IAASB to date, and focuses on three areas:

1. developing standards, with an emphasis on those that contribute to the effective operation of the world's capital markets and those relevant to small- and medium-size entities and practices
2. facilitating and monitoring the standards' adoption
3. responding to concerns about the implementation of the standards by designing activities to improve their consistent application

The strategy and work program responds to significant developments in the environment in which audit and other assurance services are performed, and in which standards are set. It also highlights the IAASB's role in working toward global acceptance of and convergence with its standards and in establishing and maintaining relevant partnerships. It is underpinned by the IAASB's communication initiatives to keep stakeholders informed of its activities and to promote adoption and implementation of its standards.

The IAASB's Steering Committee is a standing committee that advises the IAASB on matters of strategic and operational importance and addresses administrative matters that require the IAASB's deliberation. It also acts as counsel and advisor to the IAASB chair and technical director on matters that fulfill the IAASB's objectives. The Steering Committee reports to the IAASB.

The IAASB believes that open and transparent sharing of information with its stakeholders, including national standard setters and regulators, and receptiveness to their input and feedback are critical in gaining global acceptance and adoption and ensuring continuous improvement.

The IAASB's Terms of Reference indicate that IFAC will review the effectiveness of the IAASB process at least every three years. In 2008, IFAC conducted its first triennial review and a review group gathered suggestions from the IAASB and the IAASB's CAG about changes to the IAASB's Terms of Reference, due process, and working procedures.

One of the IAASB's initiatives in its strategy and work program is the development and implementation of a process to assess the effectiveness of its standards. This process will assist the IAASB in determining whether it needs to refine its standards so they will achieve their objectives. This process will be vital to the adoption of ISAs and achieving global convergence of auditing standards. An important element of this process will be to seek the involvement of the:

- oversight bodies that monitor audit quality
- regulators
- national standard setters

These institutions' collective experience should provide important input about how standards are being implemented. Equally, audit firms will provide an important source of relevant data through the lessons learned in their own quality control reviews and inspections.

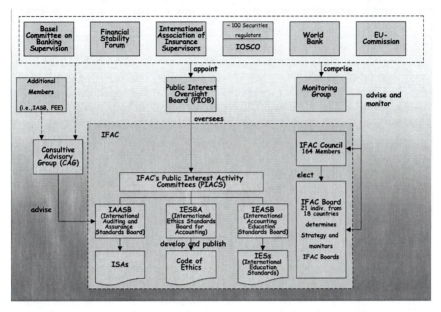

Figure 4.1 Overview of governance structure surrounding the IAASB.

3.4 The Consultative Advisory Group

The IAASB's CAG is comprised of representatives of regulators, business and international organizations, and users and preparers of financial statements who want high-quality international standards on auditing, assurance, quality control, and related services.

The Terms of Reference of the CAG state that its objective is to advise the IAASB about its agenda and project timetable for its work program, including project priorities, specific projects, and other matters as needed.

4. INTERNATIONAL STANDARDS ON AUDITING

4.1 General

High-quality standards for financial reporting, auditing, and ethics underpin the trust that investors place in financial and nonfinancial information and play an integral role in contributing to a country's economic growth and financial stability.

Investor confidence is fundamental to the efficient operation of the world's capital markets and contributes to economic growth and stability worldwide. Investors need to know that the financial information on which they base capital allocation decisions is credible. Independent auditors play a vital role in enhancing the reliability of financial information produced by companies, not-for-profits, government agencies, and other entities.

Whereas the primary responsibility for the quality of financial statements resides with company management, external auditors provide independent assurance. The rapid growth of global markets has put renewed emphasis on the need for international standards on auditing. As global integration and international investment occur more frequently, a common set of international standards presents clear benefits to investors, regulators, and audit firms. As investors seek to evaluate investment opportunities and monitor the performance of a global portfolio, they will benefit from having financial information that has been prepared using international standards.

The advantages for regulators are similar to those for investors. It is easier to accept that foreign issuers are meeting the necessary standards if they are being used for domestic purposes as well as for international ones. A regulator enforcing international standards at home may find it easier to persuade a foreign regulator to rely on the home regulator's work.

For auditing firms, international standards create efficiency because a common audit approach is used that complies with relevant standards. When auditors have overseas subsidiaries, instructing them and then relying on their work will be easier with common standards.

4.2 Development of International Standards on Auditing

Quality is the most fundamental characteristic of international auditing standards. Quality means that the standards should be understandable, based on clear principles, and provide consistent interpretation. Standards also should be capable of unambiguous translation, enforceable, and designed to achieve a high-quality audit. Most importantly, they need to be established by an international body that follows a rigorous due process with significant public input. The IAASB meets these criteria.

There is a growing acceptance of ISAs, particularly adoption and use of the standards by:

- the Financial Stability Board, which includes ISAs in its 12 Key Standards for Sound Financial Systems
- large international accounting firms that are members of the FOF
- regulatory bodies accepting financial statements audited using the ISAs for regulatory filings in their countries, or requiring the use of ISAs by including them in company law
- national accountancy bodies that have used ISAs as the basis for their national auditing standards

The ISAs are widely accepted in many jurisdictions and recognized as appropriate for many capital markets. The IAASB plans to identify and address barriers to further adoption of ISAs, and will continue to ensure that the content and breadth of proposed new standards facilitate their global acceptance and adoption. For this reason, initiatives, such as developing a framework for reviewing the effectiveness of new ISAs and participating in IFAC's work on impact assessments, have been included in the IAASB's work program.

Adoption of ISAs is well under way, based on an online chart released by IFAC in November 2009.[4] Compiled from information gathered by the Program, the chart indicates that ISAs have been adopted or used as the basis of national standards in 126 jurisdictions. The tool gives an overview of ISA adoption by jurisdiction and information about how the adoption process can vary. It also demonstrates the commitment of IFAC and its members to transparency by providing a comprehensive summary of ISA adoption to its stakeholders. IFAC members must use their best efforts to lead or actively support the adoption process within their countries. These efforts should be communicated through their CAPs that describe the current status of adoption and their planned activities.[5]

The IAASB's focus on auditing standards in recent years responded to auditors' and regulators' requests to ensure that the ISAs were high-quality standards worthy of global acceptance and would facilitate convergence. This focus led to:

- revising ISAs dealing with areas of highest audit risk to ensure that they are robust and current
- redrafting all standards to promote consistency in interpretation and international acceptance

During 2008, the IAASB approved one new standard, twelve revised and redrafted standards, and twelve redrafted standards that had not been revised. The new and revised and redrafted ISAs include requirements and guidance to strengthen practice:

- materiality in planning and performing an audit, and its use in evaluating misstatements
- risk assessment and the gathering and evaluation of audit evidence related to:
  - Accounting estimates including fair value accounting estimates and related disclosures
  - related party relationships
  - an entity's use of a service organization
- audit evidence considerations in relation to:
  - external confirmations
  - written representations including implications for engagement acceptance considerations

- using the work of others, in relation to:
  - audits of group financial statements, including the work of component auditors
  - work of an auditor's expert
- communicating with those charged with governance
- communicating deficiencies in internal control to those charged with governance and management
- auditor reporting in relation to:
  - modifications to the auditor's opinion
  - *Emphasis of Matter* paragraph in the auditor's report
- audit and reporting considerations in the context of special engagements

In the European Union, a common strategy on auditing harmonization led to the modernization of the Eighth Directive to include principles on public oversight, external quality assurance, auditor education and independence, code of ethics, auditing standards, and transparency of audit firms and their networks. A specific aspect of the revised Eighth Directive may potentially lead to the adoption of ISAs in the European Union. See Chapter 5 of this volume, "Auditing Reform in Europe," for a comprehensive discussion on the subject matter.

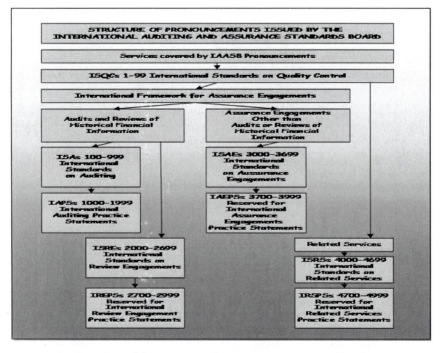

Figure 4.2   Overview of the structure of pronouncements issued by the IAASB.

4.3 The Clarity Project of the International Auditing and Assurance Standards Board

The Clarity Project, which was completed by the IAASB in March 2009, resulted in the issuance of thirty-six ISAs and one International Standard on Quality Control in a new style that is easier to understand, translate, and implement. Other major revisions also were made. The new set of clarified ISAs is effective for audits of financial statements for periods beginning on or after December 15, 2009 (2010 year-end audits).

The revised ISAs will facilitate adoption and convergence globally and provide a stable platform from which the IAASB plans to advance convergence of auditing standards. IOSCO has supported the outcome from the Clarity Project and the IAASB's efforts as noted in its November 9, 2009, *Statement on International Auditing Standards.*

With the Clarity Project completed, the IAASB has issued all of its auditing standards consistently with the drafting conventions established during that project. Because the IAASB also revised many of its auditing standards during the course of the project, the end product has created current, high-quality auditing standards.

All clarified ISAs follow the new clarity structure and have been drafted in light of the obligations and conventions set out in ISA 200 (revised and redrafted). ISA 200, *Overall Objectives of the Independent Auditor and the Conduct of an Audit in Accordance with International Standards on Auditing*, establishes the Clarity Conventions and the obligations of auditors who follow the standards. ISA 200 (revised and redrafted) clarifies that the auditor is required to understand the entire text of an ISA to apply its requirements properly. It also explains that the ISAs contain guidance for carrying out those requirements. ISA 200 (revised and redrafted) also introduces new guidance in relation to professional skepticism, professional judgment, the implications of the inherent limitations of an audit, and other matters relevant to applying the ISAs.

In Table 4.1 there is a list of the standards that were revised and redrafted, or redrafted only, during the Clarity Project:

To facilitate implementation of the revised standards, the IAASB staff has considered whether a series of modules could be developed that target specific ISAs, mainly those that have been revised and redrafted, to highlight key matters, such as:

- the IAASB's main reason for revising the ISAs
- key points of emphasis relating to new or revised requirements (or definitions), to the extent that these will result in changes to existing practice
- major viewpoints considered by the IAASB in establishing the requirements

Table 4.1   List of the Revised and Redrafted Standards during the Clarity Project

The Final Set of Clarified ISAs and ISQC 1		New, Revised and Redrafted, or Redrafted	Year Approved by the IAASB
ISA 200	Overall Objectives of the Independent Auditor and the Conduct of an Audit in Accordance with International Standards on Auditing	Revised and Redrafted	2008
ISA 210	Agreeing the Terms of Audit Engagements	Redrafted	2008
ISA 220	Quality Control for an Audit of Financial Statements	Redrafted	2008
ISA 230	Audit Documentation	Redrafted	2007
ISA 240	The Auditor's Responsibilities Relating to Fraud in an Audit of Financial Statements	Redrafted	2006
ISA 250	Consideration of Laws and Regulations in an Audit of Financial Statements	Redrafted	2008
ISA 260	Communication with Those Charged with Governance	Revised and Redrafted	2007
ISA 265	Communicating Deficiencies in Internal Control to Those Charged with Governance and Management	New	2008
ISA 300	Planning an Audit of Financial Statements	Redrafted	2006
ISA 315	Identifying and Assessing the Risks of Material Misstatement through Understanding the Entity and its Environment	Redrafted	2006
ISA 320	Materiality in Planning and Performing an Audit	Revised and Redrafted	2008
ISA 330	The Auditor's Responses to Assessed Risks	Redrafted	2006
ISA 402	Audit Considerations Relating to an Entity Using a Service Organization	Revised and Redrafted	2008
ISA 450	Evaluation of Misstatements Identified during the Audit	Revised and Redrafted	2008
ISA 500	Audit Evidence	Redrafted	2008
ISA 501	Audit Evidence—Specific Considerations for Selected Items	Redrafted	2008
ISA 505	External Confirmations	Revised and Redrafted	2008
ISA 510	Initial Audit Engagements—Opening Balances	Redrafted	2008
ISA 520	Analytical Procedures	Redrafted	2008
ISA 530	Audit Sampling	Redrafted	2008

(*continued*)

ISA 540	Auditing Accounting Estimates, Including Fair Value Accounting Estimates, and Related Disclosures	Revised and Redrafted	2007
ISA 550	Related Parties	Revised and Redrafted	2008
ISA 560	Subsequent Events	Redrafted	2007
ISA 570	Going Concern	Redrafted	2008
ISA 580	Written Representations	Revised and Redrafted	2007
ISA 600	Special Considerations—Audits of Group Financial Statements (Including the Work of Component Auditors)	Revised and Redrafted	2007
ISA 610	Using the Work of Internal Auditors	Redrafted	2008
ISA 620	Using the Work of an Auditor's Expert	Revised and Redrafted	2008
ISA 700	Forming an Opinion and Reporting on Financial Statements	Redrafted	2008
ISA 705	Modifications to the Opinion in the Independent Auditor's Report	Revised and Redrafted	2008
ISA 706	Emphasis of Matter Paragraphs and Other Matter Paragraphs in the Independent Auditor's Report	Redrafted	2008
ISA 710	Comparative Information—Corresponding Figures and Comparative Financial Statements	Redrafted	2008
ISA 720	The Auditor's Responsibilities Relating to Other Information in Documents Containing Audited Financial Statements	Redrafted	2007
ISA 800	Special Considerations—Audits of Financial Statements Prepared in Accordance with Special Purpose Frameworks	Revised and Redrafted	2008
ISA 805	Special Considerations—Audits of Single Financial Statements and Specific Elements, Accounts, or Items of a Financial Statement	Revised and Redrafted	2008
ISA 810	Engagements to Report on Summary Financial Statements	Revised and Redrafted	2008
ISQC 1	Quality Control for Firms that Perform Audits and Reviews of Financial Statements, and Other Assurance and Related Services Engagements	Redrafted	2008

5. OUTLOOK

Global activities related to international auditing standard setting continue. The Financial Stability Board stated its support for international financial standards. The IOSCO and the IFAC also reiterated their support for convergence of international auditing standards.

However, even if there was global adoption by all jurisdictions and regions of a single set of high-quality auditing standards, this would only be an intermediate step towards the ultimate goal of global consistency for conducting audits of financial statements. A challenge remains to reconcile existing differences between countries, regions, and jurisdictions concerning the litigation environment, enforcement, oversight, ethical behaviors, and values that affect the auditing process.

The information contained herein is of a general nature and is not intended to address the circumstances of any particular individual or entity. Although we endeavor to provide accurate and timely information, there can be no guarantee that such information is accurate as of the date it is received or that it will continue to be accurate in the future. No one should act upon such information without appropriate professional advice after a thorough examination of the particular situation.

NOTES

1. See Section 3.4 of this chapter for a discussion about the IAASB's CAG.
2. See Section 4.3 of this chapter for a discussion about the IAASB's Clarity Project.
3. See Section 2.4 of this chapter for a discussion about the PIOB.
4. IFAC press release, November 3, 2009, available at www.ifac.org.
5. The objective of the Program is to support IFAC members and associates in developing and incorporating the standards of IFAC and IASB into national standards and, thereby, encouraging continuous improvement by professional accountancy organizations through an ongoing assessment of their commitment to use best efforts to adopt and support adoption of international financial reporting, auditing, ethical, education, and public sector accounting standards, as well as to operate or otherwise support robust quality assurance and investigation disciplinary mechanisms.

REFERENCES

Erchinger, H., and W. Melcher. 2008. *Anwendung, Entwicklung und Zukunft der International Standards on Auditing (ISA): Eine aktuelle Bestandsaufnahme im Kontext globaler und nationaler Neuerungen, Die Wirtschaftsprüfung 20.*
International Auditing and Assurance Standards Board. 2008. *July. Strategy and work program 2009–2011.* www.ifac.org.

International Federation of Accountants. 2010. *Handbook of international quality control auditing, review, other assurance, and related services prononcements.* www.ifac.org.

International Organization of Securities Commissions. 2009. *IOSCO statement on international auditing standards.* November 9. www.iosco.org.

Jui, L. 2007. *Speech at AICPA National Conference on Current SEC and PCAOB Developments in Washington D.C.* December 10. www.sec.gov.

Thomadakis, S. B. 2006. Overseeing standards of audit, education and ethics for the accounting profession. Presentation to the Presidents Committee of IOSCO, Hong Kong, June 7. www.ipiob.org.

———. 2007. The process and assessment of international standards for audit. Presented at the IOSCO 32nd Annual Conference, Mumbai, April 12. www.ipiob.org.

5 Auditing Reform in Europe

Chiara Saccon

1. INTRODUCTION

The aim of this chapter is threefold. First, I analyze the recent reform of the statutory audit in Europe, which has been partially driven by the well-known accounting scandals of the twenty-first century in the US and Europe. In particular, I emphasize the changes in the regulations that are aimed to ensure the reliability and accuracy of audited accounts. The EU efforts to harmonize auditing led to the modernization of the Eighth Directive by including principles of public oversight, external quality assurance, auditor education and independence, code of ethics, transparency of auditing process in it. This transformation supposedly makes an auditing the important part of the overall corporate governance (CG) function.

Second, in this chapter I also analyze the implementation process by EU member states, and specifically improper delays, disparities, and omissions in transposition. And lastly, I examine the adequacy of the directive instrument as a tool used for harmonization as it generates minim level of harmonization and allows room for national regulation diversity.

2. STATUTORY AUDIT IN THE EUROPEAN REGULATION

Since the 1970s the European Union has attempted to harmonize company law and accounting through various directives, which are European laws that member states are obliged to incorporate into their own national laws. Three EU directives have been issued that have major financial reporting consequences. They are:

- Fourth Directive (1978), basically addressing format and content of financial statements[1]
- Seventh Directive (1983), addressing the issue of consolidated financial statements[2]
- Eighth Directive (1984), covering various aspects of the qualifications of professionals authorized to carry out legally required (statutory) audits[3]

The requirement to undertake a statutory audit was first included in the Fourth Directive under which companies "must have their annual accounts audited by one or more persons authorized by national law to audit accounts" (Article 51.1 [a]). The Seventh Directive extended this requirement to the company's filing consolidated financial statements. It was not until 1984, however, that the Eighth Directive specified common standards for the firms undertaking statutory audit, including minimum requirements regarding the educational background and experience of auditors. In particular, to be approved to carry out statutory audits of accounting documents an individual must have university entrance level, theoretical instruction, practical training, examination of professional competence conducted by a university, and final examination organized by the state (Eighth Directive, Article 4). In order to satisfy the practical training requirement, a trainee must complete a minimum of three years practical training in *inter alia* the audit of annual accounts, consolidated accounts, or similar financial statements. At least two-thirds of such practical training must be completed under an individual approved by the state (Eighth Directive, Article 8). The examination of professional competence must guarantee the necessary level of theoretical knowledge of subjects relevant to the statutory audit and the ability to apply such knowledge in practice (Eighth Directive, Article 5). The theoretical knowledge must cover subjects like auditing, financial and management accounting, and related regulations (Eighth Directive, Article 6). Equivalent qualifications possessed, such as significant experience or membership of professional associations, exempted candidates from examination.

In most countries the new provisions introduced no great changes in the qualification requirements. These provisions, however, set up a qualification standard in the countries with the smallest numbers of accountants, such as Germany and Denmark (Nobes and Parker 2008, 244), and resulted in increased government involvement in the areas previously regarded a domain of the professional bodies (Woolf 1997, 348). New provisions gave the authorities of the member states an ability to grant an approval to the individuals of good repute to perform the statutory auditing of accounting documents where such audit was required by community law. Following the Eighth Directive, the approved individuals had to carry out the audits with professional integrity and independency. This directive, however, does not define independence. Some guidance was included in the 1978 directive proposal but it was deleted later in the 1984 final text (Van Hulle and Van der Tas 2001, 868).

Overall, the lack of precision in the Eighth Directive has led to the inevitable differences in national legislations and, in some areas, to an absence of legislative backing altogether (Soltani 2007, 161). For example, the Eighth Directive did not regulate the free movement of auditors and the free rendering of audit services and stopped short of including requirements as to how an audit should have been performed. Auditors' oversight was another concern never properly addressed in the directive, and in the watered-down form of the final version the directive confirmed rather than changed member states' existing practices (Nobes and Parker 2008, 196).

In the prevailing opinion the Auditing Directive brought about limited harmonization between European countries as the number of issues remains unresolved (Dewing and Russell 2004, 296). First, there are constraints related to the existing differences in laws, regulations, and in mutual recognition of professional qualifications, preventing the existence of the unified European market in auditing services. Second, auditing practices remain heterogeneous across Europe. Third, high-profile corporate failures, both in Europe and in the US, call into question the role and independence of the statutory auditor and validity of the auditing services.

To solve the aforementioned problems the European Commission (EC) in 1996 organized a wide-ranging reflection on the scope and the need for further action at the EU level on the statutory audit function. The European interventions consisted of a Green Paper[4] on the role, position, and responsibilities of auditors (EC 1996), a communication on the future direction of the statutory audit in the EU (EC 1998), a recommendation setting out minimum standards for external quality assurance system for statutory audits (EC 2000), a study on the civil liability of statutory auditors (EC 2001), and a recommendation setting out fundamental principles and specific requirements on the independence of statutory auditors (EC 2002). In these interventions aimed at improving audit quality and auditor independence as well as creating a single market for European audit service, the EC promotes proposals for closer cooperation with the accounting profession rather than legislative actions (Dewing and Russell 2004, 297).

The corporate failures season in US and Europe generated a wide ranging response by the EC. The response identified financial reporting, statutory audit, and CG as key international policy issues and summarized current and future EU policy actions in each area (EC 2002). As regards statutory audit the European response focused on external quality assurance, auditor independence, and quality standards. It issued a new communication on reinforcing statutory audit in the EU (EC 2003), which formalized the outcome of previous debate on statutory audit and set out priorities in the European auditing scene. This communication announced the amending of the Eighth Directive to clarify the role and position of the auditor and defined requirements for the audit infrastructure to ensure high-quality audits, the strengthening of EU public oversight of the audit profession, and the adoption of international accounting standards for all statutory audits undertaken in the EU. In 2004 the EC proposed a revised Eighth Directive to combat fraud and malpractice in the audit of company accounts and following extensive consultation and review by committees of the European Parliament received final approval in April 2006 (European Union 2006).

3. MAIN FEATURES OF THE UPDATED AUDITING REGULATION. THE DIRECTIVE 2006/43/EC.

The Directive 2006/43/EC[5] substantially amended the previous auditing regulation in Europe. The new Statutory Audit directive is a response to accounting scandals involving European companies such as Parmalat and Ahold as well as American accounting scandals involving WorldCom, Enron, and others. These crises are perceived to be big audit failures and the new regulation is intended to reestablish confidence in the auditing process and results. The directive objectives are to ensure that investors and other interested parties can rely fully on the accuracy of audited accounts and to enhance the protection against the type of corporate scandals that occurred.

The revised directive considerably broadens the scope of the former regulation, which only dealt with the approval of statutory auditors. The new Eighth Directive requires member states to establish auditors oversight bodies; sets out rules on professional ethics and independence; requires the use in statutory audits of international auditing standards produced by an international body and endorsed by the EU; and requires the establishment of audit committees by public-interest entities and the publication of transparency reports on audit firms.

Addressing specific auditing rules contained in the directive, one can detect provisions aimed at raising the quality and transparency of auditing. Article 26 requires the application of international auditing standards in carrying out statutory audits. Reference is made to the International Standards on Auditing (ISAs) developed by the International Auditing and Assurance Standards Board (IAASB), a standing committee of the International Federation of Accountants (IFAC). In order to be applied in the EU these standards have to be endorsed by the EC. The Commission evaluation is based on the fact that they have been developed with proper due process, public oversight, and transparency and that they are generally accepted internationally. Furthermore, it is necessary that they contribute a high level of credibility and quality to the annual accounts and are conducive to the European public good. The introduction of these auditing standards is aimed at enhancing and harmonizing audit quality throughout the European Union.

Knowledge of the international accounting and auditing standards represents a new and necessary requirement for the professional competence of auditors (Article 8) and part of the candidates' examination, thus enhancing the international preparation of the profession. Furthermore, compulsory continuing education for auditors is required (Article 10) in order to ensure a high level of competence, theoretical knowledge, professional skills, and values.

Statutory auditors are subject to principles of professional ethics, covering at least their public-interest function, their integrity and objectivity, and their professional competence and due care (Article 21). They must be independent of the audited entity when carrying out statutory audits; they may inform the entity of matters arising from the audit but should abstain from the internal decision processes of it (Article 22).

The directive obliges all auditors and audit firms to undergo quality assurance reviews (Article 29). The quality assurance system has to be independent of the reviewed statutory auditors and audit firms and subject to public oversight. This quality assurance system shall have adequate resources and the funding for it shall be secure and free from any possible undue influence by auditors. Persons carrying out quality assurance reviews shall have appropriate professional education and relevant experience in auditing and financial reporting combined with specific training on quality assurance reviews. The selection of reviewers shall be effected in accordance with an objective procedure designed to ensure that there are no conflicts of interest between them and the auditor or audit firm under review. The scope of the quality assurance review shall include an assessment of compliance with applicable auditing standards and independence requirements, of the quantity and quality of resources spent, of the audit fees charged, and of the internal quality control system of the audit firm. A report, annually published, shall contain conclusions of the quality assurance review. Whereas generally the quality assurance reviews take place at least every six years, they shall be carried out at least every three years by auditors of public-interest entities. Statutory auditors and audit firms that audit public-interest entities have to publish annual transparency reports (Article 40), allowing an insight into the audit firm, its international network and other nonaudit services provided by it. This report should cover, among other things, a governance statement, a description of the internal quality control system, and a confirmation of its effectiveness by the management of the audit firm.

After the quality control system, another institutional innovation in the directive, aimed at reinforcing oversight of auditors, is represented by the public oversight system (Article 32). The directive set out common criteria for public oversight systems, in particular that they should be predominantly led and staffed by nonpractitioners, but should include a sufficient number of persons with experience and/or expertise in audits. At a European level a body called the European Group of Audit Oversight Bodies (EGAOB) has been set up so that detailed measures implementing the directive can be rapidly taken or modified and to allow for continuous monitoring of and responses to new developments. Through the external quality assurance carried out by the independent oversight bodies the revised directive put an end to the self-regulation of the audit profession.

Article 33 lays out a concept for a model for cooperation between the relevant public oversight authorities of member states: regulators in a country where an audit firm is established shall take full responsibility for supervising it, and on that basis it could work throughout Europe. However,

auditors need to prove their aptitude and knowledge of the relevant country's legislation before they can undertake statutory audits in another
member state (Articles 44, 45). The directive establishes procedures for
the exchange of information between the oversight bodies (Article 36) of
member states in investigations. In order to lay the foundations for better
cooperation with foreign oversight bodies the directive allows reciprocal
cooperation with third countries (Article 47).

Only for public-interest entities does the directive prescribe the establishment of an audit committee (Article 41). The committee with independent
members oversees the audit process, communicating directly with the auditors without going through management. This requirement strengthens the
monitoring of the financial reporting process and the statutory audit and
helps to prevent any possible undue influence of the executive management
on the financial reporting of the audited entity. To enhance the quality
of financial reporting, the auditor must communicate to the audit committee on key matters of governance arising from the audit, in particular
on any material weaknesses observed in internal control relating to the
financial reporting process. It is the single member state that determines
whether audit committees are to be composed of nonexecutive members
of the administrative body and/or members of the supervisory body of the
audited entity and/or members appointed by the general meeting of shareholders of the audit entity. At least one member of the audit committee shall
be independent and shall have competence in accounting and/or auditing.
The audit committee selects the auditor and proposes the appointment to
shareholders, and if a company dismisses an auditor it must explain the
reasons to the relevant authority in the member state concerned.

The audit committee constitution definitely represents a European
attempt in helping auditors to resist inappropriate pressure from managers
of the company they are auditing and so it is a key element within the CG
framework.

4. INTERNATIONAL CONVERGENCE IN AUDITING: AN ONGOING PROCESS

Specific aspects of the revised Eighth Directive are intended to lead directly
to an international convergence in statutory audits.

A first aspect relates to the requirement that all statutory audits in the
EU observe ISAs.

At present, several countries in Europe use national auditing standards
that are heavily influenced by ISAs (Kohler et al. 2008, 121) or represent
a mere transposition of them, sometimes reflecting the numbering too
(Cadeddu and Portalupi 2009, 15). This previous ISAs experience in Europe
would certainly make the adoption of these standards easier but this experience is often a partial one because not all the ISAs are applied as national

auditing standards. Furthermore, the set of ISAs that the EC will take into consideration for adoption is not the existing one but that stemming from the reexamination process of ISAs that IAASB commenced in 2004 and concluded in 2009. This reviewing project, commonly referred to as the "Clarity Project," concerned the structure of auditing standards. Important considerations included the extent to which the standards include explanatory guidance as well as requirements, and the language used to describe steps that are expected to be performed. The project involved wide consultation with stakeholders as the decision taken shaped new ISAs at a critical point in their development—when they were being considered for endorsement by the EU. In the meantime a committee of the EGAOB has been reviewing and commenting on the IAASB clarity's standards as they were developed.

The process to make ISAs mandatory in the EU is still uncertain as to both time and procedures. The EC has yet to determine the mechanism to be used for endorsing the ISAs for use in Europe; it may differ from that used to endorse International Financial Reporting Standards (IFRS).

Very recently the EC published two independent studies. One looks at the costs and benefits that would result from an adoption of ISAs in the European Union and the other compares international with US auditing standards.

In line with Article 26, ISAs should be adopted only if, among other conditions, they contribute to a high level of credibility and quality of audited financial statements. The first study[6] evaluates whether the adoption of the clarified ISAs would allow this condition and analyzes costs and benefits arising at the audit engagement audit firm and audit client levels, as well as those arising for audit regulators, audit markets, and capital markets. The study concludes that an adoption of the clarified ISAs would result in quantitative and qualitative benefits for companies, investors, and regulators stemming from high-quality and harmonized audits in the European Union. On that basis the EC launched in June 2009 a public consultation to determine whether ISAs should be adopted in EU. The second study[7] is aimed at identifying potential differences between ISAs and the auditing standards of the US Public Company Accounting Oversight Board (PCAOB) and their implications for those European companies which are US foreign registrants. The comparative analysis concludes that the number of areas for which substantive differences are perceived is limited.

Auditing has long moved beyond national borders and the crisis has shown how much markets interact with each other. However, the crisis has also highlighted the lack of cooperation and coordination between authorities. The new Eighth Directive introduces a model of international cooperation with third countries as regards the auditing public oversight and inspections but it needs to be based upon mutual trust and mutual assistance. The EC very recently adopted a decision recognizing the adequacy of the auditor oversight systems in Canada, Japan, and Switzerland and allowed EU member states' public oversight bodies to cooperate with their counterparts in these countries (EC 2010a). The EU's aim has always been to move towards full reliance on the audit inspections of the public oversight bodies in third countries. This would mean that auditors from these countries would no longer have to be inspected by European public oversight bodies, as Europe could rely on the audit inspections carried out by their counterparts in these countries. In return, European oversight bodies would expect the same treatment for EU audit firms. Putting in place this model of cooperation would go a long way towards restoring the confidence of investors, but it has to be based upon mutual trust (McCreevy 2009).

5. MEMBER STATES TRANSPOSITION

Noting that the Statutory Audit Directive was adopted in response to the US and European crises and that the current financial crisis highlights the importance of high-quality accounting and auditing practices, the slowness of the adoption process in Europe is surprising. The period for transposition expired on June 2008 but as of January 2009 only twelve member states had transposed the directive in full. It was fifteen in March, and the number increased to twenty-one in May, whereas six member states made a partial transposition and in July and November no further changes emerged.[8] Austria, Ireland, Italy, and Spain were referred to the European Court of Justice over their failure to notify the EC of all their national measures transposing the Statutory Audit Directive into national law. Between November 2009 and January 2010 European member states made significant progress on the directive transposition: Austria, Estonia, Italy, and Luxembourg adopted the remaining national implementing measures transposing the Statutory Audit Directive (EC 2010b). Currently Spain and Ireland are late with the transposition.

The implementation process of the revised Eighth Directive is being carefully monitored by the European Parliament that has never assumed this role before. During its monitoring activity Parliament highlighted specific problems related to the member states transposition. Some member states have not yet implemented Article 41, under which they must require public-interest entities to set up an audit committee, despite this requirement being an important means of guaranteeing the independence of statutory audit of companies' annual accounts.

The system of public oversight required by Article 32 has been gradually introduced in almost all member states despite significant difference. A public oversight system is legally established in twenty-six member states where the persons in charge of its governance have been appointed. The public oversight system had adequate and independent financial resources to perform its activities in 2009 in twenty-five member states and had necessary human resources in twenty-four of them. Currently, Cyprus is the only member state that has not yet legally established a public oversight system (EC 2010b).

It has to be remembered how important it is that cooperation, required under the directive, between public oversight authorities should actually materialize because intensive cooperation among them fosters convergence between member states and can prevent additional administrative burdens resulting from different national procedures and requirements. Inevitably, the relevance of the regulation impact shows the effect of previous national auditing regulatory frameworks and practices. In the Netherlands, as a reaction to the accounting scandals in the US and Europe, the regulatory power was transferred from the professional bodies to an oversight body called the Authority for the Financial Markets (AFM), which is responsible for independent oversight of statutory auditors and audit firms in public practice (Meuvissen and Wallage 2008, 182).

Regarding the application of ISAs, some research states that existing national auditing standards are substantially in line with them (Niemi and Sundgren 2008, 85) but others show that there is important diversity in the wordings of audit reports among different EU countries. In this scenario the undue delay in the approval of ISAs in the EU could have an adverse effect on the regulatory environment, resulting in further fragmentation, which is contrary to the general objective of the directive.

6. FUTURE DEVELOPMENTS

The development of the regulatory auditing process is still under way in Europe.

To be decided is the mechanism to be used for endorsing the ISAs for use in Europe, their partial or full adoption, and the delay in their approval.

The gap for the setting up of adequately resourced independent public oversight of auditors should be closed and the coordination required under the directive between national public oversight bodies should be strengthened, because intensive cooperation between these authorities will improve convergence between member states, will prevent additional administrative burdens resulting from different national procedures and requirements, and will allow for mutual recognition with third countries' oversight authorities.

The success of any new regulation as measured by a resulting regulatory framework representing a mechanism that provides confidence in the reliability of financial markets and services generally, and of statutory audits quality and independence in particular, is dependent on the degree to which such aforesaid regulation is implemented and interpreted, generating full, homogeneous, and timely transposition and enforcement.

NOTES

1. Fourth Directive of July 25, 1978 (78/660/EEC), on the annual accounts of certain types of companies.
2. Seventh Directive of June 13, 1983 (83/394/EEC), on consolidated accounts.
3. Eighth Directive of April 10, 1984 (84/253/EEC), on the approval of persons responsible for carrying out the statutory audits of accounting documents.
4. A *Green Paper* is a discussion document released by the EC intended to stimulate debate and launch a process of consultation, at the European level, on a particular topic. A Green Paper usually presents a range of ideas and is meant to invite interested individuals or organizations to contribute views and information.
5. Directive of May 17, 2006 (2006/43/EC), on statutory audit of annual accounts and consolidated accounts.
6. EC (2009b).
7. EC (2009a).
8. The EC drew up several "Scoreboard on the Transposition of the Directive on Statutory Audit (2006/43/EC)"s in 2008 and 2009 (EC 2009c, 2009d, 2009e, 2009f, 2009g) based on the information provided by member states.

REFERENCES

Cadeddu, L., and A. Portalupi. 2009. *Il processo di revisione contabile.* Milan: IlSole24Ore.

Dewing, I. P., and P. O. Russell. 2004. Accounting, auditing and corporate governance of European listed countries: EU policy developments before and after Enron. *JCMS: Journal of Common Market Studies* 42 (2): 289–319.

European Commission. 1996. Green paper on the role, position and liability of statutory auditors within the European Union. www.ec.europa.eu

———. 1998. Statutory audit in the European Union, the way forward. Commission Communication OJ C 143.

———. 2000. Minimum standards for external quality assurance system for statutory audits. Commission Recommendation 2001/256/EC.

———. 2001. Study on civil liability of statutory auditors. www.ec.europa.eu

———. 2002. Statutory auditors' independence in the EU: A set of fundamental principles. Commission Recommendation 2002/590/EC.

———. 2003. Reinforcing the statutory audit in the EU. Commission Communication OJ C 263.

———. 2009a. *Evaluation of the differences between International Standards on Auditing (ISA) and the standards of the US Public Company Accounting Oversight Board (PCAOB).* Maastricht: Maastricht Accounting, Auditing and Information Management Research Center.

———. 2009b. *Evaluation of the possible adoption of International Standards on Auditing (ISAs) in the EU.* Duisburg: University of Duisburg-Essen.

———. 2009c. January. Scoreboard on the transposition of the directive on statutory audit. 2006/43/EC.

———. 2009d. March. Scoreboard on the transposition of the directive on statutory audit. 2006/43/EC.

———. 2009e, May. Scoreboard on the transposition of the directive on statutory audit. 2006/43/EC.

———. 2009f. July. Scoreboard on the transposition of the directive on statutory audit. 2006/43/EC.

————. 2009g. November. Scoreboard on the transposition of the directive on statutory audit. 2006/43/EC.

————. 2010a. Commission Decision of February 5, 2010, on the adequacy of the competent authorities of certain third countries pursuant to Directive 2006/43/EC of the European Parliament and of the Council OJ 6.2.2010.

————. 2010b. February. Scoreboard on the transposition of the directive on statutory audit. 2006/43/EC.

European Union. 1978. Directive 78/660/EEC.

————. 1984. Directive 84/253/EEC.

————. 1983. Directive 83/349/EEC.

————. 2006. Directive 2006/43/EC.

Kohler, A. G., K. Marten, R. Quick, and K. Ruhnke. 2008. Audit regulation in Germany. In *Auditing, trust and governance. Regulation in Europe*, ed. R. Quick, S. Turley, and M. Willekens, 111–43. London: Routledge Taylor and Francis Group.

McCreevy, C. 2009. *Audit Working papers—Statement Charlie McCreevy Commissioner for the Internal Market and Services, MEMO/09/79.* www.ec.europa.eu.

Meuvissen, R., and P. Wallage. 2008. The Auditing profession in the Netherlands. In *Auditing, trust and governance. Regulation in Europe*, ed. R. Quick, S. Turley, and M. Willekens, 168–85. London: Routledge Taylor and Francis Group.

Niemi, L., and S. Sundgren. 2008. Developments in auditing regulation in Finland. In *Auditing, trust and governance. Regulation in Europe*, ed. R. Quick, S. Turley, and M. Willekens, 78–97. London: Routledge Taylor and Francis Group.

Nobes, C., and R. Parker. 2008. *Comparative international accounting.* 10th ed. Harlow, UK: Prentice Hall.

Soltani, B. 2007. *Auditing. An international approach.* Essex: Prentice Hall, Pearson Education Limited.

Van Hulle, K., and L. Van der Tas. 2001. European Union. Group accounts. In *Transnational accounting*, 2nd ed., vol. 1, ed. D. Ordelheide and KPMG, 879–952. Bath: Palgrave.

Woolf, E. 1997. *Auditing today.* 6th ed. Harlow, UK: Prentice Hall.

6 The Impact of Mandatory Adoption of IFRS on Income Statement and Balance Sheet Properties

Gary Grudnitski and François Aubert

In this chapter we report the results of conducting a two-stage investigation on the effects and consequences of mandatory adoption of International Financial Reporting Standards (IFRS) in France, Germany, Italy, Portugal, Spain, Sweden, and the United Kingdom. In the first stage we determine the impact of mandatory adoption of IFRS by identifying differences in key accounting measures computed under IFRS and in accord with a country's local generally accepted accounting principles (LG). In the second stage of our analysis we address whether there is support for the proposition that the adoption of an IFRS-reporting regime produces quality accruals in these countries.

1. ADOPTION OF REGULATION NO. 1606/2002

The European Parliament and the Council of the European Union (EU) adopted Regulation No. 1606 on July 19, 2002. The regulation mandated adoption of IFRS by (with a few exceptions) EU publicly traded companies preparing their financial statements on a consolidated basis on or after January 1, 2005. It aimed at "contributing to the efficient and cost-effective functioning of the capital market" and enabling EU companies "to compete on an equal footing for financial resources" on European and World capital markets. To facilitate the transition to IFRS, the International Accounting Standards Board (IASB) in June of 2003 issued IFRS 1. IFRS 1 sets out the procedures a company must follow when it adopts for the first time IFRS as the basis for preparing its general purpose financial statements. From a disclosure perspective, IFRS 1 stipulates the presentation of one year of comparative information in a company's first financial statements under IFRS (Deloitte 2004). This meant that companies transitioning from LG to IFRS for the first time in 2005 had to present their 2005 and 2004 financial statements in accord with IFRS 1. IFRS 1 also requires reconciliations[1] between LG and IFRS in a company's first IFRS financial statements.

2. EFFECTS ON KEY ACCOUNTING MEASURES

Data for our investigation was obtained using the ISIN identifiers and Reuters Instrument Codes (RIC) from the FactSet, Reuters, and Compustat databases. Data for the following accounting variables were collected for each company adopting IFRS for the first time in fiscal year 2005: total revenue (TR); net income before extraordinary items (NIBEI); earnings per share (EPS); total assets (TA); discretionary accruals (DA); tangible book value per share (TBVS); net operating cash flow (OCF); and return on assets (ROA).

As shown in Table 6.1, two sets of descriptive statistics consisting of the mean, standard deviation and the first quartile, median, and third quartile values were computed by country for each variable. The first set of descriptive statistics came from accounting values constructed under IFRS for 2004 (the year prior to transition); the second set used accounting values produced by applying the LG of each country for 2004.

3. CONSEQUENCES OF ADOPTION
ON ACCRUALS QUALITY

On a country-by-country basis we investigated the quality of accruals produced under IFRS. The context for this assessment was a statistical model focusing on a comparison between the associations of operating cash flows to accrual numbers produced using IFRS and LG. Specifically, following the model suggested by Wysocki (2005), we regressed operating cash flows of a company against changes in its accruals (the model of Jones 1991). The model is estimated using IFRS and LG accruals:

$$DA_i = \alpha_0 + \alpha_1 OCF_i$$

where DA is the absolute change in accruals[2] calculated under IFRS and LG, and OCF is the operating cash flow of a company both scaled by TA.

As shown in Table 6.2, a regression statistic, R-squared, represents the degree of association between the variables constructed under the alternative reporting regimes; its accompanying F-statistic indicates the likelihood the degree of association is statistically different from zero.

To address whether IFRS produce accruals of higher quality than LG, a statistic is generated to represent the differential association between the dependent variable of IRFS and LG accounting values for accruals. This statistic, calculated as the change in R-squared, represents whether the degree of association between accruals and cash flow is statistically different from zero. It is constructed as follows:

$$F = (R^2_{IFRS} - R^2_{LG})/((1 - R^2_{IFRS})/(n - d.f._{IRFS}))$$

where n is the number of observations (companies in a country) and d.f. are the degrees of freedom used by the estimation equation.

Table 6.1 Descriptive Statistics

Statistic	TR	NIBEI	EPS	TA	DA	TBVS	OCF	ROA
Panel A: France (349 companies)								
LG								
Mean	2391.929	59.582	0.088	7056.414	-0.105	18.671	236.652	0.834
Std. Dev.	9117.747	459.976	0.953	58155.220	0.435	22.071	997.284	0.978
Quartile 1	25.767	-0.473	0.009	17.149	-0.168	5.097	0.820	0.226
Median	98.606	1.927	0.055	72.355	-0.092	11.331	7.251	2.421
Quartile 3	531.603	17.053	0.099	461.509	-0.046	23.399	58.593	5.333
IFRS								
Mean	2369.114	91.380	0.112	7412.975	-0.074	40.470	245.826	2.003
Std. Dev.	9446.343	560.998	0.936	61884.180	0.397	109.013	1110.255	9.781
Quartile 1	22.744	0.077	0.019	17.148	-0.134	3.873	0.505	0.614
Median	89.962	2.949	0.066	73.945	-0.078	12.416	5.429	3.127
Quartile 3	498.010	20.215	0.114	485.777	-0.041	31.091	44.927	6.272
Panel B: Germany (1.489 companies)								
LG								
Mean	2139.164	22.248	0.060	6824.789	-0.114	17.024	206.568	0.151
Std. Dev.	9684.303	299.628	0.390	53815.570	0.272	17.526	1184.130	18.223
Quartile 1	15.477	-2.535	-0.001	16.612	-0.166	5.476	0.358	-0.988

(continued)

Table 6.1 (continued)

Median	82.793	0.367	0.058	64.679	-0.104	13.322	9.853	1.661
Quartile 3	387.004	6.976	0.112	288.045	-0.002	19.977	47.989	5.334
IFRS								
Mean	2052.130	63.082	0.022	6923.612	-0.130	16.977	204.122	0.118
Std. Dev.	9633.804	378.966	0.442	53844.740	0.193	31.255	1266.468	17.329
Quartile 1	15.476	-0.709	-0.001	17.388	-0.166	3.118	0.912	-1.586
Median	73.388	1.246	0.062	64.984	-0.096	10.562	10.786	1.976
Quartile 3	347.953	10.406	0.113	303.786	-0.015	17.226	44.907	5.526
Panel C: Italy (132 companies)								
LG								
Mean	2304.455	69.186	-0.013	7839.531	-0.106	5.152	242.881	0.827
Std. Dev.	8131.932	453.889	0.277	31545.390	0.111	6.005	1505.544	6.284
Quartile 1	68.176	-0.625	0.009	109.041	-0.131	1.426	1.733	0.171
Median	249.179	5.013	0.042	384.330	-0.095	3.295	15.594	1.233
Quartile 3	898.644	28.422	0.081	1848.050	-0.040	6.679	49.504	3.468
IFRS								
Mean	2302.629	93.907	0.008	7689.985	-0.091	5.109	248.581	1.586
Std. Dev.	8241.149	550.452	0.220	32270.530	0.081	6.583	1501.994	7.152
Quartile 1	67.624	0.054	0.002	105.626	-0.125	1.368	1.422	0.244
Median	243.191	6.488	0.051	393.897	-0.075	3.125	13.882	1.685
Quartile 3	944.740	39.003	0.092	1844.269	-0.040	6.641	55.008	4.413
Panel D: Portugal (27 companies)								
LG								
Mean	1415.729	61.895	n/a	6235.414	-0.063	n/a	36.374	1.500

(continued)

Std. Dev.	2070.621	116.271	n/a	14644.490	0.012	n/a	64.762	4.547
Quartile 1	144.629	-1.811	n/a	141.583	-0.068	n/a	6.470	0.596
Median	504.757	8.076	n/a	526.984	-0.059	n/a	18.008	1.616
Quartile 3	1440.980	93.489	n/a	4664.302	-0.056	n/a	51.276	3.828
IFRS								
Mean	1415.729	61.895	n/a	6235.414	-0.063	31.225	36.374	1.500
Std. Dev.	9633.804	378.966	0.442	53844.740	0.193	31.255	1266.468	17.329
Quartile 1	15.476	-0.709	-0.001	17.388	-0.166	3.118	0.912	-1.586
Median	73.388	1.246	0.062	64.984	-0.096	10.562	10.786	1.976
Quartile 3	347.953	10.406	0.113	303.786	-0.015	17.226	44.907	5.526
Panel F: Spain (76 companies)								
LG								
Mean	1956.699	166.403	0.129	9782.076	-0.062	n/a	44.704	3.364
Std. Dev.	5102.982	449.448	0.309	53346.420	0.064	n/a	44.841	9.089
Quartile 1	95.649	2.576	0.055	104.100	-0.079	n/a	12.996	1.405
Median	342.891	21.418	0.084	539.316	-0.030	n/a	44.704	3.023
Quartile 3	1183.198	116.347	0.099	2937.868	-0.024	n/a	76.411	5.824
IFRS								
Mean	2094.114	183.578	0.113	10517.150	-0.067	60.335	61.061	2.328
Std. Dev.	5515.622	492.533	0.331	60319.580	0.028	0.000	70.351	14.839
Quartile 1	82.486	3.528	0.036	109.756	-0.084	60.335	11.315	1.189
Median	337.524	23.477	0.076	518.425	-0.062	60.335	61.061	3.133
Quartile 3	1163.270	130.336	0.094	2963.194	-0.049	60.335	110.807	6.407

(*continued*)

Table 6.1 (continued)

Panel G: Sweden (164 companies)

LG

Mean	7975.837	335.181	0.039	18741.570	-0.103	34.044	795.955	0.087
Std. Dev.	23397.210	1603.241	0.228	130127.500	0.121	43.160	3011.373	18.789
Quartile 1	163.927	-20.463	0.012	79.631	-0.156	11.154	-5.495	0.652
Median	644.150	8.880	0.062	360.201	-0.083	20.930	29.393	4.246
Quartile 3	2714.500	111.746	0.106	1857.000	-0.039	40.200	199.298	7.981

IFRS

Mean	8358.719	644.402	0.051	19068.240	-0.069	29.056	839.416	0.914
Std. Dev.	24217.590	2214.083	0.282	129876.900	0.084	34.694	3052.363	18.817
Quartile 1	183.301	-2.612	0.026	79.631	-0.091	8.147	-6.953	0.573
Median	804.643	29.874	0.077	380.891	-0.059	17.600	26.223	4.900
Quartile 3	3038.943	265.077	0.124	1998.700	-0.029	34.521	264.367	8.860

(continued)

Panel G: United Kingdom (541 companies)

LG

Mean	829.248	40.166	0.006	3498.501	0.044	183.920	115.159	-3.026
Std. Dev.	6001.819	455.343	0.096	39347.440	1.961	209.111	813.643	30.646
Quartile 1	2.483	-0.640	0.000	7.957	-0.130	58.738	-0.263	-1.390
Median	14.751	0.542	0.000	45.974	-0.084	119.809	1.403	2.104
Quartile 3	124.112	6.091	0.001	189.372	-0.057	221.476	17.400	6.244

IFRS

Mean	844.991	50.329	0.008	3587.931	0.044	220.423	112.575	0.014
Std. Dev.	6642.062	493.143	0.116	39696.820	1.962	799.137	840.888	34.059
Quartile 1	2.356	-0.534	0.000	7.979	-0.129	48.912	-0.474	-0.941
Median	14.456	0.668	0.001	45.682	-0.084	114.991	1.061	3.762
Quartile 3	118.712	6.468	0.002	194.823	-0.057	236.842	14.379	9.984

Note: This table provides descriptive statistics for selected income statement and balance sheet data constructed under national GAAP (LG) and IFRS. Financial statement data includes: TR. NIBEI. TA. OCF. EPS. TBVS. DA. and ROA (NIBEI/TA). The currency for all countries except Sweden (Krona—SEK) and the United Kingdom (Pound Sterling—GBP) was the euro. For each sample the descriptive statistics include the mean. standard deviation. and the first quartile. median. and third quartile values.

Table 6.2   Accruals Quality by Country

Country	IFRS			LG			$R^2_{IRFS} - R^2_{LG}$
	α_0	α_1	R^2	α_0	α_1	R^2	
France	.024	.012	.010	.029	.005	.008	
349 firms	(0.81)	(0.42)	[1.19]	(0.95)	(0.17)	[0.91]	
Germany	-.136	-.000	.002	-.138	-.000	.000	
1,489 firms	(4.72)	(-1.06)	[1.13]	(-3.28)	(-0.55)	[0.30]	
Italy	.010	.391	.057	-.032	1.224	.067*	
132 firms	(0.20)	(0.91)	[2.57]	(-0.58)	(2.16)	[3.08]	
Portugal	-.011	.464***	.660***	-.027	.522***	.620***	.040
27 firms	(-0.26)	(3.83)	[14.91]	(-0.63)	(3.84)	[12.50]	[3.06]*
Spain	.129	.036	.110*	.115	.111	.068	.042
76 firms	(2.16)	(0.19)	[2.98]	(2.51)	(0.42)	[1.76]	[3.54]*
Sweden	.153	-.134	.016	.158	-.177	.017	
164 firms	(3.88)	(-0.82)	[0.86]	(4.05)	(-0.99)	[0.92]	
United Kingdom	.056	-.201	.083***	.060	-.249	.091***	
541 firms	(3.43)	(-1.57)	[16.19]	(3.66)	(-1.61)	[18.00]	

Note: Statistics calculated only for countries in which $R^2_{IFRS} > R^2_{LG}$. A single asterisk (*), A double asterisk (**), and a triple asterisk (***) indicate F-statistics significant at the $\rho \le 0.10$, $\rho \le 0.05$, and $\rho \le 0.01$ level. respectively.

In assessing whether accruals quality produced under IFRS was better or higher quality than under the LG, two conditions had to be met. First, the difference in R-squared estimated using IFRS and LG had to be positive (i.e., $R^2_{IFRS} > R^2_{LG}$). Second, this positive difference in R-squares had to be significantly different than zero as measured by the F-statistic calculated according to the preceding equation.

4. COUNTRY ANALYSIS

In the paragraphs that follow we discuss the results of our investigation for companies from the seven countries. The discussion for each country is comprised of two parts. In the first part, large differences in key accounting variables constructed under IFRS and that country's LG are identified. In the second part, the results of our analysis of the quality of accruals under IFRS are presented both on an absolute and relative (to LG) basis.

4.1 France

France had 349 companies switching to IFRS in 2005. Panel A of Table 6.1 presents descriptive statistics on the key accounting variable constructed under IFRS and LG. Of significance is the difference in NIBEI constructed under LG and IFRS. Panel A of Table 6.1 lists an average NIBEI for French firms under LG of approximately €59.6MM compared to €91.4MM under IFRS. Also, small first quartile losses (€.5MM) under LG appear to be changed to small profits (€.1MM) under IFRS. Finally, because average TA calculated under the two accounting regimes are similar, substantial differences (.8 to 2 percent) in the key variable of ROA seem to be due to differences in NIBEI.

Also of note is the difference in average TBVS. Under IFRS it is more than double that calculated using LG (i.e., approximately €40.5MM to €18.7MM). One possible contributing factor to the difference in average TBVS is that French GAAP uses historical cost rather than fair value in valuing assets. Another factor that perhaps exacerbates this gap is the percentage of banks and financial institutions in the French subsample (approximately one-sixth of the firms in this subsample operate in the "finance" FactSet industry classification), and the differential impact fair value accounting had on these types of entities.

Panel A of Table 6.2 presents statistics on the association between accruals and cash flows under alternative accounting regimes. It reports a positive statistical association between accruals and cash flows was not found for accruals constructed under either IFRS or LG.

4.2 Germany

Germany had 1,489 companies switching from German GAAP to IFRS in 2005. Panel B of Table 6.1 presents descriptive statistics on the key accounting measures constructed under IFRS and LG. Of noticeable difference is the mean value for NIBEI under LG and IFRS. Specifically, the mean value of NIBEI under LG and IFRS is €22.2MM and €18.7MM, respectively, for the German firms in our sample. Surprisingly, this difference in net income between accounting regimes did not impact average returns as the ROA under LG and IFRS is identical.

Panel B of Table 6.2 reports on the association between accruals and cash flows under alternative accounting regimes. This panel reports results for the association between accruals and cash operating flows similar to those found for the French subsample of companies.

4.3 Italy

Panel C of Table 6.1 notes 132 companies switching to IFRS from Italian GAAP in 2005. Except for the mean LG loss of just over 1 percent, descriptive statistics on the key variables are comparable to those obtained for French firms. Notice that the mean ROA constructed under IFRS was double that using LG. Panel C of Table 6.2 shows that there is a statistical association between accruals and cash flow for these variables constructed under IFRS and LG. However, because the degree of association (i.e., R^2) is about the same, we cannot conclude that one regime produced higher quality accruals than the other.

4.4 Portugal

The sample for Portugal had the fewest number of firms (twenty-seven). Also, values for EPS and TBVS were not available in our data bases. Because of higher NIBEI values constructed under IFRS (mean values of €91.6MM compared to €61.9MM under LG), Panel D of Table 6.1 lists average EPS of 2.1 percent under IFRS as compared to 1.5 percent under LG. Additionally, first quartile NIBEI values increased from a loss of €1.8MM under LG to a profit of €4.3MM under IFRS.

Notably, Panel D of Table 6.2 reports on a strong statistical relationship between accruals and cash flow for both LG and IFRS. And, importantly, this panel shows that the degree of association is higher for IFRS than LG, and this difference in association between the two accounting regimes is statistically significant (i.e., different from zero).

4.5 Spain

Panel F of Table 6.1 shows similar values for all variables (except missing TBVS under LG) constructed under LG and IFRS for seventy-six Spanish firms. The notable exception is ROA variable. For the only time, EPS under LG is greater than EPS under IFRS (i.e., 3.4 to 2.3 percent). Although it is difficult to speculate on the principal cause of this reversal it may be due to the percentage of banks and financial institutions in the Spanish sample and the valuation of their long-term assets and liabilities, a fair value basis allowed by IFRS.

Panel F of Table 6.2 reports on a statistical relationship between accruals and cash flow constructed on the basis of IFRS. Because the association between accruals and cash flow under IFRS is statistically significant, whereas the association between these variables constructed under LG is not, we are led to conclude that accruals of Spanish companies under IFRS are of higher quality than those constructed under Spanish GAAP.

4.6 Sweden

The descriptive statistics for the monetary variables in Panel G of Table 6.1 for 164 Swedish firms are expressed in terms of krona (kr or SEK) instead of euros. Of importance is the difference in NIBEI constructed under LG and IFRS. Panel G of Table 6.1 lists an average NIBEI for Swedish firms under LG of approximately kr335.2MM compared to kr644.4MM under IFRS. Also, small first quartile losses (kr20.5MM) under LG appear to be reduced to very small losses (kr2.6MM) under IFRS. Finally, because average TA calculated under the two accounting regimes are similar, substantial differences (.1 to .9 percent) in the key variable of ROA seem to be mainly because of differences in NIBEI.

Statistics on the association between accruals and cash flows under alternative accounting regimes for Swedish firms mirror those found for French firms. Panel G of Table 6.2 indicates neither a positive statistical association between accruals under IFRS and cash flows nor one that is statistically different from that attained when accruals are computed using LG.

4.7 United Kingdom

For the 541 UK companies that make up our last subsample the monetary variables of Panel H of Table 6.1 are expressed in millions of pounds (£ or GBP) instead of euros. Of significance is the overall improvement under IFRS in the performance measure of ROA (i.e., approximately 3 percent).

Panel H of Table 6.2 reports on the association between accruals and cash flows under UK GAAP and IFRS. Panel H of this table indicates a statistical association between accruals and cash flow for both UK GAAP and IFRS, although the degree of association is not statistically different between the two. Notable is the value derived under both accounting regimes for the coefficient, α_1. As this coefficient represents the contemporaneous correlation between accruals and cash flows, some researchers (Wysocki 2005) believe that the larger negative valve derived under LG (i.e., $\alpha_{LG} = -.249$ compared to $\alpha_{IFRS} = -.201$) suggest greater earnings' smoothing activities and is consistent with the evidence of earnings management found by Leuz, Nandab, and Wysocki (2003).

NOTES

1. The reconciliations consisted of equity at the date of transition (beginning of the prior year) and at the beginning of the current reporting period (end of the prior year). Reconciliation was also required of the net profit or loss for the year prior to the current reporting period.
2. Specific values for DA were calculated by subtracting operating cash flow from operating income.

REFERENCES

Deloitte. 2004. *First time adoption: A guide to IFRS 1.* http://www.deloitte.com/dtt/cda/doc/content/A%20guide%20to%20IFRS%201_first%20time%20adoption%202004.pdf.

European Commission. 2002. Regulation (EC) No 1606/2002 of the European Parliament and of the Council on the Application of International Accounting Standards. *Official Journal of the European Communities* 243:1–4. http://eur-lex.europa.eu/LexUriServ/LexUriServ.do?uri=OJ:L:2002:243:0001:0004:EN:PDF.

Jones, J. 1991. Earnings management during import relief investigations. *Journal of Accounting Research* 29:193–228.

Leuz, C., D. Nandab, and P. Wysocki. 2003. Earnings management and investor protection: An international comparison. *Journal of Financial Economics* 69:505–27.

Wysocki, P. 2005. Assessing earning and accrual quality: US and international evidence. MIT Working Paper.

Part III

Analysis of Changing Institutional Environments, New Accounting Policies, and Corporate Governance Practices in Selected Countries

Part III of the monograph contains the analyses of institutional environments, IFRS adoption, and national corporate governance (CG) practices in seven European countries: France, Germany, Italy, Sweden, UK, Portugal, and Spain. The purpose of the analyses is to evaluate the recent developments in accounting and identify the link between accounting CG practices and performance.

In particular the issues discussed in Part III include:

- international convergence in accounting, changes in objectives of financial reporting, and in characteristics and constraints of decision-useful information
- economic resources and claims on them and the usefulness of income measure for valuation purposes and how legal and tax rules impact the internationalization of national accountings
- evaluation of new CG regulations and practices, governance characteristics, and disclosure

7 Analysis of Changing Institutional Environments, New Accounting Policies, and Corporate Governance Practices in France

Pascale Delvaille

1. ACCOUNTING

1.1 International Convergence in Accounting

1.1.1 Standardization of Accounting Practices in France

As in many European countries, French accounting principles and accounting rules are enacted by the national legislature. The primary source of this legislation is the Commercial Code (*Code de Commerce*), which includes provisions based on different laws and decrees (*Règlements, Lois and Décrets.*). Articles L.123–12 to L 123–28 of the code provide a framework of general accounting rules, which are applicable to all forms of business enterprises (Nobes and Parker 2008, 304). Another set of articles, L. 233–1 to L. 233–27, applies to groups' consolidated accounts. Other important sources are ministerial orders (*Ordonnances*) and recommendations (*Recommandations* and *Avis*) prepared by different organizations, such as national standard setters (*Conseil National de la Comptabilité* [CNC] and *Comité de la Réglementation Comptable* [CRC], which merged into the *Autorité des Normes Comptables* [ANC] in 2009), the accounting profession (*Ordre des experts comptables, Commissaires aux comptes*), and the financial market regulation authority (*Autorité des marchés financiers* [AMF]) for listed companies. French accounting is also influenced by tax laws (*Code Général des Impôts* [CGI] and *Lois de Finance*). In 2007, there were a total of three million business enterprises, approximately 1.5 million of which have unlimited liability (sole proprietorships and general partnerships), with the other half composed of companies with limited liability. A limited liability company may take a form of a *Société à responsabilité limitée* (SARL), a *Société Anonyme* (SA), and, in rare cases, a *Société en commandite par actions* (SCA). Less than one thousand companies are publicly traded and, to be listed on the stock exchange, the company must take the form of either an SA with a minimum share capital of €275,000 (compared to €37,000 for the other companies) or an SCA. Only a minority of SAs are

listed on a stock exchange.[1] At the beginning of 2007, the number of regis-
tered companies classified by categories was 1,500,000 SARL and 133,000
SA, equal to 8 percent of the total number of limited liability companies
(Bertrel et al. 2009, 716). The different forms of companies listed on the
French stock exchange and their governance characteristics are presented
in the second section of this chapter.

The accounting requirements that apply depend on the legal form of the
business entity. In this chapter, we focus primarily on companies with limited liability such as SARL and SA. Due to the concept of a legal entity, all
business enterprises, that is, sole proprietorships, partnerships, or corporations, must prepare individual or separate financial statements covering the
legal entity (*Comptes sociaux*). These statements must comply with French
GAAP and serve as a basis for the determination of dividends for shareholders and for calculating the taxable income.

Internationalization of French Accounting

The internationalization of French accounting is primarily focused on
consolidated financial statements. Whereas certain accounting principles
related to consolidations of listed companies were developed in the 1960s
and 1970s, the harmonization of the requirements for consolidated financial statements truly began in the 1980s with the implementation of the
European Union's Seventh Directive. The Seventh Directive prompted the
French accounting authorities to revise their own accounting principles for
consolidated financial statements, particularly those related to evaluation
methods, to align French GAAP to International Financial Reporting Standards (IFRS) principles. Consequently, there were several options available
to companies seeking to measure their assets and liabilities for consolidation purposes that were different from those applied in individual financial
statements. For example, the use of the revaluation of assets, the capitalization of financial interest, and the recognition of gains on foreign exchange
transactions (not realized on the closing date) were made possible. The
convergence between French rules for consolidated accounts and international, especially Anglo-Saxon, standards resulted from two elements: the
pressure of capital markets and the lobbying of large French companies
that were listed in the US and therefore had to prepare a reconciliation of
earnings and stockholders' equity from French GAAP to US GAAP. As a
consequence, for example, the principle of substance over form was introduced in the group financial statements to better satisfy the needs of both
national and international equity investors. This internationalization of
consolidated financial statements compared to individual financial statements was possible because the consolidated financial statements are not
the basis for dividend and tax payments; these are legally based on individual financial statements only.

These changes in French GAAP reflected the new relationships between the state and the accounting profession (Colasse and Standish 1998)—and the increased influence of financial markets—requiring more detailed information in the financial statements of multinational groups.

For consolidated financial statements, the French legislature has issued specific regulations, first in 1999 (*Règlement CRC 99–02*) and then regularly amended.[2] In contrast to Germany and the United Kingdom, standards for consolidated financial statements are not published by a private committee.

Unlike reforms in Germany, the French reform of 1998 did not succeed[3] in allowing companies to use international accounting standards (i.e., IFRS or US GAAP) instead of national rules in preparing group financial statements. As a result, the French authorities decided to enhance the convergence of local rules with international standards both in individual and in consolidated financial statements, including changes in the recognition and measurement of items such as provisions and tangible assets, depreciation and impairment, especially between 2002 and 2005. However, differences between French GAAP and international standards still remain (Delvaille, Ebbers, and Saccon 2005; Alexander, Delvaille, and Saccon 2010). In summary, the convergence of French GAAP with IFRS has been achieved in some areas (*Règlements*, CRC), but for other areas, an amendment of law and decrees remains necessary.

Since the decision of the European Commission (EC) requiring all listed European companies to prepare their consolidated financial statements in accordance with IFRS from 2005 onwards (EC Regulation on IAS No. 1606/2002), France, as with other member states, has the option to prescribe IFRS for other types of statements or companies. Given the French tradition of codified law, it is not surprising that the EU option (for member states to apply IFRS to nonlisted groups and individual financial statements) has not completely been transposed in French law by the regulatory authorities. A partial use of the option has been approved for consolidated financial statements of nonlisted entities. French GAAP is still mandatory for all individual financial statements. Consequently, in France today, three levels of GAAP exist:

- French GAAP for individual financial statements
- French GAAP for consolidated financial statements of nonlisted groups (if they do not use IFRS)
- IFRS for listed groups

The possibility of introducing a simplified version of international standards, especially for small and medium-size entities (SMEs) in France was under debate for several years. The French standard setter CNC, the *Ordre des Experts comptables* (OEC), which is playing a key role in the debate, and several organizations, such as the National Statistics Institute (*Institut National de la Statistique et des Etudes Economiques* [INSEE]) or the Tax Authority Body (*Direction Générale des Impôts* [DGI]), have expressed major reservations against applying IFRS in individual entity accounts, as they also serve as the basis of companies' tax returns (Delvaille, Ebbers, and Saccon 2005). In 2008, the CNC conducted a survey of the expectations and needs of SMEs, including field tests. The analysis of the accounting environment of the 678 SMEs in the sample confirms that individual financial statements are initially used for tax purposes. The companies estimate that separating accounting and tax rules would be expensive for them, whereas the benefit to be gained is not clear (CNC 2008). The same survey shows in the area of financial reporting that using the IFRS for SMEs (for example, in the case of leasing, the discounting of long-term provisions and construction contracts) can improve the relevance of information for both internal decision making and external communication. A study conducted by Mazars at the European level enhances a particularity of the French companies: 76 percent of the respondents find it difficult to interpret IFRS (Mazars 2008). Therefore, the French regulators do not want to authorize IFRS for SMEs in the near future.

1.1.2 Changes in Financial Reporting Objectives

Under French GAAP, individual financial statements have to meet three objectives:

- profit determination
- information disclosure
- legal proof[4]

The profit determination and information disclosure objectives can be contradictory. For example, if the market value of an asset increases beyond its historical acquisition cost, then many agree that the right information—depending on the type of asset under consideration—would be to present this asset as having a (higher) market value on the balance sheet, whereas in most GAAP systems, for profit determination reasons, such a markup is not allowed, save for a very limited number of exceptions. Because (in this and other cases) it is not possible with one set of financial statements to achieve both objectives at the same time, there has to be a hierarchy. The French legislature does not explicitly address this issue, but the accounting rules themselves and their practical application show that the profit determination objective dominates the information disclosure objective in cases of conflict. Providing information is only important as long as it does not restrict the profit determination objective (as defined in the following lines).

Among the many environmental elements that influence a given country's GAAP, we can name two that are essential in France and that have led to the importance of the profit determination objective: the primary way in which companies finance and the link between financial and tax accounting.

Regarding the first element, stock markets are much less important to company financing for French companies than for Anglo-Saxon companies, especially the US. The large majority of French businesses are privately and not publicly owned. Consequently, equity financing plays a limited role in companies' financing strategy and is often limited to retained earnings. Debt financing is the primary source of external financing, and because these private companies have only restricted access to bond markets, they use bank financing. Because rules are made for the primary users or beneficiaries, French GAAP is predominantly bank-oriented or, more generally, creditor-oriented. In this setting, the accounting rules are one element of law-based creditor protection tools.

Because it is in the interest of creditors that assets and profits of their clients not be overstated and that their liabilities not be undervalued, the principle of prudence logically has a central position in French GAAP. Determining accounting profits in a prudent way avoids the distribution of exaggerated and fictitious dividends based on paper but not on realized profits. This approach leads to the prescription of an asymmetric treatment for gains and losses: Unrealized profits cannot be accounted for (see our earlier example of increases in market value beyond the acquisition cost), whereas unrealized losses must be anticipated as soon as they are known. Therefore, the principle of prudence leads to a worst-case presentation of the company's situation (on a going-concern basis), and the creditors do not have any bad surprises beyond what is presented in the financial statements (at least in theory).

Given this situation, net income under French GAAP should on average be lower than the net income based on a more shareholder-oriented GAAP, such as IFRS. A study by Ernst and Young (2005) for French companies shows that the average impact on their net income for fiscal year 2004 from their changing from French GAAP to IFRS was + 34.3 percent. A similar result is presented in a study by Mazars (2005). For 81 percent of the French sample companies, Mazars finds a positive impact on their net income for fiscal year 2004 from switching to IFRS. Overall, the impact of this transition is rather strong: For 22 percent of companies, the change is higher than 50 percent of their net income for 2004, although the absolute amounts remain "reasonable," with the impact being €50 million or less for 45 percent of the companies (Delvaille and Hossfeld 2006).

In addition to the way in which companies finance, the second reason for the importance of the profit determination objective is the link between financial and tax accounting. Indeed, the financial net income is the starting point for the calculation of taxable profits, and in tax returns, only some differences are reconciled for the rather limited cases where financial accounting and tax accounting rules collide. Based on this link, companies try as much as possible to integrate tax rules into their financial statements to minimize reconciliations and trouble with tax authorities. In this context, the principle of prudence is of course well accepted by these companies, because it leads to lower taxable profits.

The previous paragraphs explained that profit determination is more important in French GAAP than it is in information disclosure. This statement applies to individual financial statements under French GAAP but not to consolidated financial statements under French GAAP. It is legally impossible for a French company to pay dividends if it does not present an accounting profit (and does not have retained earnings) in its individual financial statements. This legal requirement is very reasonably applicable to legal entities. However, in French company law, groups are not considered to be legal entities. Therefore, dividend and tax laws do not apply to groups. They are legally not entitled to pay dividends, and they are not required to provide tax returns.

As a consequence, the legal question of profit determination is not relevant for consolidated financial statements.[5] Therefore, French accounting regulators have more flexibility regarding consolidated financial statements because there are no company law or tax law impacts. We can thus state that the information disclosure objective is more important than the profit determination objective for consolidated financial statements.

1.1.3 Changes in Characteristics and Constraints of Decision-Useful Financial Reporting Information

The major change in the international regulation of consolidated financial statements took place with Regulation (19)99–02, "Consolidated Accounts of Commercial Companies and Public Enterprises," issued by the CRC. Regulation 99–02 abandoned certain "traditional" French accounting characteristics and treatments for consolidation purposes but did change them for individual financial statements.

First, the principle "substance over form" was introduced and explicitly mentioned. Indeed, in coherence with the objective of consolidated financial statements of providing information about economic entities and without legal restrictions regarding dividends or income tax, the approach to accounting for transactions based on their legal form was no longer necessary. However, the application of this principle is not as far reaching as it is in US GAAP or IFRS.

Second, Regulation 99–02 states that in the consolidated financial statements, the "effect of accounting entries carried out solely for the application of tax legislation" must be eliminated. On the one hand, because consolidated financial statements are not used to determine taxable income, tax considerations should not and do not influence the accounting rules for consolidation. On the other hand, this is also a reaction to criticism of French or, more broadly, other continental European countries' GAAP systems, particularly by the US accounting community; the latter has consistently complained about the negative tax influence on French (European) financial statements, which makes it difficult to extract decision-useful information.

Third, the matching principle (matching expenses with revenue) was for the first time explicitly mentioned in a regulation. Although this mention could not be considered a fundamental change (such as the previous two points), it represented a slight shift away from the traditional French accounting, where the dominant approach was to account expenses in the period of their consumption. Today, even if the matching principle has been abandoned in IFRS, it remains in French GAAP.

In addition to the aforementioned fundamental changes in the approach to consolidated financial statements and in line with "substance over form," Regulation 99–02 introduced preferential methods for certain accounting issues. Preferential methods indicates that these methods are preferred compared to the traditional French methods in these areas. The proposed methods are all in line with IFRS. Initially, there were five preferred methods; Regulation 2004–06 added two additional methods.

- The costs of retirement and their comparable benefits (e.g., severance payments; supplementary retirement allowances; medical coverage; and recognition of long service, sickness, and provident benefits) for the benefit of active and retired personnel, chargeable to the enterprise, should be provided for and systematically taken into account in calculating profits or losses over the term of the activity of employees. Accounting for pension benefits is optional in French GAAP, and companies have traditionally not accounted for them, instead only providing information in the notes.
- Finance leases should be capitalized on the balance sheet of the lessee. In addition, capital gains on sale-leaseback transactions should be spread over the term of the contract, where the item is once more leased, directly or through an intermediary, within the context of a finance lease transaction. In traditional French GAAP, capitalizing financial leases is not allowed; following the legal approach, these contracts are treated as rentals.Debt issuance costs, redemption premiums and issue premiums should be spread systematically over the life of the debt. This accounting treatment is only partially new. Premiums are already spread over the life of the debt in traditional French GAAP (but not necessarily based on the effective interest method). For debt issuance costs, their treatment is optional (immediate expense or spread over time) in traditional French GAAP.

- Currency translation differences related to monetary assets and liabilities denominated in foreign currencies should be recorded in profits or losses during the period to which they relate. Currency translation differences are put in the balance sheet in traditional French GAAP, and only losses impact the income statement by means of a provision (expense) for pending currency losses (principle of prudence). Regulation 99–02 allows, in this case, accounting for unrealized translation gains in the income statement.
- Transactions partially completed at the close of the financial year (the provision of services or the supply of goods) should be accounted for according to the percentage-of-completion method. Although the percentage-of-completion method is allowed under traditional French GAAP, in practice companies use only the completed contract method. The preference for the former represents (another) break of the principle of prudence, as it leads to the recognition of unrealized revenues.
- Regulation 2004–06 indicated the preference for the method wherein the cost is expensed compared to traditional French GAAP, which allows these costs to be capitalized and amortized.
- Finally, development costs can be capitalized (under conditions similar to IAS 38). This change is only a partial one from traditional French GAAP, where in exceptional circumstances it was permitted to capitalize development and applied research costs.

1.2 Economic Resources and Claims on Them

French accounting regulation follows the clean surplus concept when measuring a company's performance. There is one exception to this approach: The French commercial code allows all tangible and financial noncurrent assets to be revalued. This is a holdover from the times when France had high inflation in the 1940s, 1950s, and 1970s and the government imposed regular revaluations based on a price index; the last of these legal revaluations took place in 1976. In financial accounting, the revaluation amount is included in a revaluation reserve within equity. Up to 1976, this reserve was not included in taxable income. Since then, the French tax laws have treated it as a taxable profit.[6] Aside from this rule, there are no "other comprehensive income" items; indeed, the concept itself is not known in French GAAP.

As previously mentioned, French GAAP as part of company law is primarily creditor-oriented (i.e., bank-oriented). However, the French approach is not focused solely on this user group; rather, it is much broader to satisfy other stakeholders, such as employees. Anecdotal evidence is provided by the fact that companies with more than fifty employees have to have a profit-sharing scheme. The way how this bonus is presented in the income statement is specific. In fact, it is not included in personnel expenses; rather, it is presented separately as the third last line, immediately before income tax and net income. This spot down the income statement seems to indicate that the item is closer to profit appropriation than it is to profit determination, underlining the message that employees should receive their share of profits.

Additional hard evidence for this approach of providing information not only to creditors (i.e., banks) but also to other users is illustrated by the large amount of accounting-related information that (certain) companies have to disclose in addition to financial statements, among others:

- For a company's work council, elected union representatives, employees, shareholders, and government labor authorities: a social report covering labor-related subjects such as employment, compensation, working conditions (hygiene, security, length, organization, etc.), and education.
- For auditors, a company's work council and its supervisory board (if there is one, see the following chapter): a prospective income statement and a financial plan for the next year as well as a retrospective statement presenting available-for-sale assets and due debts.
- For shareholders, the total compensation of the five or ten employees, depending on the size of the company, with the highest payments.

Even the way in which the accounting regulator is set up is influenced by this stakeholder approach; the composition of the newly created ANC shows that all stakeholders have to be implicated:

- There are sixteen people in the decision-making body (*collège*). In addition to representatives of the government and financial market authorities, nine people are nominated because of their economic and accounting knowledge after the consultation of the companies and the accounting profession. There is also one union representative.
- Also, twenty-five people are members of a consultative committee, representing the "economic and social world." Two of these members must be union representatives.

2. CORPORATE GOVERNANCE

2.1 Regulation and the Scope of Corporate Governance

2.1.1 Definition of CG in France

Defining CG specifically for France is not an easy task, as there is no official definition under French company law. Nevertheless, we can use a broad definition from Charreaux:

Corporate governance includes all of the mechanisms that restrict directors' power and influence their decisions, that is, that "govern" their behavior and define the scope of their discretionary power.[7] (quoted in Wirtz 2008, 9; our translation)

Given France's tradition of codified law, the main rules for CG are set by law, in particular the 1966 French Company Law. France is also highly influenced by the common rules set at the European level (directives) and then transposed into laws at the national level. However, even if there is a common skepticism of the French toward self-regulation, France has been influenced by the Anglo-Saxon CG system, and a set of recommendations has progressively appeared.

These recommendations are CG codes (CGC) giving guidelines about best practices in CG and are generally issued by representative bodies of the public firms. Even if some of these guidelines have become legally binding through their introduction into laws, most of them remain nonmandatory and are based upon the "comply-or-explain" principle.

There has been a rapid trend for the adoption of reference codes in the CG practices of French listed firms. In 2009, more than eight listed firms out of ten firms complied with the AFEP-MEDEF code,[8] that is, the reference code (AMF 2009). Moreover, "soft laws" such as the AFEP-MEDEF code have been accepted by official bodies like the French AMF.

An important feature of CG is the structure of the governing bodies of a company. Today, the French Company Law included in the 2000 Commercial Code basically defines three possibilities for the CG system:

- A *unitary board* or one-tier system (*système moniste*) with a single *Président Directeur Général* (PDG), who has the role of chairman and CEO. This is the traditional French system that is still in place today in most listed companies. The important level of power given to the PDG is in line with the French tradition of centralized power (Mallin 2007, 172). This unitary board is called a *Conseil d'Administration* in French.
- A *two-tier model* (*Système dualiste*)—closer to the German model— with a supervisory board (*Conseil de Surveillance*) and a management board (*Directoire*). In this case, the roles of chairman (*Président*) and CEO (*Directeur Général*) are clearly separated. This case is not very common. The choice between the Anglo Saxon one-tier model, with a single *Conseil d'Administration* at the top, and the German two-tier model, with a separated *Conseil de Surveillance* and *Directoire*, had already been introduced in the 1966 Companies Law.
- A *third model*, introduced by a law passed in 2001, called the New Economical Regulation Law (*Nouvelles Régulations Economiques* [NRE]), which maintains the traditional unitary board model (*Conseil d'Administration*) while separating the functions of chairman and CEO. It is an important change in the French model, as it splits the

historical PDG function into two functions (Richard and De Pitray 2007). France is one of the only systems in the world offering this option (Hopt and Leyens 2004).

In order to identify which model French companies actually use, Table 7.1 summarizes the CG structure of French companies listed in the CAC 40 (as of August 2009).

The two-tier system is actually applied by only 2–3 percent of all publicly traded corporations and only about 20 percent of the CAC 40 companies (Hopt and Leyens 2004, 16). Using a larger sample of 281 French listed companies, a study shows that 65 percent of these firms had chosen the one-tier system with a single PDG, whereas 35 percent chose one with a clear separate role (Ernst and Young 2009).

2.1.2 The Different Laws and Codes on Corporate Governance in France

Codes

In addition to the general CG systems defined by law, French CG principles are also based on different "codes" or sets of recommended best practices.

The first code called Viénot I—so named because it was prepared by Marc Viénot, former PDG of Société Générale[9]—was published in 1995, three years after the famous Cadbury Report in the UK. This code introduced a set of best practices regarding CG. It was then revised in 1999 with the publication of the Viénot II report.

The third report, headed by another PDG of Société Générale, the Bouton Report, was published in 2002 right after the Enron scandal. It followed the principles introduced by the Viénot Reports, adding new rules regarding the board's roles, responsibilities, and accountability.

The Viénot (1995, 1999) and Bouton (2002) Reports were jointly summarized in 2003 by the Association of French Private-Sector Companies (*Association Française des Entreprises Privées* [AFEP]) and the French Companies Movement Association (*Mouvement des Entreprises de France*

Table 7.1 Governance Structure of CAC 40 Listed Companies

Corporate Governance System	% Companies in the CAC 40
One-tier system with PDG	40%
One-tier system with the Chairman and CEO functions separated	30%
Two-tier system	20%
Other (company not incorporated in France)	10%

[MEDEF]) making up the AFEP-MEDEF Corporate Governance Code. This code is now the reference code for CG practices in France. This code was revised in December 2008, in a context of financial crisis. Some of the rules about remuneration or independent administrators have been tightened (AFEP-MEDEF 2008).

The AFEP-MEDEF code is based on the "comply-or-explain" principle and, according to an AMF study with a sample of eighty French listed companies (AMF 2009), is followed by 80 percent of the listed companies. Moreover, if 67 percent of the companies in the sample do not comply with some of the AFEP-MEDEF code, 80 percent of them explain why.

Finally, MiddleNext, the small and midcap association, published in 2009 its own CGC specifically designed for this type of company (Middle-Next 2009). Most of the principles of the AFEP-MEDEF Report are used but some of them have been adapted for the midcaps where the shareholding structure is generally very concentrated.

Laws

In addition to these codes, the government has also introduced new laws about CG to modernize the 1966 Companies Law. As noted earlier, the 2001 NRE Law (*Nouvelles Régulations Economiques*) introduced the option of separating the functions of chairman and CEO.

Another important law is the Financial Security Law (*Loi de Sécurité Financière* [LSF]) passed in August 2003, which established the AMF through the merger of the Stock Exchange Commission (*Commission des Opérations de Bourse* [COB]) and two other stock exchange regulatory bodies. As far as CG is concerned, one of the missions of the AMF is to study the CG practices of French listed firms every year. The AMF reports whether corporations comply with the rules/codes like the AFEP-MEDEF Corporate Governance Code. The AMF publishes every year a report called the *AMF Report on Corporate Governance and Internal Control*, which is available on the AMF website.

The last important law to mention is the Law for the Trust and Modernization of the Economy (*Loi pour la confiance et la modernisation de l'économie* [LME]) passed in 2005. The law aims at tightening the different disclosure requirements on CEOs' remuneration.

Finally, an important element of CG regulation stems from the interaction between French and European legislation. In 2008, two European directives were transposed into French law:

- the Eighth Directive, which concerns the legal auditing of listed firms and the control of financial publications
- the Corporate Governance Directive, which states that any listed company must refer to a CGC and follow the "comply-or-explain" principle (see Chapter 3 of this volume, "New Corporate Governance Rules and Practices," for the details)

Other

The French Institute of Directors (*Institut Français des Administrateurs* [IFA]) is another important player in the French CG system. It was created in 2003 by the Paris Chamber of Commerce and a group of private organizations. Its objectives are to represent the directors and provide them with relevant support. This is an important step toward the further professionalization of the directors' function.

2.1.3 A Stakeholder Model

In French companies, we find a CG system that considers the interests of different stakeholders such as employees, creditors, customers, or suppliers.

Following the European continental model of stakeholders, the Viénot I Report defines the notion of "the firm's social interest" (*Intérêt social de l'entreprise*), regarding all stakeholders as the prevailing interest of the firm over, for example, the maximization of share value for shareholders alone. Therefore, companies have a responsibility not only toward their shareholders but to society as a whole.

> In the Anglo-Saxon countries, emphasis is placed on the fastest maximization of share value, whereas in the European continental model, particularly in France, the emphasis is placed on the general interest of the company and its relationship to society as a whole. (Viénot 1995, quoted in Wirtz 2008, 33; our translation)

Another distinctive characteristic of the French system is the strong presence of unions and employee representation in the management of companies. Even if there is a trend toward decreasing the number of representatives from trade unions, the unions still possess great power in France. The "Social Partners" (*Partenaires Sociaux*) are an important element in the French stakeholder model.

> One of the characteristics of French commercial law is the possibility of having people from the company's work council (*Comité d'entreprise*) on the board with a consultative function and one or several employee(s) as directors as soon as the employees have more than three percent of the incorporated social capital of the firm. (AFEP-MEDEF 2008, 11; our translation)

This board structure could somehow limit the ability of the board to discuss strategic questions (Charkam 2008; Desnoulez 2009).

However, with the globalization of economies and financial markets, particularly since the 1980s, this French model has tended to converge toward the Anglo-Saxon model. This trend is reinforced by the strong presence of international investors in the equity of French companies. According to the *Banque de France*, at the end of 2006, 46.2 percent of the capitalization of the CAC 40 was owned by foreign investors, and this proportion continues to grow (+12.2 points since 1997). This characteristic of the shareholding structure of French listed companies also explains the early movement toward the definition of clear CG rules (Wirtz 2008, 66).

2.2 *Governance Characteristics*

2.2.1 *Missions of the Boards, Level of Power, and Responsibilities*

The AMF, in its 2009 report on internal control and CG, quotes the definition used by one French listed company on the board's functions and responsibilities:

> The board elaborates the strategy of the firm, sets the orientations of the business and checks their effective enforcement, decides whether the functions of chairman and CEO should be separated or kept unified, nominates the administrators, decides on the powers of the management board, validates the orientations set by the chairman in his *Rapport du Président*, appropriately controls, checks and monitors the procedures and reports of management control, certifies the financial statements and is responsible for providing good and reliable information to the financial market and the shareholders. (AMF 2009, 26; our translation)

On the other hand, the official definition under French company law is the following:

> The board of director sets the orientation of the business and checks the effective enforcement. Within the limits of the General Assembly's prerogatives and the legal status of the firm, the board is responsible for addressing any issue regarding the business and should make decisions to ensure that the business functions appropriately. The board is entitled to control and monitor anything whose control or monitoring it considers to be necessary. The chairman or CEO of the firm is required to communicate any relevant or necessary information to the directors for them to comply with their responsibilities. (Code de Commerce, Art. L. 225–35; our translation)

In order for directors to comply with their responsibilities, the successive CGC, from the Viénot I Report in 1995 to the most recent AFEP-MEDEF code (2008), recommend the creation of different committees and the presence of independent directors.

As far as independent directors are concerned, a definition is clearly stated in the AFEP-MEDEF code. This definition is summarized by the AMF for firms listed on Euronext, stating that independent directors are those "who are not in a situation where the independence of their judgment could be distorted or where there could be a real or potential conflict of interest" (AMF 2009, 34).

In addition to the number of independent directors (at least one-third of the board), companies are also encouraged to publish information on their directors and disclose how their experience and skills contribute to the business.

Regarding committees, any listed company must have, by law, an audit committee with at least one independent director (*Ordonnance* of December 8, 2008, implementing the Eighth European Directive).

The other committees that are recommended by the AFEP-MEDEF code but are not imposed by law are as follows:

- a committee to evaluate the accounts
- an internal audit committee
- a committee to select the external auditors
- a remuneration committee
- a nomination committee (which could belong to the remuneration committee)

According to the AMF, most of the listed companies have remuneration committees, and this proportion is increasing. Indeed, more than 90 percent of the Euronext A-compartment companies have such a committee, whereas they were only 42 percent a year earlier (AMF 2009, 39). Many companies have also a strategy committee even if the latter does not appear in the AFEP-MEDEF code.

In the stakeholder model, emphasis is placed on the interests of all the stakeholders and not only on share value maximization. The board of directors is therefore accountable for identifying, measuring, and making decisions on all the risks that could impact any of the stakeholders.

2.2.2 Auditing

As in most countries, France has two main auditing functions:

- an internal one, performed by the company itself through its internal audit team, which reports to the audit committee
- an external one by professional firms (the *commissaires aux comptes*)

On average, there are 3.6 people on the audit committees, who meet 5.3 times a year (AMF 2009, 41). The audit committee (*comité d'audit* or *comité des comptes*) must be created by the board, and there must be at least one independent director (*Ordonnance n° 2008–1278*, December 8,

2008). However, the AFEP-MEDEF code recommends having at least two-thirds of independent directors on the audit committee.

The main objectives of the audit committee are to validate the corporate accounts and to ensure that the financial information published by the company is reliable and understandable.

> The audit committee is responsible for all of the issues related to the elaboration and control of the accounting and financial information. (Code de commerce, Art. L. 823–19; our translation)

The audit committee is also responsible for interacting with the external auditors and to ensure that the external auditors work in an independent and trustful context. It is also responsible for the internal audit team's outputs.

As far as external auditing is concerned, in 2004, only 42 percent of the French listed companies were audited by one of the Big Four auditing firms (Pigé 2008, 169). Another distinctive characteristic of the French model is the presence of many independent auditing firms. French groups have always been required to appoint two auditing firms, which has enabled independent auditing firms to survive.

2.2.3 Conflict of Interests

One conflict of interest arises from the typical French unitary board where a single person assumes the cumulative functions of CEO and chairman. This combination is sometimes subject to criticism because the power could be too concentrated and the risk less mitigated. This criticism explains the introduction of the two-tier model, which separates the two roles. However, even if the functions of chairman and CEO are split, the chairman is usually a former CEO (Heidrick and Struggles 2009). Nevertheless, this centralization of power is traditional in the French environment.

The French system has also often been criticized because of its "elitism" linked to the French *Grandes Ecoles* system with its powerful networks. Chabi and Maati (2006) even talk about "the small world of CAC 40," where only very few intermediaries are necessary for two directors to meet. A large majority of board members comes from a limited number of higher education institutions (business schools, engineering schools, etc.).

Another conflict of interest arises from the board's responsibility for both the "social interest" of the firm and the information and value generated for the shareholders. In France, CGC consider the "social interest" of the firm (Wirtz 2008). This interest should indeed prevail over the directors' interests. Successive CGC have therefore tried to reduce this potential conflict between the directors and the company or its owners.

In order to reduce this potential conflict of interests, the AFEP-MEDEF code also encourages boards to have a sufficient number of independent directors[10] (see Table 7.2).

Table 7.2 Number of Independent Directors Recommended by the Codes, Adapted from Wirtz (2008) and AFEP-MEDEF (2008)

		1995	1999	2002	2008
Code		Viénot I	Viénot II	Bouton	AFEP-MEDEF
On the board					
		2	1/3	1/2	1/2 or 1/3
On the committees					
	Auditing	1	1/3	2/3	2/3
	Remuneration	N/A	1/2	1/2	1/2
	Nomination	1	1/3	1/3	1/2

2.2.4 Evaluating Board Performance

As far as board performance is concerned, the AFEP-MEDEF code recommends that boards regularly evaluate their ability to meet expectations, fulfill their missions, and achieve their goals. According to the same code, the board should carry out an unofficial self-evaluation at least once a year and an official one every three years. It should also revise its composition and working procedures accordingly. The evaluation of the board has three objectives (AFEP-MEDEF 2008, 14):

- assessing the way in which the board operates
- ensuring that important questions are suitably prepared and discussed
- measuring the performance of each director and his contribution to the board's efficiency

In practice, however, this evaluation of board performance is not regular enough in France, as only 62 percent of the companies evaluate the board performance every year. Moreover, even if companies communicate about this evaluation, very few action plans are actually disclosed in the CG documentation (AMF 2009, 5). According to the 2008 report, 70 percent of the boards from the Euronext A-compartment are assessed every year, the percentage was less for smaller companies.

In addition to these self-assessment mechanisms, boards are also rated by external companies. In France, every year since 2004, the *Agence Economique et Financiers* [AGEFI] [11] has given an annual reward for the company with the best CG (*Grand Prix du Gouvernement d'Entreprise*), rewarding companies for their CG practices and especially for their boards' performance.

There is an ongoing debate in France regarding the directors, board members, and PDGs' remuneration, as the 2009 Henri Proglio case showed.[12] As recommended by the AFEP-MEDEF code, most boards have a remuneration committee, which is the only body responsible for fixing the remuneration of its members. Moreover, half of the remuneration committee's members must be composed of independent directors.

The global amount of remuneration for the board is voted during an annual general meeting by the shareholders, and the remuneration committee is then responsible for sharing it according to different criteria (AFEP-MEDEF 2008, 22). The compensation of the board members should include a fixed and a variable component. By law, the remuneration of the board members must be disclosed in the firm's annual report.

One striking point about the board's composition in France is the under-representation of women. According to the AMF (2009) report, the share of women in these boards was only 10.6 percent at the end of 2008.

2.2.5 Disclosure on Corporate Governance

Clear disclosure on CG practices is an important requirement for financial analysts and financial markets. The Financial Communication Observatory (OCF) underlines that information on CG practices is critical for allowing financial analysts to understand how particular companies are managed (OCF 2009, 44). Solomon (2007, chap. 6) also explains the importance of CG disclosure in capital markets.

According to the Federation of European Accountants (FEE 2009), there are two key approaches to CG reporting:

- There is a *descriptive approach*, where the company describes its CG principles.
- There is a *comply-or-explain approach*, where the company mentions a CGC and explains why it has not followed some of the recommendations. Most French listed companies follow this second approach.

In 2006, a European directive was published requiring companies to add a CG statement to their annual report. This statement must contain information about the CG practices of the company (Fourth Directive, Appendix 1, 46a, in FEE 2009) as follows:

- a reference to a CGC or relevant explanations of CG practices
- following the "comply-or-explain" principle
- the description of the internal control mechanisms and risk management procedures
- information about the shareholding structure, the way the board is appointed, and the powers of the board members
- information about shareholders' meetings and rights
- information about the different management bodies and committees

These requirements have been transposed primarily in the French Commercial Code but are also included in the AFEP-MEDEF code, which is applied by 80 percent of French listed companies (AMF 2009, 31). In addition, French commercial law also obliges the PDG or chairman (in cases where the functions of chairman and CEO are separated) to publish a president's statement (*Rapport du Président*) attached to the annual report, where the chairman has to explain the way the board works and whether it complies with its mission statement. Furthermore, the remuneration of the members of the board must be disclosed and justified.

Finally, there are growing concerns and requirements about nonfinancial reporting standards. Companies are increasingly pressurized to be socially responsible, and French companies are very advanced in this trend toward corporate social responsibility. French companies have to comply with European laws and with all the requirements mainly enforced in the 2001 NRE Law (Delbard 2008).

2.3 Corporate Governance and Income Management

In France, as outlined earlier, the financial statements of individual entities are based on French GAAP, which are very close to the taxation rules, under which transactions are recorded mainly on their legal form, as opposed to their economic substance. For example, the accounting for provisions and accruals, including their reversals in subsequent accounting periods, may be justified under the prudence concept, but the real motivation is often to "manage" the taxable income. In France, there are many SMEs, which are predominately owned by families or a small group of shareholders, for whom "profits," as such, may not be their primary objective. Family-owned companies often have a long-term perspective, and more importance is given to the company's capacity to generate internally the financing sources (*autofinancement*) and to the preservation of an adequate equity base. This longer-term perspective also reflects the underlying concepts of French commercial law, which provides protection for employees and creditors.

Indeed, the safeguarding of employees' rights—employment and remuneration—is embedded in French legislation. For example, any company that employs more than fifty persons is obliged to set up a profit-sharing scheme (*Plan de Participation*) for its employees, which is based on detailed formulae relating to the company's results and its net worth or equity.

Moreover, legislation also exists regarding company equity. For example, companies are obliged to maintain a positive shareholders' equity, and if the equity base turns negative due to losses, shareholders must formally decide how to reconstruct the equity base within two years and/or decide to liquidate the company. The importance of a company's equity base is also reflected in legislation, which requires the constitution of "a legal reserve" (*réserve légale*) as part of the shareholders' equity. This "legal reserve" is funded by an annual allocation of profits (5 percent) until the reserve reaches 10 percent of the company's share capital.[13]

However, within a group of companies, the compulsory application of a uniform GAAP among the subsidiary entities does tend to reduce the practice of income smoothing. Moreover, under IFRS or French consolidation GAAP, the concepts applied are based more on the economic substance of transactions as opposed to pure legal form, thus limiting the practice of income smoothing.

Notwithstanding the application of IFRS, for consolidated financial statements, certain observers consider that income smoothing is still possible, particularly when estimates and judgment are required for asset valuations, impairment tests, and the determination of goodwill. The exploratory study of Tort (2006) on French companies confirms that the management of accounting income fundamentally depends on particular objectives, such as profit maximization/optimization strategies (usually for listed companies), policies of control (for independent companies), and income smoothing (for subsidiaries of a group).

In general, the international financial reporting framework includes some indisputable contributions to neutralize the effects of smoothing strategies, notably including the following:

- the introduction of fair value, which tends to favor, conversely, a certain volatility of earnings
- the conceptual framework's principle of neutrality or absence of bias in the establishment of accounts and the determination of results at the end of the fiscal period (Tort 2006)

Essentially, the issues of governance and income smoothing relate to the question of transparency and adequate disclosures in financial statements. In analyzing financial statements, it is important to know and understand the underlying accounting concepts that have been applied and the regulatory context of the company's reporting. Although it is considered that these aspects are common among all countries, in France it is important to distinguish the relevant accounting and reporting concepts that apply to the different reporting entities.

NOTES

1. This number amounted to less than seven hundred on the Euronext, totaling a market capitalization of €1,056 billion at the end of 2008 (www.euronext.com).
2. A discussion on the development on the evolution of the CRC structure versus the new accounting regulation authority (*Autorité des Normes Comptables* [ANC]) created in 2009 is presented in the following.
3. At that time, large French enterprises were lobbying the government for permission to draw up their accounts directly in accordance with international

accounting standards. The government agreed to this demand and passed a law doing so in April 1998, which released French listed enterprises from the obligation to follow French law for the preparation of their consolidated accounts. However, the necessary decree for application prepared by the French Accounting Regulation Committee (CRC) was not published prior to 2005; the eventual publishing coincided with the application of the corresponding EU regulation.

4. Companies have to keep their accounting records for ten years. This objective only becomes important in cases of litigation; as a result, we provide no further comments on it here.

5. Again, we stress the legal point. Economically, of course, French groups and their investors monitor their performance, particularly net income, based on consolidated numbers.

6. Therefore, French companies no longer revalue.

7. "La gouvernance recouvre l'ensemble des mécanismes qui ont pour effet de délimiter les pouvoirs et d'influencer les décisions des dirigeants, autrement dit, qui 'gouvernent' leur conduite et définissent leur espace discrétionnaire."

8. The AFEP and the MEDEF are two associations of public firms: the Association of French Private-Sector Companies (*Association Française des Entreprises Privées* [AFEP]) and the French Companies Movement Association (*Mouvement des Entreprises de France* [MEDEF]). They represent and lobby for their members. MEDEF is the largest entrepreneurs' organization in France; the MEDEF represents more than seven hundred thousand companies, of which 90 percent are SMEs with fewer than fifty employers. The MEDEF is a privileged partner in the dialogue with decision makers and the government. It is also an essential partner in the dialogue between unions and management (see http://medef.typepad.com/medef_en/missions.html). AFEP has about one hundred members representing 1,100 billion euros of turnover and 4.8 million jobs. The AFEP brings together almost all of the "bosses" (chief executives/senior executives) of the Paris stock index "CAC 40" and the large French companies. It is one of the most powerful business lobbies in France (see www.journaldunet.com/economie/enquete/afep, accessed November 2006).

9. Société Générale is one of France's leading banks and a member of the AFEP.

10. Furthermore, the AFEP recommends that a director be unable to accumulate more than three mandates at the same time, whereas the maximum today for one person is five, not including mandates for foreign companies.

11. The AGEFI is a press company that specializes in finance.

12. Henri Proglio is a well-known French chief executive. There has been an important debate regarding the remuneration he receives from his two positions with EDF and Veolia.

13. Similar but more specific regulations exist for certain business sectors such as banking and insurance.

REFERENCES

Alexander, D., P. Delvaille, and C. Saccon. 2010. Corporate governance and accounting: Analogies and differences in the European regulatory harmonization process. Paper presented at the EAA annual congress, Istanbul, May.

Autorité des marchés financiers. 2009. *AMF 2009 report on corporate governance and internal control, December. Autorité des Marchés Financiers.* www.amf-france.org (accessed January 30, 2010).

Association Française des Entreprises Privées-Mouvement des Entreprises de France. 2008. *Code de gouvernement d'entreprise des sociétés cotées, Décembre.* www.code-afep-medef.com (accessed January 15, 2010).

Bertrel, J.-P., A. Medina, M.-P. Fenoll-Trousseau, and D. Fasquelle. 2009. *Droit de l'entreprise 2009/2010: L'essentiel pour comprendre le droit.* Lamy: Rueil-Malmaison.

Bouton, D. 2002. *Pour un meilleur gouvernement des entreprises cotées, MEDEF.* http://archive.medef.com/medias/upload/1509_FICHIER.pdf (accessed January 30, 2010).

Chabi, S., and J. Maati. 2006. The small world of the CAC 40. *Banques et Marchés* 82:41–53.

Charkam, J. 2008. *Keeping better company: Corporate governance ten years.* Oxford: Oxford University Press.

Code de Commerce, 2010. www.legifrance.gouv.fr (accessed January 15, 2010).

Colasse, B., and P. Standish. 1998. De la réforme 1996–1998 du dispositif français de normalisation comptable. *Comptabilité-Contrôle-Audit* 2 (4): 5–27.

Conseil National de la Comptabilité. 2008. *IFRS for SMEs—Survey of the expectations and needs of SMEs including field tests, July, Conseil National de la Comptabilité.* www.bercy.gouv.fr/directions_services/CNCompta/rapports_etudes (accessed February 15, 2010).

Delbard, O. 2008. CSR Legislation in France and the European regulatory paradox: An analysis of EU CRS policy and sustainability reporting practice. *Corporate Governance* 8 (4): 397–405.

Delvaille, P., G. Ebbers, and C. Saccon. 2005. International financial reporting convergence: Evidence from three Continental European countries. *Accounting in Europe* 2:137–64.

Delvaille, P., and C. Hossfeld. 2006. Implementation of the IFRS by French listed companies: Implications for external and internal reporting. Paper Presented at the European Accounting Association Annual Congress, Dublin, March.

Desnoulez, A. 2009. Comparative analysis of corporate governance in France and the United Kingdom. ESCP Europe Berlin Research Paper.

Ernst and Young. 2005. *Passage aux IFRS—Les pratiques des grands groupes européens.* Meylan: CPC.

———. 2009. *Panorama des pratiques de gouvernance des sociétés cotées françaises.* http://www.ev.com/FR/fr/Services/Advisory/Risk/Enterprise-wide-Governance--Risk-and Compliance/Panorama-des-pratiques-de-gouvernance-des-soci%c3%A9r%C3%A9s-c%C3%B4t%C3%A9es-fran%C3%A7aises-2010 (accessed January 30, 2010)

Federation of European Accountants. 2009. Discussion paper for auditor's role regarding providing assurance on corporate governance statements, FEE.

Financial Communication Observatory. 2009. *Financial communication: Framework and practices. Observatoire de la Communication Financière.* www.observatoirecomfi.com (accessed January 30, 2010).

Heidrick and Struggles. 2009. *Corporate governance report 2009—boards in turbulent times.* www.heidrick.com/Publications/Reports/PublicationsReports/CorpGovEurope2009.pdf (accessed January 31, 2010).

Hopt, K. J., and P. C. Leyens. 2004. *Board models in Europe. Recent developments of internal corporate governance structures in Germany, the United Kingdom, France, and Italy.* ECGI. January. http://papers.ssrn.com/sol3/papers.cfm?abstract id=487944 (accessed December 15, 2009).

Mallin, C. 2007. *Corporate governance.* 2nd ed. Oxford: Oxford University Press.

Mazars. 2005. *IFRS: La Communication Financière des Groupes Français en 2004,* Paris. www.mazars.com (accessed December 23, 2009).

————. 2008. *Les Normes IFRS pour les PME: Perceptions et Attentes à Travers l'Europe.* www.mazars.com (accessed December 23, 2009).

MiddleNext. 2009. *Code de gouvernement d'entreprise pour les valeurs moyennes et petites. Première édition* www.middlenext.com (accessed January 30, 2010).

Nobes, C., and R. Parker. 2008. *Comparative international accounting.* 10th ed. Harlow: Pearson Education Limited.

Pigé, B. 2008. *Gouvernance, Contrôle et Audit des Organisations.* Paris, *Economica.*

Richard, B., and H. De Pitray. 2007. Président Directeur Général ou Président et Directeur Général? *Revue Française de Gouvernance d'Entreprise* 1:27–34.

Solomon, J. 2007. *Corporate governance and accountability.* Chichester: Wiley.

Tort, E. 2006. A case study of earnings management practices. *European Financial and Accounting Journal* 1 (4): 16–41.

Viénot, M. 1995. *Le conseil d'administration des sociétés cotées.* Paris: CNPF-AFEP.

————. 1999. *Rapport du comité sur le gouvernement d'entreprise,* AFEP-MEDEF. http://www.cg.org.cn/theory/zlyz/vienot19997.pdf (accessed January 31, 2010).

Wirtz, P. 2008. *Les meilleures pratiques de gouvernance d'entreprise* Paris: La Découverte.

8 Analysis of Changing Institutional Environments, New Accounting Policies, and Corporate Governance Practices in Germany

Axel Haller and Martin Wehrfritz

1. INTERCONNECTIONS BETWEEN ECONOMIC ENVIRONMENTS, ACCOUNTING, AND CORPORATE GOVERNANCE

In approaching the task of investigating latest developments in financial reporting and corporate governance (CG) in Germany, a closer look has to be made at the German financial system in general. Traditionally in Germany, stock markets play a comparatively smaller role than, for instance, in Anglo-Saxon countries (Schmidt 2004). Only a relatively small number of companies in Germany are publicly traded on capital markets and ownership is very concentrated. The bulk of German business entities, in particular the small ones, are held privately. As far as financing of companies is concerned, equity financing plays a minor role whereas bank financing is still predominant. Indicators for this fact are a relatively low rate of private share ownership and a relatively low equity ratio of German enterprises of around 18 percent on average (although it has to be said that parts of this low ratio are due to differing accounting standards; Working Group on External Financial Reporting of the Schmalenbach-Gesellschaft-Deutsche Gesellschaft für Betriebswirtschaft 1995). On the other hand, a distinctive instrument of financing for German corporations are accrued liabilities, provisions, and deferred credits, whereupon the majority are allotted to pensions that have to be capitalized under German generally accepted accounting principles (GAAP). Apart from that, banks are often creditors and at the same time investors in large stock corporations because deposits are often used to acquire extensive holdings. Also, they exert influence by using proxy rights assigned by individual shareholders who are not interested in attending the general meetings. To sum up, the German financial system can be characterized as typically relationship-based or as an insider system in contrast to an outsider or arm's-length system as, for example, in the US (Vitols 2005).

Apart from the financial system, the other major cultural specific influencing factor on financial accounting and CG in Germany is the legal system. Germany is a country with a code law system, where the major part of the legal regime is based on deductively developed written law. This applies also to the field of financial accounting and CG. Most of the regulation is incorporated in specific codes and acts that are developed and passed by political institutions (parliament and government). Only a little standardization has been done by private bodies. This judicial characteristic relates directly to the overall cultural system in Germany that can be characterized as being "state focused," in contrast to the predominantly "individualistic culture" in the US, which tends to leave regulation to a large part to private parties (regulation through contracts or private institutions/standard setters).

Connected to these factors and characteristics, the external control mechanism, which is exercised by market forces outside of a company that put pressure on the management of being replaced in case of poor performance, plays a minor role (primarily because of the minor importance of the capital market for companies and individuals) compared to internal corporate control (Werder and Talaulicar 2006). The German CG system is predominantly based on internal control mechanisms and represents a standard example of an insider-controlled system. One of the major characteristics of this control system is the two-tier governance structure, which is laid down in the Stock Corporation Act (*Aktiengesetz* [AktG]) and divides up in a management board (*Vorstand*) and a supervisory board (*Aufsichtsrat*; see the following).

Because of the growing internationalization of business in the past, the following sections will address the question whether the surrounding conditions have changed in the last few years in Germany, both in the area of financial reporting and CG.

2. ACCOUNTING

2.1 International Convergence in Accounting

2.1.1 Standardization of Accounting Practices in Germany

As mentioned earlier, in contrast to countries where accounting principles are developed by private standard-setting bodies, accounting rules in Germany are mainly enacted by the legislature and codified in law, namely, the German Commercial Code (*Handelsgesetzbuch* [HGB]). Apart from that, major sources of the accounting regime are so-called principles of proper accounting (*Grundsätze ordnungsmäßiger Buchführung* [GoB]) that supplement written law. Those principles have arisen from different sources, such as the accounting practice, court decisions (primarily by tax courts), and the accounting literature (commentaries). Moreover, there are standards for consolidated financial statements published by the private

German Accounting Standards Committee (GASC). German GAAP are therefore all codified rules and noncodified principles, standards, and norms that have to be observed when a company's financial statements are compiled (Haller 2003; Leuz and Wüstemann 2004).

Because of the legal approach of German GAAP and the EU accounting regime (Fourth and Seventh EU Directive; see Chapter 5 of this volume, "Auditing Reform in Europe"), accounting requirements depend on the legal form of the business entity. German accounting generally distinguishes between entities with unlimited liability (sole proprietorships and general partnerships), i.e., the owners have unlimited liability for all the obligations of the business, and entities with limited liability (foremost stock corporations, so-called *Aktiengesellschaften* [AG], and limited liability companies, so-called *Gesellschaften mit beschränkter Haftung* [GmbH]), i.e., there is no unlimited personal liability for any owner. Business vehicles with limited liability are exposed to much stricter accounting regulations than those with unlimited liability. Only their financial statements are required to be audited (except little companies), and they must be filed with the Commercial Register (for a detailed analysis of differential reporting in Germany, see Eierle 2005). In the following, this chapter will focus primarily on companies with limited liability, i.e., privately held and public stock corporations.

Due to the legal entity concept, every business undertaking, i.e., sole proprietorship, partnership, or corporation, has to prepare individual financial statements for the legal entity (*Jahresabschluss*). These statements still have to comply with German GAAP—despite the increasing importance of International Financial Reporting Standatds (IFRS) in the German accounting regime (see later)—and are an immediate link to legal consequences like the determination of payouts to the owners and tax payments. This strong connection between financial accounting and tax accounting is a typical element of the German accounting framework. Via the principle of congruency (*Maßgeblichkeitsprinzip*), computation of taxable income is directly related to income resulting from financial accounting. This principle was always based on the (fairness) idea that the taxable income should be based on the performance figure determining the dividend disbursements to the equity holders (Haller 1992; Leuz and Wüstemann 2004). Moreover, the principle allows especially small companies to compile only one set of accounts (the so-called *Einheitsbilanz*) for both financial and tax purposes, which significantly reduces costs for the preparation of company accounts. Nevertheless, one part of the principle of congruency has been abolished recently as discussed below.

On the other hand, consolidated financial statements (*Konzernabschluss*) have to be prepared by groups, i.e., companies that are able to exert control over one or more subsidiaries. Until the initiatives of the European Union in the last years, German GAAP was basically required for those statements, too. However, Germany was one of the first countries in the EU to allow the voluntary application of internationally accepted accounting principles (i.e., IFRS or US GAAP) instead of German GAAP in group accounts. This option was introduced in 1998 by the enactment of the Capital Raising Facilitation Act (*Kapitalaufnahmeerleichterungsgesetz* [KapAEG]) in order to alleviate globally active corporations which were exposed to the pressure of applying more investor-oriented principles due to cross-listings or market needs (Haller 2002). Until then, these companies were forced to compile two parallel sets of financial statements (or at least additional reconciliations), which resulted in high expenses and failure to explain two different reported amounts of net income. Another step that enforced the drive of internationalization of accounting in Germany was the obligation to apply internationally accepted accounting principles for mostly venture capital–financed, growing firms listed on a new segment of the German Stock Exchange, the New Market (*Neuer Markt*), which existed between 1997 and 2003.

The peak of the internationalization process of accounting in Germany was—as in other countries of the EU—the so-called IAS-Regulation (EC No. 1606/2002), which obliged all publicly traded European companies to prepare their consolidated accounts according to IFRS from 2005 onwards (apart from a few exemptions, especially those companies that reported under US GAAP at that time, with the suspension of the application of IFRS until 2007). The member state options of this regulation to prescribe (or allow) IFRS for other types of companies and/or financial statements were transformed very cautiously in Germany. All non-publicly-traded companies can opt to use IFRS in their consolidated accounts, whereas individual accounts have to be compiled under German GAAP (however, it is allowed to file individual financial statements complying with IFRS with the Commercial Register in addition to the ones under German GAAP). Therefore, apart from distinguishing on the one hand between entities with limited and those with unlimited liability, and on the other hand between individual and group financial statements, another clear differentiation between publicly traded and non-publicly-traded companies concerning the relevance of accounting rules has characterized accounting regulation in Germany for the last few years.

Whilst Germany was one of the leading non-US countries as regards corporations compiling their consolidated accounts according to US GAAP beginning with the former New Market in 1997 and the Capital Raising Facilitation Act in 1998, US GAAP have now become unattractive for German corporations because of the IAS-Regulation and the acceptance of IFRS from foreign private issuers by the Securities and Exchange Commission (SEC; since the end of 2007 through SEC Release No. 33–8879).

All in all, there has been an advancing internationalization in group accounting of German publicly traded companies since 1997. The following figure depicts, for companies traded on the major indices of the Frankfurt Stock Exchange, the share of US GAAP, IFRS, and German GAAP, respectively, in each year between 1997 and 2009 and particularly shows the spread of IFRS in the last few years (some US GAAP accounts have still been prevalent since 2007 because the concerning company is US-based or EU-based, having US GAAP accounts as primary financial statements in the annual report and just supplementary IFRS accounts outside the annual report for legal reasons).

Considering what has been said, the internationalization of German accounting primarily focused on consolidated financial statements. On the contrary, accounting rules for individual accounts were not subject to major modifications in the past until recently. The Fourth and Seventh Directives of the European Union, which aimed to harmonize accounting rules throughout Europe, were implemented in Germany in a very conservative way by the Implementing Act (*Bilanzrichtliniengesetz* [BilRiLiG]) in 1985 (Haller and Eierle 2004). Member state options were exercised to keep with long-lasting German accounting traditions. Finally in May 2009, German accounting law underwent extensive revisions by the Accounting Law Modernization Act (*Bilanzrechtsmodernisierungsgesetz* [BilMoG]), which can be regarded as a considerable step in the convergence process of the German accounting regime to international financial reporting (see the following).

Along with the internationalization of the German accounting regime for publicly traded companies and against the background of the development of the IFRS for SMEs by the IASB, which was finally published in July 2009, there has been an intense discussion about whether convergence towards international accounting should also take place for non-publicly-traded firms, especially SMEs. Studies show that although a remarkable number of German SMEs have material cross-border

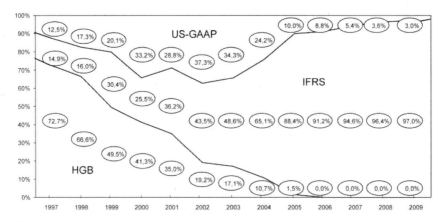

Figure 8.1 Use of international and national accounting standards in group accounts of major publicly traded companies in Germany between 1997 and 2009 (based on Zwirner 2009).

business activities in terms of export and import of goods and services as well as investments in foreign subsidiaries, financing through equity or foreign borrowings happens quite rarely (Eierle, Haller, and Beiersdorf 2007). This is one reason why the German accounting community does not regard the IFRS for SMEs as being relevant for the major part of German SMEs. In addition, its application is expected to be too costly and complex for German SMEs. This is in line with the opinion of banks as a major user group of financial statements of SMEs. According to a recent study, 46 percent of the banks that were interviewed see no or only little need for customers to present internationally comparable financial statements. Nevertheless, this assessed need for such information increases with the number of customers as well as with the share of foreign customers (Haller et al. 2008).

2.1.2 Changes in Financial Reporting Objectives

As already mentioned (see section 1 of this chapter), partly because of the fact that loans by banks are the main source of finance for German entities, the general concept of the firm in Germany is much more stakeholder-oriented than shareholder-oriented. This materially influences the objectives of financial accounting (in particular with regard to individual accounts). Besides the creditors, German financial statements serve the interests of the shareholders, the tax authority, and other stakeholders like employees, customers, suppliers, and even the whole society (Haller 2003). The introduction of the Public Disclosure Act (*Publizitätsgesetz* [PublG]) in 1969, which subjects nonlimited entities that exceed certain thresholds in terms of size to the same strict financial reporting regulations as limited liability companies, was hence grounded in the idea that big entities are meant to assume social responsibility. In this respect, financial reporting in Germany has a broader focus than in Anglo-Saxon countries, where primarily the interests of shareholders are focused on (Haller and Walton 2003).

Taken this specific socioeconomic environment into account—and therefore given the fact that German financial statements do not only serve one major interest group—as the investors in other countries, there are several objectives of financial reporting in Germany that try to balance the interests of the involved parties. Apart from the basic aim of stewardship, these can be identified as providing information and income calculation. The latter includes the sub-goals of the protection of creditors and minorities and the derivation of taxable income.

Creditors are interested in the preservation of capital in order to ensure their interest payments and payments of principle. Because of the overwhelming importance of bank financing in Germany, accounting law aims to protect creditors by bordering the distribution of profits to shareholders. Thus, assets and liabilities are valued cautiously and profits are calculated on a conservative basis that is sensitive to risks (principle of prudence). This is confirmed by studies analyzing the effects of the transition of German publicly traded companies from German GAAP to IFRS at the beginning of 2005. For instance, according to one study, equity under IFRS was on average 19.6 percent higher than that reported under German GAAP and net income in 2004 increased by 15.4 percent after IFRS adoption (Haller, Ernstberger, and Froschhammer 2009). Other studies deliver comparable results for Germany (Leker, Mahlstedt, and Kehrel 2008; Küting and Zwirner 2007) and international studies show that this holds especially compared to Anglo-Saxon countries where the effects are the opposite way, i.e., for instance, equity is on average lower under IFRS compared to local GAAP of those countries (Hellman et al. 2010).

This reasoning holds also for SMEs with limited liability that are not listed on the stock market but for which essentially the same accounting principles are relevant as for big stock corporations in Germany. This stands in contrast to, for instance, the US, where only those companies that are subject to the requirements of the authorities of capital markets—and therefore need the auditor's opinion—have to adhere to US GAAP.

Notwithstanding this clear tendency towards conservative accounting rules, there are also regulations that avoid the undervaluation of net assets by the management by an overinterpretation of the principle of prudence. This serves the interests of minority shareholders by guaranteeing an appropriate level of reported income available for distribution.

The third purpose of income calculation in German financial statements—besides creditor and minority protection—is to derive taxable income, because, as already mentioned, the tax accounts are closely tied to the commercial accounts (principle of congruency). Although this principle primarily affects the tax accounts, it also has an influence on the commercial financial statements. An optimized tax strategy requires appropriate actions in the commercial accounts and therefore strengthens the conservative valuation in this set of financial statements (Working Group on External Financial Reporting of the Schmalenbach-Gesellschaft-Deutsche Gesellschaft für Betriebswirtschaft 1995; Haller 1992). However, a part of this principle has been abolished lately by the Accounting Law Modernization Act (BilMoG—see the following).

All these goals are an outflow of the stakeholder-oriented approach in Germany, which indicates that the financial statements should address and serve the interests of all stakeholders of a firm. This is in sharp contrast to Anglo-Saxon countries where the main objective is to give a fair presentation of the financial situation of an entity in order to provide decision-useful information to the investors.

Nevertheless, the true and fair view principle has been imposed by the directives of the European Union on Germany. However, it has no dominant influence on recognition and measurement but should be guaranteed by the information given in the notes to the accounts. According to the German legislator, this ensures more reliable and objective financial accounting figures because of less individual judgment and interpretation, whereas relevance is achieved by additional information in the notes (Haller 2003).

The pass of the Accounting Law Modernization Act (BilMoG) in May 2009 represents a major change of the German financial accounting regime. There was a clear shift to a gaining importance of the information function of financial accounting at the expense of the principle of prudence. According to the German legislator, this reform should adapt German accounting rules to international accounting rules in order to make an equivalent alternative to internationally accepted accounting principles like IFRS or US GAAP out of reformed German GAAP. In addition, the act also enlarges the instruments of individual accounts of publicly traded companies, which are not required to present consolidated accounts, by a Statement of Cash Flows and a Statement of Changes in Equity, which provide important information not only to shareholders. These additional instruments had already been introduced for consolidated accounts by the Accounting Law Reform Act (*Bilanzrechtsreformgesetz* [BilReG]) in 2004.

2.1.3 Changes in Characteristics and Constraints of Decision-Useful Financial Reporting Information

As already mentioned, German accounting law traditionally has the characteristic of delivering decision-useful information by providing reliable and objective data, determined on a prudent basis. This implies that income is only recognized if it is definitely realized, assets are valued conservatively on a lower-cost or market basis, and all potential risks and future losses that can be anticipated reliably are recognized through liabilities. This stems, as already said, from additional goals of accounting (preservation of capital, protection of creditors) that go beyond the information of investors. Nevertheless, the Accounting Law Modernization Act (BilMoG) of 2009 represents a shift in the focus of these objectives. The relevance of decision-useful financial reporting information has been strengthened by the amendment of various rules, whereas reliability has suffered some loss of the great importance it possessed before the reform. The act amended and added, amongst other things, concrete recognition and measurement rules in the German Commercial Code (HGB). For instance, according to Article 248 (para. 2 HGB), companies are now allowed to recognize development cost as an intangible asset, which was not allowed to be recorded in the past because it was asserted that their values could not be determined objectively (e.g., as based on a purchase). The prior option to recognize goodwill resulting from a business combination was changed to an obligation to do so (Article 246, para. 1 s. 4 HGB). Measurement of provisions has become more relevant because future cost increases have to be included according to Article 253 (para. 1 s. 2 HGB), which were not under former rules. Also, the often criticized rule to include only direct costs for the valuation of self-generated inventories and fixed assets has been altered. The reform act prescribes that indirect costs related to material and manufacturing have to be included in costs of conversion (Article 255, para. 2 s. 2 HGB).

The second major component of the reform was the abolishment of various overt accounting options that were also typical for German GAAP. The possibility to recognize future impairment losses on assets on the basis of a "reasonable commercial assessment" has been withdrawn as well as the option to recognize provisions for operating expenses without an obligation to a third party.

However, the reform has not brought a turn from historical cost to fair value accounting. The long tradition of German accounting of only calculating profits that have been definitely realized persists. Historical acquisition or production costs are still the maximum value to be capitalized (Article 253, para. 1 s. 1 HGB). Fair values (e.g., replacement costs or market values) above amortized costs are still not permitted, except for an exceptional rule for trading securities of banks that can be measured on a fair value basis (Article 340e, para. 3 s. 1 HGB).

This shift to a stress of relevant information and the recognition of less objective accounting figures is compensated by distribution restrictions in order to protect creditors. For instance, the profit from recognizing development cost cannot be distributed to shareholders as long as the amount of distributable retained earnings is smaller than the amount of capitalized development cost. The same applies to recognized deferred tax assets.

Another essential reform piece of the Accounting Law Modernization Act is the abolishment of one element of the principle of congruency, namely, the "principle of converse congruency." According to this principle, specific income-reducing tax benefits were allowed in the tax statements but could only be used if they were equally applied in the commercial accounts. Therefore, the tax law had an important effect on financial accounting. The abolishment of this principle represents an incisive break with one part of the connection between tax accounting and financial accounting that has existed since 1874, when the first tax laws of German states (Bremen and Saxony) referred to commercial accounts to compute tax payments (Haller 1992; Ballwieser 2001). It helps to disentangle the distortion of commercial accounts by politically motivated allowances, promotes the informational content of German financial statements, and might represent the first step towards a set of stand-alone tax accounts that are totally independent of the commercial financial accounts. The latter would represent a situation that would break entirely with the long tradition of the principle of congruency.

2.2 Economic Resources and Claims on Them

German accounting law strictly adheres to the clean surplus concept, which means that the equity change (excluding transferals from and to the equity holders) over the lifetime of an entity (so-called "total income") always equals the sum of reported net incomes shown in the profit and loss accounts of each of the individual periods. The only exception exists in the consolidated accounts where currency translation effects do not touch the profit or loss account. Hence, the concept of comprehensive income that includes "other comprehensive income" as an element is largely unknown in German financial accounting. This implies that profit or loss includes all changes in equity besides transactions with shareholders. According to a recent study, investors attach more importance to changes of the profit of a corporation compared to those of the dividend or the cash flow. However, this does not hold for institutional investors who equally lay stress on all three figures (Ernst, Gassen, and Pellens 2009).

In Germany there is no requirement to report earnings per share (EPS) like, e.g., under IFRS or US GAAP, with one exemption within the German Accounting Standards (GAS), which are only applicable to group accounts under German GAAP. However, German corporations presented similar figures on a voluntary basis in the past (for the most used ratio, see Busse von Colbe, Becker, and Berndt 2000). Since the IAS-Regulation and the requirement for German listed corporations to adhere to IFRS, listed parent companies present earnings per share according to IAS 33.

As already said, the peculiarities in German accounting law had an important influence on companies' performance measure. The principle of conservatism and the principle of congruency were the main drivers of low levels of reported profit and a high rate of "internally generated equity" through undervaluation (so-called "creation of hidden reserves") as an instrument of financing. In the past, the biggest change in the single accounts was the abolishment of the principle of converse congruency (see the preceding), which will lead to financial reporting that is less distorted by tax law. The fact that conservatism in German accounting law still persists, especially regarding the reluctance to adopt fair value accounting in the Accounting Law Modernization Act, is due to a politically affected legislative process. The global financial crisis and the criticism on the potential pro-cyclical effects of fair values were the main reasons why the reform of German accounting law fell short on this issue.

3. CORPORATE GOVERNANCE

3.1 Regulation and the Scope of Corporate Governance

Because of the underlying Continental European legal system and a different socioeconomic environment, the German CG system differs from the Anglo-Saxon one in many aspects. German law can be characterized as civil or code law in contrast to common law like, e.g., in the US. As German GAAP, CG regulations are primarily codified in law, e.g., in the German Commercial Code (HGB), Stock Corporation Act (AktG), Limited

Liability Company Act (GmbH), etc. The legal structure of the German stock corporation (AG), which stands at the center of the CG debate, has been basically untouched since the enactment of the Stock Corporation Act in 1969. Thus, the CG structure of large corporations in Germany was also relatively stable over time. In addition to codified rules, the German legislator assigned the task to develop standards for good and responsible CG to a newly founded government commission (*Regierungskommission Deutscher Corporate Governance-Kodex*, the so-called *Cromme-Commission*, named after its former chairman Gerhard Cromme) in 2002, after various private initiatives had already proposed voluntarily applicable codes. This commission published a nonlegislative code on CG (German Corporate Governance Code) for the first time in 2002. The code has been revised several times since then and is in effect as amended on May 26, 2010 (for the details of the code see Chapter 3 of this volume, "New Corporate Governance Rules and Practices"). The code includes standards of best practice and is legally fixed in the Stock Corporation Act (Nietsch 2005). Article 161 of the Stock Corporation Act requires a declaration of conformity with the code for publicly traded companies, which includes an obligation of "comply-or-explain," which means that either the company keeps to the recommendations of the code or it has to explain why it does not follow the respective recommendation. However, the code comprises a lot of regulations that are already binding rules enacted in the Stock Corporation Act. Therefore, many argue that the German Corporate Governance Code has not changed the structure of German CG fundamentally. It rather plays an explanatory role and is seen as a "marketing instrument" to promote German corporations' shares to international investors (Noack and Zetzsche 2005). The great majority of German stock corporations adhere to the code. According to a recent study, in 2009 96.3 percent of the so-called "DAX 30 companies," which are the thirty biggest German stock corporations in terms of market capitalization, complied with the recommendations of the code and 85.4 percent with the suggestions (Werder and Talaulicar 2010). Apart from codified and noncodified rules, CG is also prevalent as factual CG through certain processes between the involved parties in the governance or the ownership structure of a corporation.

As a result of the aforementioned prevailing stakeholder concept of the firm in Germany, another specific characteristic of the German CG system is the integration of creditors and employees into the governance of corporations. As already explained, banks have an important influence on corporations not only as shareholders, but also as big lenders and as holders of proxy rights of their clients. Apart from that, codetermination by employee representatives is mandatory in corporations, whereas the extent depends on the size of the company (Schmidt 2004). This major participation of employee representatives in the decision making of companies is regulated in three laws, the Montan Participation Act (*Montan-Mitbestimmungsgesetz*) of 1951, the Industrial Constitution Act (*Betriebsverfassungsgesetz*) of 1952, which was transformed into the Third-Contribution Act (*Drittel-beteiligungsgesetz*) of 2004, and the Participation Act (*Mitbestimmungsge-setz*) of 1976, and reflects the responsibility of a company to its employees (Haller 2003).

The scope of CG in Germany becomes obvious when looking at the German Corporate Governance Code. It includes no concrete definition of CG but it says that it "presents essential statutory regulations for the management and supervision (governance) of German listed companies and contains internationally and nationally recognized standards for good and responsible governance" (para. 1, German Corporate Governance Code). This is a broader approach of CG than that of other authors who, for instance, take a shareholder-oriented position and claim that CG has to serve foremost the interests of the investors (e.g., Shleifer and Vishny 1997).

3.2 Governance Characteristics

3.2.1 Recent Regulations

There have been several legal changes and new regulations on CG in Germany during the last two decades and an accompanying debate on "good" CG (Steger and Hartz 2005). Most of the regulations were legislative measures. Figure 8.2 displays legislative acts, nonlegislative rules, and other pronouncements of the German legislator concerning CG regulation, of which only some can be treated in this chapter. It shows that the frequency of activities has increased significantly in recent years.

Because of criticisms that accused this system of being outdated, the German legislator passed a number of acts in recent years promoting the stock market, debundling concentrated ownership and cross-holdings amongst corporations. In 2002, the Fourth Financial Market Promotion Act extended the power of the recently established Federal Financial Supervisory Authority (*Bundesanstalt für Finanzdienstleistungsaufsicht* [BaFin]), which monitors securities trading.

In 2004, the Accounting Enforcement Act (*Bilanzkontrollgesetz* [BilKoG]) set up an external financial reporting enforcement system on a two-tier basis. The first tier consists of the so-called Financial Reporting Enforcement Panel (*Deutsche Prüfstelle für Rechnungslegung* [DPR]), which is organized under private law and conducts investigations of financial statements because of raised suspicion (a so-called reactive audit) and by random samples (a so-called proactive audit). At the second tier is the BaFin, which continues the examination and can enforce accounting mistakes if a company is unwilling to cooperate (Ernstberger, Stich, and Vogler 2008). In addition to the established enforcement system, enforcement takes place through CG. The management is obliged to ensure proper application of accounting law, the supervisory board has to examine the financial statements, and the statutory audit plays an important role. The

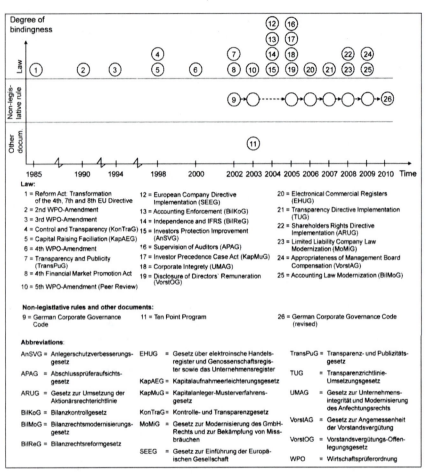

Figure 8.2   Regulatory activities in Germany concerning corporate governance issues.

Law for the Strengthening of Control and Transparency (*Kontroll- und Transparenzgesetz* [KonTraG]) in 1998 and the Law on Transparency and Publicity (*Transparenz- und Publizitätsgesetz* [TransPuG]) in 2002 aimed to improve the monitoring process of the management board by the supervisory board. Furthermore, a tax reform in 2000, which exempted capital gains from the disposal of cross-shareholdings from corporate tax, aimed at unwinding cross-holdings amongst corporations. However, low share prices in the years after the stock market bubble around the turn of the millennium averted widespread sales (Werder and Talaulicar 2006).

As already mentioned, most rules of the new German Corporate Governance Code just replicated legal bindings of German corporate law. Moreover, most of the new regulations were introduced because of the obligation to implement directives of the European Union. However, because these directives are always compromises between the countries with either an Anglo-Saxon or a Continental European background, they do not dictate rules that break with either one of the two systems, in this case with the respective CG systems. For instance, the regulation of the European Commission on the Statute for a European company (*Societas Europae* [SE]), which aimed to harmonize law on the legal structure of corporations across Europe, includes the choice for the companies between the single-tier and the two-tier governance model. The German companies that have so far adopted the SE as their legal form (for instance, Allianz SE, BASF SE, MAN SE, etc.) have kept their two-tier governance structure. Therefore, notwithstanding these new regulations and legal changes in recent years, many argue that the German CG system has not undergone a fundamental change towards the Anglo-Saxon, outsider-oriented one (Nietsch 2005; Werder and Talaulicar 2006).

3.2.2 Auditing

There have been major legislative activities in Germany recently concerning auditing as an instrument of external CG, which is legally required for all (except small) companies with limited liability (mainly AG, GmbH) and for large entities, which fall under the PublG (see section 2 of this chapter). In this respect, the Sarbanes-Oxley Act (SOX) of 2002, which was a reaction to a number of accounting and auditing scandals in the US (in particular the Enron case), was a main driver for these reforms and partly served as a role model for the German legislator. Also, the new US regulations resulted in rulings of the EU that had to be implemented by the EU member states and therefore also by Germany.

The most important regulatory initiative of the EU was the amendment of the directive on statutory audit of annual accounts and consolidated accounts, the so-called modernized Eighth Directive, in 2006, which included rules on the auditing profession's oversight, auditor's independence, and auditing standards (for details, see Chapter 5 of this volume, "Auditing Reform in Europe").

The German government followed the international trend with the publication of the Ten Point Program to Foster the Integrity of Companies and Investor Protection (*10-Punkte-Programm zur Stärkung der Unternehmensintegrität und des Anlegerschutzes*) in 2003, which included an announcement of several acts concerning capital market conditions and CG, in particular auditing. The first legislative act following the Ten Point Program was the Law on the Supervision of Auditors (*Abschlussprüferaufsichtsgesetz* [APAG]), which established a private board comparable to the PCAOB (the so-called *Abschlussprüferaufsichtskommission* [APAK]). The APAK is provided with information and inspection rights for the quality assurance of statutory audits and is also the responsible body for cooperation with auditing oversight authorities of other countries (Haller, Ernstberger, and

Kraus 2006). Even though the accounting profession through the Chamber of Public Accountants (*Wirtschaftsprüferkammer* [WPK]) is still responsible for oversight of German auditors in the first step, the APAK oversees the WPK's actions and is the final decision authority. Another law, the Accounting Law Reform Act (BilReG), was passed in 2004 and made fundamental revisions to German regulations on auditor's independence. It concretized circumstances when an auditor shall not carry out a statutory audit because of financial or personnel relationships with the client (e.g., financial interests in the audited entity). The BilReG also introduced a cap for income earned from one single client and its subsidiaries of 30 percent and 15 percent of total income respectively depending on whether the client is an "ordinary" entity or an "entity of public interest" (those are entities raising capital in an organized market—this differentiation in audit requirements according to companies of public interest and others was new for Germany and relates to the amended Eighth EU Directive). Moreover, the rule of internal rotation of statutory auditors, the disclosure of fees distinguishing between different services, and interdiction of carrying out audit and certain nonaudit services at the same time were established by the act. In 2009, the Accounting Law Modernization Act (BilMoG) introduced the obligation for publicly traded companies (with some exemptions) to establish an audit committee that is responsible for issues of accounting and risk management and auditor engagement amongst others. Also, the mandatory application of International Standards on Auditing (ISAs) was prescribed for every statutory audit, as soon as those standards are endorsed by the European Union.

These regulatory activities can be seen as spillover effects by SOX; that is to say, there was a one-sided process of convergence in external CG, namely, Germany shifting towards regulations of the US, in particular of SOX (Haller, Ernstberger, and Kraus 2006). Most of the new rules resulted from the implementation of the amended Eighth EU Directive. Particularly these regulations on caps on income earned from one client and on auditors' rotation have led to an increasingly concentrated audit market in Germany. This concentration also stems from the mandatory IFRS application in group accounts for publicly traded companies, because the big accounting firms are able to handle the specialization in different accounting standards. In 2008, already around 82 percent of the accounts of 160 German corporations that are contained in the selection indices DAX, MDAX, SDAX, and TecDAX (the major trading indices) of the Frankfurt Stock Exchange were audited by the Big Four accounting firms (Petersen, Zwirner, and Boecker 2010).

3.2.3 Power and Responsibilities of Top Management

As already stated, the German stock corporation has a two-tier system with a management board (*Vorstand*) that is responsible for the executive management of the company and a separate supervisory board (*Aufsichtsrat*) for monitoring and advising the management board. All members of the management board are jointly accountable for the management of the company. A member of the management board can never be a member of the supervisory board of the same company and vice versa. The chairman of the management board represents the board without the right to instruct other board members (Werder and Talaulicar 2006). Besides other duties, the management board is responsible for the presentation and publication of financial statements and has to pass it to the supervisory board for examination together with the long form audit report of the statutory auditor. Whereas both the management board and the supervisory board are responsible to agree on the individual annual accounts, there is no such agreement on the consolidated accounts that are nevertheless reviewed by the supervisory board. Because of the prevalent codetermination in Germany, the supervisory board is made up by up to one-half of employee representatives (depending on the size of the company), whereas the other half are shareholder or bank representatives. However, the chairman of the supervisory board is typically a representative of the shareholders who has a tie-breaking vote.

The inclusion of various stakeholders in the supervisory body of a company is often referred to as the continental approach of a network-oriented governance that strengthens the effectiveness of monitoring (Koehler et al. 2008). Recently, there have been several legislative acts that intended to promote internal CG by the supervisory board. In 1998, the KonTraG aimed to improve management supervision by the obligation to establish an early warning system. The Law on Transparency and Publicity (TransPuG) prescribed a specific number of board meetings, committees, and information to be presented to the supervisory board by the management board. Since the enactment of the Accounting Law Modernization Act (BilMoG) in 2009, a publicly traded company has to make sure that one member of the supervisory board has distinct expertise in financial reporting or auditing. Furthermore, the Accounting Law Modernization Act clarified and stressed the responsibility of the supervisory board for internal control mechanisms.

3.2.4 Conflict of Interests

Governance of German corporations is characterized by a clear distinction between execution of management and supervision. This separation is embodied by the two boards. Information asymmetries, which are the main reason for the agency problem, are reduced via private communication channels rather than by public disclosure (Ball, Kothari, and Robin 2000). That is why CG in German corporations is often said to be insider controlled (Leuz and Wüstemann 2004).

However, misapplications of the dualistic board system have taken place. It is still very common in German corporations for the former chairman of the management board to become the chairperson of the supervisory board.

This was often criticized because of conflicts of interests. It is said that these former chairmen could try to hugger-mugger past faults under their tenure of office and that a strategic realignment of the company could be impeded. In recent years, the German legislator announced several times regulations to break with this tradition but to date no bill has been passed. Another criticism addresses the problem that some executives hold too many positions in different supervisory boards of other firms; doubts as to whether they can fulfill their monitoring function adequately are appropriate.

3.2.5 Evaluating Board Performance

In German corporations, compensation of the management board is determined by the supervisory board. In July 2009, the German government passed the Act on the Appropriateness of Management Board Compensation (*Gesetz zur Angemessenheit der Vorstandsvergütung* [VorstAG]), which, amongst other things, obliges the whole supervisory board instead of a remuneration committee to vote on the remuneration of the management board. This is, however, often criticized as being counterproductive because the installation of a committee made up by experts is seen as superior in determining appropriate compensation. Until the enactment of the VorstAG, there were only recommendations in the German Corporate Governance Code for how the members of the management board of German corporations should be remunerated. The compensation of the board members shall include a fixed and a variable component. The variable component should include one-time and annually payable components linked to the business performance as well as long-term incentives cognizant of risk elements. The individual components as well as the compensation in total must be appropriate. This was codified by the aforementioned VorstAG, that aims for a greater focus on incentives concerning the company's long-term development in executive remuneration.

In practice, management board remuneration is based on different aspects. Besides a fixed amount, contracts usually base variable components on the overall performance of the entity, i.e., the growth of the company, reported income, or market value. Stock options are also very common as a variable component of compensation. However, the VorstAG includes a rule whereupon the vesting period must amount to a minimum of four years.

3.2.6 Disclosure on Corporate Governance

Since 2002, listed corporations in Germany have been obliged to make a declaration of conformity with the German Corporate Governance Code, including a list of recommendations that were not applied. This requirement was introduced by an amendment of the Stock Corporation Act by the Law on Transparency and Publicity from 2002 (TransPuG).

In 2009, the Accounting Law Modernization Act (BilMoG) enlarged this disclosure requirement for listed corporations by demanding a "declaration of governance" (Article 289a HGB), which is more detailed and includes more information on CG. This declaration has to be included into the management review (the so-called *Lagebericht*), a reporting instrument supplementing the financial statements, which is mandatory for all companies with limited liability (as in all member states of the EU, according to the Fourth and Seventh Directive). From 2009 onwards, this declaration must include explanations in case of deviations from recommendations of the Corporate Governance Code. In addition to that, companies have to report on essential CG practices that exceed what is required by law alongside with an indication where these are accessible for the general public. Moreover, the company has to describe the functioning of the management board and the supervisory board as well as the composition and the functioning of the committees. Further, the Accounting Law Modernization Act (BilMoG) introduced the obligation for listed corporations to report in their financial statements on the characteristics of their internal control and risk management systems in regard to the accounting processes and the responsibility of the supervisory board to monitor them. Thus, the German legislator tried to stimulate corporations to implement appropriate internal control systems and to grapple with their effectivity.

The recommendation of the German Corporate Governance Code to disclose the individual remuneration of each member of the management board was very rarely complied with in the past. As a consequence, the German legislator passed the Law on Disclosure of Management Board Compensation (*Gesetz über die Offenlegung der Vorstandsvergütungen* [VorstOG]) in 2005, which dictates the publication of management board compensation on an individual basis. The disclosure of each board member's compensation should facilitate the evaluation whether the remuneration of the concerned board member is appropriate. Also, such a disclosure should help to avoid excessive executive compensation, which is currently discussed as being incriminatory for the balance between the different participants in governance of corporations. Nevertheless, if three-quarters of the shareholders in attendance at the general meeting vote for an opting-out clause, the company is not obliged to follow this particular disclosure requirement.

Reporting about nonfinancial success factors of the business has become more and more common in Germany because the conviction that nonfinancial factors can have a considerable influence on a firm's performance is increasing, and the legislator has required this type of information in the management review (*Lagebericht*) if it is perceived to be material. In addition to the disclosure in the management review, large companies in particular have started to present separate so-called "sustainability reports" or "corporate social responsibility reports" on a voluntary basis (Institut für ökologische Wirtschaftsforschung/future e.V. 2007), in order to react to the growing expectation of the stakeholders with regard to the role of companies in establishing a sustainable development of society.

3.3 Corporate Governance and Income Management

The goal of creditor protection via preservation of capital in German accounts is mainly achieved by conservative accounting. Besides this objective, prudent calculation of profits leads to hidden reserves, which is meant to be an appropriate instrument of internal financing for companies in order to strengthen their financial stability. The principle of congruency and the former principle of converse congruency have also been main drivers for a relatively low reported income. In the past, income smoothing was the primary goal of corporations in reporting income.

Profits of sole proprietorships and partnerships with unlimited liability of the owners can be distributed completely. In contrast, the shareholders of corporations do not have full access to reported profits. The restriction of profit distribution of stock corporations is codified in Article 58 of the Stock Corporation Act (AktG) and serves the goal of the preservation of capital. First of all, a specific amount of legal reserves as a percentage of common stock have to be established. Furthermore, bylaws of the company can require additional reserves to be retained. The amount of distributed income is not only decided by the management of the company, but also by the shareholders in the general meeting. However, in general only 50 percent of the reported profit is at the shareholders' disposal. They can decide whether to disburse it or transfer it to retained earnings. The other half is at the management's discretion to either put it in the retained earnings or to leave it up to the shareholders' discretion. This is another reason for prudent calculation of income, because shareholders are always entitled to half of reported income and the management must be sure that these payouts are definitely realized (Working Group on External Financial Reporting of the Schmalenbach-Gesellschaft-Deutsche Gesellschaft für Betriebswirtschaft 1995). Further, the preservation of capital is partly achieved by several rules that are dispersed in the German Commercial Code that restrict profit distribution for specific recognized assets. As already mentioned (section 2 of this chapter) this is the case for profits from recognized deferred tax assets as well as capitalized development expenses. These amounts are not allowed to be disbursed to the shareholders, as long as the freely disposable retained earnings are lower than the recognized tax assets and/or expenses.

Another aspect is the strict separation between the individual accounts for the entity and the consolidated accounts for the group. Profit distribution is still dependent on the income in the individual accounts. The introduction of IFRS had no influence on the legal determination of payouts. However, practitioners see more relevance for disclosed income in the consolidated financial statements and try to harmonize reported income figures of the two sets of accounts within the legal tolerance (Pellens, Gassen, and Richard 2003).

REFERENCES

Ball, R., S. Kothari, and A. Robin. 2000. The effect of international institutional factors on properties of accounting earnings. *Journal of Accounting and Economics* 29: 1–52.

Ballwieser, W. 2001. Germany—individual accounts. In *Transnational accounting*, 2nd ed., ed. D. Ordelheide and KPMG, 1217–1351. New York: Palgrave.

Busse von Colbe, W., W. Becker, and H. Berndt. 2000. Ergebnis je Aktie nach DVFA/ SG. In *DVFA/SG earnings per share*, 1–123, 3rd ed. Stuttgart: DVFA/SG.

Eierle, B. 2005. Differential reporting in Germany—a historical analysis. *Accounting, Business and Financial History* 15 (3): 279–315.

Eierle, B., A. Haller, and K. Beiersdorf. 2007. Final report of the survey on the ED-IFRS for SMEs among German SMEs. Berlin: BDI/DIHK/DRSC.

Ernst, E., J. Gassen, and B. Pellens. 2009. Verhalten und Präferenzen deutscher Aktionäre: Eine Befragung von privaten und institutionellen Anlegern zum Informationsverhalten, zur Dividendenpräferenz und zur Wahrnehmung von Stimmrechten. *Studien des Deutschen Aktieninstituts, Heft 42*, ed. v. Rosen. Frankfurt am Main: DAI.

Ernstberger, J., M. Stich, and O. Vogler. 2008. Economic consequences of the German reforms on the enforcement of IFRS. University of Bochum Working Paper.

Haller, A. 1992. The relationship of financial and tax accounting in Germany: A major reason for accounting disharmony in Europe. *International Journal of Accounting* 27: 310–23.

———. 2002. Financial accounting developments in the European Union: Past events and future prospects. *European Accounting Review* 11 (1): 153–90.

———. 2003. Accounting in Germany. In *International accounting*, 2nd ed., ed. P. Walton, A. Haller, B. Raffournier, 91–128. London: Thomson.

Haller, A., and B. Eierle. 2004. The adaptation of German accounting rules to IFRS: A legislative balancing act. *Accounting in Europe* 1 (1): 27–50.

Haller, A., J. Ernstberger, and M. Froschhammer. 2009. Implications of the mandatory transition from national GAAP to IFRS—empirical evidence from Germany. *Advances in Accounting, Incorporating Advances in International Accounting* 2 (25): 226–36.

Haller, A., J. Ernstberger, and C. Kraus. 2006. Extraterritorial impacts of the Sarbanes-Oxley Act on external corporate governance—current evidence from a German perspective. *Corporate Ownership and Control* 3(3): 113–27.

Haller, A., J. Löffelmann, K. Beiersdorf, H. Bolin, B. Etzel, and K. Haussmann. 2008. Financial reporting from the perspective of banks as a major user group of financial statements. Empirical results and implications for the further development of an international financial reporting standard for private entities. Berlin: DRSC.

Haller, A., and P. Walton. 2003. Country differences and harmonization. In *International accounting*, 2nd ed., ed. P. Walton, A. Haller, B. Raffournier, 1–34. London: Thomson.

Hellman, N., S. Gray, R. D. Morris, and A. Haller. 2010. The impact of IFRS on international financial analysis: The significance of country differences in a comparative study of UK, Australian, Dutch, French, German and Swedish companies. Stockholm School of Economics Working Paper.

Institut für ökologische Wirtschaftsforschung/future e.V. 2007. Nachhaltigkeitsberichterstattung in Deutschland—Ergebnisse und Trends im Ranking 2007. Münster: Iöw/future.

Koehler, A. G., K.-U. Marten, R. Quick, and K. Ruhnke. 2008. Improvements driven by internationalization. In *Auditing, trust and governance—developing regulation in Europe*, ed. R. Quick, S. Turley, and M. Willekens, 111–143. London and New York: Routledge.

Küting, K., and C. Zwirner. 2007. Analyse quantitativer Reinvermögenseffekte durch die Anwendung der IFRS—Modellierte Berechnungsmethodik und empirische Befunde. *Zeitschrift für internationale und kapitalmarktorientierte Rechnungslegung* 7 (3): 142–54.

Leker, J., D. Mahlstedt, and U. Kehrel. 2008. Auswirkungen der IFRS-Rechnungslegungsumstellung auf das Jahresabschlussbild. *Zeitschrift für internationale und kapitalmarktorientierte Rechnungslegung* 8 (6): 379–88.

Leuz, C., and J. Wüstemann. 2004. The role of accounting in the German financial system. In *The German financial system*, ed. J. P. Krahnen and R. H. Schmidt, 450–81. Oxford: Oxford University Press.

Nietsch, M. 2005. Corporate governance and company law reform: A German perspective. *Corporate Governance: An International Review* 13 (3): 368–76.

Noack, U., and D. Zetzsche. 2005. Corporate governance reform in Germany: The second decade. *European Business Law Review* 16 (5): 1033–64.

Pellens, B., J. Gassen, and M. Richard. 2003. Ausschüttungspolitik börsennotierter Unternehmen in Deutschland. *Die Betriebswirtschaft* 63: 309–32.

Petersen, K., C. Zwirner, and C. Boecker. 2010. Der Wirtschaftsprüfungsmarkt in Deutschland. Ergebnisse einer Analyse in DAX, MDAX, SDAX und TecDAX. *Zeitschrift für internationale und kapitalmarktorientierte Rechnungslegung* 4: 217–24.

Schmidt, R. 2004. Corporate governance in Germany: An economic perspective. In *The German financial system*, ed. J. P. Krahnen and R. H. Schmidt, 386–424. Oxford: Oxford University Press.

Shleifer, A., and R. W. Vishny. 1997. A survey of corporate governance. *Journal of Finance* 52 (2): 737–83.

Steger, T., and R. Hartz. 2005. On the way to "good" corporate governance? A critical review of the German debate. *Corporate Ownership and Control* 3 (1): 9–16.

Vitols, S. 2005. Changes in Germany's bank-based financial system: Implications for corporate governance. *Corporate Governance: An international Review* 13 (3): 386–96.

Werder, v. A., and T. Talaulicar. 2006. Corporate governance developments in Germany. In *Handbook on international corporate governance. Country analyses*, ed. C. A. Mallin, 28–44. Cheltenham, Northampton: Edward Elgar Publishing.

———. 2010. Kodex Report 2009: Die Akzeptanz der Empfehlungen und Anregungen des Deutschen Corporate Governance Kodex. *Der Betrieb* 63 (16): 853–61.

Working Group on External Financial Reporting of the Schmalenbach-Gesellschaft-Deutsche Gesellschaft für Betriebswirtschaft. 1995. German accounting principles: An institutionalized framework. *Accounting Horizons* 9 (3): 92–99.

Zwirner, C. 2009. Weitere Zunahme der Bedeutung der IFRS. Eine empirische Untersuchung zur Entwicklung der Rechnungslegung am deutschen Kapitalmarkt. *Zeitschrift für Internationale Rechnungslegung* 10: 425–29.

9 Analysis of Changing Institutional Environments, New Accounting Policies, and Corporate Governance Practices in Portugal

*Gabriela Gueifão and
Mohamed Azzim Gulamhussen*

1. ACCOUNTING

1.1 International Convergence in Accounting

1.1.1 Standardization of Accounting Practices in Portugal

Portuguese accounting rules' history began in the 1970s when tax authorities, after approving corporate tax law (*Código da Contribuição Indústrial* [CCI]), gave some directions about the elements the financial statements would have to show. At the same time an accounting commission (*Comissão de Normalização Contabilística* [CNC]) was created with the goal of developing and regulating an accounting system for all companies, dependent on approval by law-decree, giving birth to general principles of proper accounting (*Princípios Contabilísticos Geralmente Aceites* [PCGA]). These accounting principles included a set of codes for accounts designated as *Plano Oficial de Contabilidade* (POC; see, amongst others, Bento and Machado 2009; Borges, Rodrigues, and Rodrigues 2007).

POC was codified into law in 1977 after publication in the official journal of the state (*Diário da República* [DR]) by Law-Decree 47/77 of February 7. After joining the EU in 1986, a new set of accounting rules had to be designed on the basis of the directives emanating from the EU. POC was revised in 1989 with the objective to translate the Fourth (78/660/CEE) and Seventh (83/349/CEE) EU Directives into POC, which was subsequently approved by Law-Decree 238/91 of July 21, 1991. At the same time, corporate tax law was also revised with the issuance of a new tax code designated as *Imposto sobre o Rendimento de Pessoas Colectivas* (IRC), integrally substituting the old CCI. Additionally, in order to develop or clarify some accounting matters, from 1991 until 2002, twenty-nine accounting directives (*Directrizes Contabilísticas* [DC]) were issued and approved by law-decree. In this context, Portuguese accounting practice comprised codified rules and noncodified principles that had to be observed when compiling financial statements. The hierarchy of the Portuguese accounting system when evaluating an accounting fact was, until 2005, POC, DC, and finally International Accounting Standards/International Financial Reporting Standards (IAS/IFRS) issued by the International Accounting Standards Board (IASB), when the first two sets of rules were not applicable.

It is important to highlight the fact that, in Portugal, financial accounting and tax reporting are intertwined. The accounting system is based not according to accounting principles and rules, but to tax rules, in order to avoid extra costs of adjusting financial statements in view of tax reporting. A good example relates to asset depreciation rates: tax law–issued depreciation rates for all tangible and intangible assets. The company can use management rates (based on the asset's life expectancy) when accounting depreciation. If those rates are different from the ones according to tax law, adjustments have to be made in order to calculate tax income as well as deferred taxes. The majority of Portuguese companies normally follow tax law rates in order to avoid such adjustments.

In Portugal, individual businesses as well as fully established companies have to prepare individual financial statements for tax purposes, to be reported to the tax authority (*Direcção Geral de Contribuiçoes e Impostos* [DGCI]) on a yearly basis. Those financial statements have to comply with the Portuguese PCGA respecting the aforementioned hierarchy, and are considered by the tax authorities as well as by other stakeholders to portray a true and fair view of the company's value; this way they are the base for the calculation of the payout ratio to owners and income taxes. As stated earlier, this connection between financial accounting and tax accounting (like in Germany) is a typical element of the Portuguese accounting environment.

In legal terms, sole proprietorships as well as corporations have to be formalized according to *Código das Sociedades Comerciais* (CSC) to attain legal capacity. The two most important types of companies in the Portuguese market are the privately owned companies and the publicly owned companies. To be formalized, privately owned companies have to subscribe a minimum of €5.000 of initial share capital and have at least one partner whereas publicly owned ones have to subscribe a minimum of €50.000 of initial share capital and have at least five shareholders (as per CSC). Both companies are obligated to have an organized accounting system in accordance to POC, needing a certified accountant (*Técnico Oficial de Contas* [TOC]) for the disclosure of statutory financial statements and tax reporting. In some companies, depending on the total assets, total revenues and number of employees, an external auditor (*Revisor Oficial de Contas* [ROC]) may be required to certify those statutory accounts. Both types of companies have to deposit their statutory accounts with public authorities and companies with listed securities also have to publish them.

Until 2005 group companies, companies that control one or more business entities, had to prepare consolidated financial statements according to POC. In the case where those groups companies had to present their financial statements in other financial markets or to the parent company located in a different country, the financial statements had to be translated and adjusted according to different accounting systems—like US generally accepted accounting principles (GAAP) or IAS/IFRS—which resulted in totally different income outputs and performing ratios, conveying to the stakeholders a different message of the company's performance, depending on the set of rules applied. One example of this is the Portuguese bank BCP that in the late 1990s presented high losses according to US GAAP and large gains according to POC.

This incongruence saw a solution in 2005 through the EU Regulation EC No. 1606/2002, which mandated all listed European companies to prepare their consolidated financial statements according to IAS/IFRS from 2005 onwards, leaving nonlisted companies the option to use IAS/IFRS in their consolidated financial statements, with individual accounts having to be presented under Portuguese PCGA for taxation (Gueifão 2007).

Portuguese PCGA differs in many ways from the IASB accounting standards, especially concerning consolidated accounts. In the face of this issue, in 2007 CNC, with the approval of the Portuguese government, began the setting of a different accounting system for all types of companies regarding individual accounts, named *Sistema de Normalização Contabilística* (SNC), which substituted POC in January of 2010. This system is similar to IASB with the issuance of standards (NCRF) instead of rules accounting and principles, main feature of POC, translating IAS/IFRS accepted by the EU into the Portuguese PCGA, with the necessary adjustments due to our economical specificity, moving forward into the conceptualization, internationalization, and convergence of the Portuguese accounting system.

The new Portuguese accounting system was approved on July 13, 2009 by law decree 158/2009 and contains a conceptual framework (inexistent in POC), 28 NCRFs and a chart of accounts. In light of this, Tax Law (IRC) was also revised on the same date by Law-Decree 159/2009. Following these changes, from 2010 onwards Portuguese listed group companies have to comply with IASB rules approved by the EU in their consolidated statements (already done since 2005) and SNC rules in their individual statements. All other companies, independent of type, have to comply with all SNC rules with the exception of sole proprietorships businesses and micro-small companies, which have to comply with a specific SNC rule (SNC-PE), created especially for these types of companies.

1.1.2 Changes in Financial Reporting Objectives

Like other continental European countries, stock markets in Portugal play a comparatively smaller role than, for instance, in Anglo-Saxon countries. A relatively smaller number of companies in Portugal are listed in the stock exchange, the most important one being Euronext where PSI-20 is the most important index, which only represents twenty companies; but even these have a low free float.

The majority of domestic business entities are privately held; 95 percent of those are considered micro-small companies. Due to this aspect of the Portuguese economic infrastructure, equity financing plays a minor role in the financing of companies, meaning bank financing is the major source of outside funding. In light of this aspect, creditors, mainly banks, are interested in the preservation of capital in order to ensure reimbursement of interest and loaned capital. Because of the high importance of bank financing in Portugal, business law aims to protect creditors by limiting the distribution of profits to shareholders (5 percent of net profit has to be allocated as a legal reserve until 20 percent of share equity amount), and accounting principles are based on the principle of prudency, meaning assets and liabilities are valued cautiously and profits are calculated on a conservative basis. This is confirmed by analyzing the effects of the transition of Portuguese publicly traded companies from Portuguese PCGA to IFRS at the beginning of 2005. According to Gueifão (2007), although equity under IFRS is on average 7.78 percent lower than what was reported under Portuguese PCGA, net income increased by 11.42 percent after IFRS adoption. Broadly speaking, the Portuguese financial system can be characterized as an insider and conservative system in contrast to an outsider fair-valued one, for example, the Anglo-Saxon system (see also Esperança, Gama, and Gulamhussen 2003)

Financial statements should serve the interests of the shareholders, creditors, tax authorities, and other stakeholders like employees and the local society, amongst others, and balance their information requirements. Although they are expected to be used by the aforementioned institutional entities, the main use has been, up until presently, for tax authorities, for determination of taxable income, and banks, for the purpose of securing or renewing loans. Calculation of taxable income is based on the principle of congruency; i.e., financial statements for tax purposes are tied to the company accounts. This reasoning holds especially for micro- and medium-size companies that are not listed in the capital markets but for which essentially the same accounting principles are relevant, as for large companies. This contrasts to, for instance, the US, where companies need only to fulfill requirements of the Securities and Exchange Commission (SEC), and therefore, needing an opinion from an auditor, have to adhere to the local GAAP.

The role of information for the use of several stakeholders has in recent years been changed by the introduction of the regime of *Informação Empresarial Simplificada* (IES) in 2007 by Law-Decree 8/2007 of January 17, whereby financial statements of all firms are available not only to the tax authorities (for taxation and reporting purposes), but also to statistical bureaus, mainly *Instituto Nacional de Estatística* and *Banco de Portugal,* in order to develop statistical information, and other public authorities (in order to register and deposit statutory accounts), this way ending the problem of all companies having to report to those entities separately and only when they were asked to, multiplying the work and costs associated. The IES report serves all those entities through a single reporting mechanism.

Presently, the approval of the new accounting system for all Portuguese companies (SNC), similar in concept and structure to IASB accounting standards, to comply from 2010 onwards, represents a major change of moving from the disclosure of financial statements for the sole purpose of taxation and creditor assurance, present in the majority of Portuguese companies, and thus a more insider and conservative view of reporting, to the disclosure of financial statements based on accounting standards close to the stakeholders' interests, a more outsider and fair-value view of reporting. This leads also, and more importantly, to a change of mentality of all accounting professionals as well as management.

1.1.3 Changes in Characteristics and Constraints of Decision-Useful Financial Reporting Information

The Portuguese financial reporting rules have a clear objective of delivering useful, objective, and reliable information compiled on a prudent basis. In this environment, income and costs are recognized when realized, assets are valued on a historical-cost basis, and risks are allowed by establishing liabilities. Such compilation of financial statements highlights the importance of, for example, preservation of capital, as stated earlier, whose relevance spans the requirement of information of investors making it relevant to creditors as well.

Over the years, financial reporting in Portugal has gone through some important changes. For example, in the older POC (DL 47/77) like the new POC (DL 410/89) revaluation of assets was allowed (DC nr. 16). The high inflationary period that characterized the Portuguese economy led to a higher frequency of reevaluation of assets, defying the principle of congruency across years in the compilation of financial statements. In order to control this, Portuguese tax authorities issued reevaluation rates for certain types of assets, in certain years, to be considered as tax deductible, thus limiting the assets' revaluation process. This represented a major constraint on the usefulness of the information reported, once free reevaluation of assets was also permitted, the corresponding costs were not tax deductible, making the decision of reevaluating or not a certain asset, a matter of paying more taxes or not. In recent years, and especially after the accession to the EU and the low inflation levels experienced by the economy on account of the convergence criteria, this has led to an abolishment of the practice of reevaluation of assets, thus the disappearance of such constraint.

An interesting change that has been observed in the compilation of financial statements relates to the principle of specialization. The older POC (DL 47/77) foresaw the possibility of specialization through the use of a specific item—deferred costs. In the revised POC (DL 410/89), new items were created—deferred costs and income, and accruals in costs and income—increasing the level of accuracy of reporting. Of particular relevance here is a dispute that emerged between tax authorities and some large companies. Large companies used these latter developed items to account deferred salaries, especially the ones relating to holidays. Tax authorities did not see this level of specialization as necessary. However, the courts ruled in favor of companies, making specialization an important ingredient of the compilation of financial statements over the years and to all types of companies.

Finally, the older POC, for example, treated leasing as only operational, but the recent POC foresees the possibility of accounting for both operational and financial leasing (DC nr. 25), leading to an increase in the usefulness of that information.

However, the reforms have not brought a turn from historical cost to fair value accounting. The long tradition of Portuguese accounting of only calculating profits that have been definitely realized persists. Historical acquisition or production costs are still the maximum amount to be capitalized. Fair values (e.g., higher replacement costs or market values) above amortized costs are still not permitted (DC nr. 13).

Nevertheless, this system slightly changed in the beginning of 2010, as mentioned earlier. With SNC, fair value accounting can be applied, with certain limitations, opening the path towards an outsider view of reporting and representing a major change and a major concern at the same time as to the form and basis of its application and consequent taxation. In that regard, the Corporate Tax Code IRC was revised in order to limit fair value accounting, where applied, for tax purposes, thus, in a certain way, again providing constraints to the decision of using or not using fair value accounting.

1.1.4 Economic Resources and Claims on Them

Portuguese accounting rules adhere to the clean surplus concept, in which total income over multiple accounting periods should equal the sum of reported incomes of the individual accounting periods. The only exception exists in the consolidated financial statements where currency translation effects, among other things, do not touch the profit or loss account. Hence, the concept of comprehensive income—profit and loss account includes all changes in equity besides transactions with shareholders—is an element less familiar in the domestic reporting environment. Studies on the value-relevance of comprehensive income compared with net income shows that the former is more relevant than the latter, although the difference is minimum (see, amongst others, Vistas 2007). With SNC compliance, one of the main novelties is the introduction of a Statement on Changes in Equity, inexistent in POC as a statement but only as a note (Note 40 of the Notes), wherein the recognition of gains and losses directly in equity mandated in several SNC standards is shown without going through results, moving from a clean surplus perspective to a dirty surplus one, giving the comprehensive income concept, until now unknown in Portuguese accounting, a new and fresh beginning.

The peculiarities of Portuguese accounting had an important influence on company performance measures. The application of PCGA has over the years shown low levels of reported profit and low equity levels due to the prudence principle. Conservatism in Portuguese accounting rules still persists and will persist, even with the new SNC accounting system in which some standards limit the use of fair value accounting, like in Germany. Although some SNC standards permit the use of fair value accounting with certain limitations, on a day-to-day basis, companies will continue to use the conservative perspective, i.e., historical cost, mainly due to difficulties of computing and subjectivity in calculating fair values where a market doesn't exist, making fair calculation very difficult to implement. Also the recent global financial crisis and the fear of the potential pro-cyclical effects of fair values strengthen the reasons why the reform of Portuguese accounting system fell short on this issue.

The Portuguese accounting system is presently changing from a set of rules and accounting codes (simple rule of debit and credit using a chart of accounting codes [POC]) to a set of standards (policies and rules are defined, levels of report are prescribed, and limitations are identified), from a tax point of view to a stakeholder point on view, from a historical perspective to a limited fair value but a more extensive reporting one. This new system that began in 2010 has led presently to changes, reevaluations, and recognitions of accounting facts that the older system prevented. This change is also presently leading Portuguese tax authorities to rethink corporate taxation in light of the new accounting system. Companies are presently diagnosing the differences between accounting systems (POC versus SNC) and their impact on equity and net income as well as preparing themselves for a more accurate and complete reporting when compared with the old one. In view of these fundamental changes a new reevaluation of corporate governance (CG) is presently under way (see the Ante-Project of Corporate Governance from February of 2009, from the Portuguese Institute of Corporate Governance).

2. CORPORATE GOVERNANCE

2.1 Regulation and the Scope of Corporate Governance

Comissão de Mercados e Valores Mobiliários (CMVM) was instituted in 1991 to supervise securities, derivatives, and financial markets. It was mandated to establish rules that must be complied with regarding disclosure, attributions of board members, and related matters. Supervision by CMVM guarantees investor protection; efficiency of financial market functioning; information control; systemic risk prevention; and independence from any entity subject or not to its supervision.Despite the institution of CMVM in 1991, CG principles were first introduced only in October 1999 with the approval of a set of recommendations regarding a system of rules of conduct that had to be observed in the exercise of management and control of listed companies. These early recommendations (and the more recent ones as well) did not impose a rigid model. They permitted naturally the coexistence of two types of systems: one supported on external control and another supported on internal control.

CMVM considers that an adequate CG policy ought to guarantee transparency; ensure the protection of shareholders and creditors; hold the chief executive officers (CEOs) responsible for not achieving company goals and for the violation of laws; not prevent the maximization of company performance; be in accordance of international CG regulations; and be adjusted to the country's reality. Based on this first approach, in 1999 a recommendation was issued that mandated all companies to inform the market about the degree of achievement of those recommendations.

In 2001 the relevance of this information was strengthened by mandating all listed companies to report if, and to what degree, they complied with those recommendations or, if not, to explain why they didn't, i.e., a motto of "comply-or-explain," enabling markets to eventually penalize companies with doubtful governance options. Nevertheless, an appropriate market reaction is only possible if the governance model of each listed company is known in detail. To this effect all listed companies were encouraged to publish a report on CG along with the management report or within it. Information requirements were heightened, enforcing, although to a limited extent, the disclosure of posts held by board members in other companies; evolution of share prices and dividend policy; and management processes. In 2003 new recommendations were published to meet national and international standards. These recommendations required companies to disclose more information about their CG practices and in particular about board member compensation.

The domestic code does not provide any single definition but presents essential recommendations for the management and supervision of companies and includes internationally and nationally recognized standards for good and responsible CG. This is suggestive of a wider scope compared to definitions claiming that CG has to serve foremost the interests of capital suppliers.

Portuguese code of law gives companies the freedom to choose between different models. Companies can opt between the so-called monistic or dualistic system. In countries like the US and the UK companies generally adopt the monistic system; in Germany companies generally adopt a dualistic model. In the monistic system the CEO has management responsibility. In the dualistic system the board, with managers from diverse backgrounds, has the management responsibility. In the case of Portugal, companies generally adopt a model with a board of directors (that delegate daily management in an executive committee) and a supervisory board mimicking the monistic system; or a dualistic system with an executive board of directors and a general and supervisory board (Fernamdes, 2009).

Finally, Portuguese CG code (CGC) is progressively getting in line with international guidelines and laws. The CG ante-project, mentioned earlier, took into account the valuable contribution of the so-called good practices of CG that the European countries have adopted since the 1990s and all the recommendations in the CMVM CG Code. This ante-project also leaves space for the application of other codes coming from civil society to enrich the practice of good governance.

2.2 Governance Characteristics

2.2.1 Recent Regulations

In recent years the domestic capital market has been experiencing many changes in technology and financial innovation. Regulators have tried to respond to these new developments by instituting new rules and recommendations, and more importantly increasing the frequency of disclosure. An analysis of this complex network of rules and recommendations is beyond the scope of this chapter. But there are some distinguishing features that deserve attention.

Anglo-Saxon capital markets are often labeled the most developed ones. In these markets, outside control through the markets for mergers and acquisitions or leveraged buyouts, for example, plays an important role in disciplining management. In particular, such control puts pressure on the less efficient managers, enabling their substitution by more efficient managers. However, the Portuguese domestic capital market is still at a relatively early stage of development with highly concentrated ownership. This is typical of an insider-controlled market. Thus, much of the regulation has focused on internal control, although external control has also received attention due to the progressive exposure of the economy to the international environment. Efforts to increase the free float in the market have, however, not been very successful and the number of listed companies and free float remains relatively meager.

In recent years entities subject to CMVM recommendations have had to disclose more information and meet more criteria (for example, disclosure of compensation plans and audit systems) when compared with others companies. Information, in general, is more frequent and demanding than that defined in general law of CSC (see also Law-Decree 8/2007 of 17/11 that institutes the IES). Following external pressure from several stakeholders, CMVM attributions were also altered by Law-Decree 169/2008 (2/8).

New recommendations have also been introduced because of the obligation to implement EU directives. These directives do not dictate specific rules that disarticulate the local CG system. In some cases they even reinforce it, as is the case with the statute for EU companies (aimed to harmonize law on the legal structure of companies across Europe) that gives companies the option to choose between a monistic and dualistic CG model. Thus, despite increasing regulatory activity and coordination efforts amongst the several intervening entities, it is not unambiguously clear that there is a fundamental change towards the Anglo-Saxon model. On the contrary, it appears to reinforce a more pluralist approach to CG.

2.2.2 Auditing

In 2008, the government instituted Law-Decree 225/2008 (20/11) that created the *Conselho Nacional de Supervisão de Auditoria* (CNSA), a national supervisory audit council, with the responsibility of organizing public supervision of statutory auditors. It sets rules for deontology, and audit. It assesses annual plan of quality control proposed by *Ordem dos Revisores Oficiais de Contas* (OROC), a statutory auditor board, and it follows its execution.

Auditing acts as an important external governance mechanism in Portugal (see, amongst others, Bhimani, Gulamhussen, and Lopes 2009). As mentioned earlier, both sole proprietors and professional partnerships can opt for an organized accounting system or a simplified one; both need a certified accountant to prepare the financial statements. Companies need to have an organized accounting system, with a TOC, and some of them, depending on the amount of total assets, total revenues, and number of employees, face the additional requirement of having their accounts be certified by an ROC. Where the ROC has doubts about a company's ability to continue as a going concern, the professional code of conduct requires the independent auditor to disclose the uncertainty in her or his opinion. According to the rules of the chamber of ROC, independent auditors are required to proactively assess the going-concern status of a client and issue a opinion. The history of going-concern uncertainty in Portugal has been debated like in many other countries, but from the year 2000 onwards, the chamber of ROC recommends the adoption of the ISA 570.

According to the Securities Code (Law-Decree 486/1999 of 13/11) auditors registered with the CMVM should issue an opinion about the annual financial information. Therefore, the auditor should examine accounts or prospectuses submitted to CMVM (the documents and prospectuses serve different purposes and are assessed at different points in time). They should also verify other documents. Whenever account disclosure includes business and other forecasts, the auditor's report should clearly indicate his opinion on correctness and criteria adopted.

Auditors need to be registered with the OROC in Portugal. They need to demonstrate human, material, and financial resources to ensure ethics, independence, and technical skills. Auditors are liable for damages to investors or third parties resulting from errors in reports or going concern opinions. Auditors should buy insurance suitable for their duties.

In this respect, the Sarbanes-Oxley Act (SOX) of 2002, which was a reaction to a number of accounting and auditing scandals in the US, was also the main driver for reforms and partly served as a role model for European legislators of which Portugal is no exception. Also, the new US regulations resulted in rulings of the EU that had to be implemented by the EU member states and therefore also by Portugal. The most important regulatory initiative of the EU was the amendment of the directive on statutory audit of annual accounts and consolidated accounts, the so-called modernized Eighth Directive, which included rules on the auditing profession's oversight, auditor's independence, and auditing standards. In Portugal, the main regulatory activity elapses from the effects of the SOX shifting towards international standards, in particular the SOX.

2.2.3 Power and Responsibilities of Top Management

CMVM regulates CG in Portugal. CMVM regulation 7/2001 establishes that companies issuing shares for trading in regulated markets should publish a detailed report on CG. Modifications introduced by Law-Decree 76–A/2006 of 29/3 in the CSC led to changes in CMVM regulation 1/2007. The CG report should contain information on the composition of boards and description of control and risk management systems. It should mention qualification and duties of directors. Information on stock allotment should also be disclosed. Financial statements of the last five years should be available. Regarding information disclosure, there should be information on the company's business with indication of an investor support system. Early in this regulation a compliance statement is mentioned. It should point to which CMVM recommendations were adopted and which weren't. The ones that weren't fully complied are considered not adopted. There should be an explanation for no adoption. There should also be indication of the location where CG documents are available (Fernandes, 2009).

CMVM regulation 11/2003 amended 7/2001 and converted some recommendations on CG to information duties. It established mandatory information disclosure on the website. Regarding information disclosure, there should be information on stock allotment plan for workers and directors. There should also be information about the company's structure, investor support desk, reporting documents, amounts paid to auditors and to related persons, and a calendar related to the company's meetings, among other information.

Regulation 1/2010 defined the concept of *independent director*, which before was done by each company. Directors are not considered independent in cases where they have functions in a competing company, they have any other compensation from the company except from their independent management functions, or they have more than 10 percent of share capital. The objective is to create a balanced composition of board of directors.

The supervisory system is improved with adoption of a stronger independence concept. More importance is given to nonexecutive directors. Transparency is reinforced through: compensation of directors and director's qualifications. According to instruction 4/2004 (amended by 5/2008), companies that issued securities for trading purposes should send information to CMVM regarding: privileged information; periodic information; general meetings; payments of dividends, interests, and reimbursement and exercise of other rights; board members and their functions; CG; qualified holdings and para-social agreements; own–share transactions; securities transactions where they are board members; and annual summary of information disclosed.

Regulation 10/2005 defined the minimum financial information to be presented in some cases. It has three main objectives. It tries to reinforce the checks and balances system within the company, enhance transparency, and adapt midterm information to the IAS/IFRS reference.

Additionally, regarding information disclosure, CMVM Regulation 5/2008 (Regulation 5/2008 is expected to be amended following the public consultation in course) defined further information duties. It refers to: qualified holdings, deadlines for disclosure, information to be disclosed and with what frequency, own–share transactions, and identification of board members and of their transactions. In the specific case of companies that issued securities for trading purposes, annual accounts and reports should be presented, along with supervisory board opinion and a list of qualified holdings with indication of shares and percentage of voting rights. The board should also clarify any changes in financial statements, management reports, and a declaration of conformity of financial statements.

In 2007 CMVM presented a CGC with recommendations for boards regarding voting rights, information disclosure, and audit. It mentions compensation, nomination, independence, and incompatibility of board members. Besides these indications, boards themselves should evaluate governance reports and models adopted.

2.2.4 Conflict of Interests (Agency Problem)

The management of information asymmetries that cause agency problems is often accomplished through private information channels rather than public information channels. Information asymmetries are much more acute in the case of small firms, due to lower compliance requirements, than in large firms that have stringent compliance requirements and more exposure to the public in general (although in this latter case there is no enforcing legislation).

2.2.5 Evaluating Board Performance

In Portuguese listed companies, compensation of the management board is determined by a compensation committee. This can be seen as a better way of determining appropriate compensation compared to the case where it is the supervisory board that determines compensation. The CGC comprises recommendations on how board members should be remunerated. The compensation of the board members can include a fixed and a variable component. The variable component can include one-time and annually payable components linked to the company performance as well as long-term incentives cognizant of risk elements. The individual components as well as the compensation in total must be appropriate. Besides the fixed component, contracts usually base variable components on the overall performance of the entity, i.e., the growth of the company, reported income, or turnover. Stock options are also becoming very common as a variable component of compensation.

Another important aspect is the trend towards looking at nonfinancial elements of the company to remunerate. Whereas this trend is still at an incipient stage it is gaining importance, especially within the small community of nonlisted firms.

2.2.6 Disclosure on Corporate Governance

Portuguese code of law addresses many important CG issues. However, these are mostly recommendations and not binding rules. The apparent objective is to reduce information asymmetries between stakeholders and managers. It is expected that recommendations will be interpreted and followed in the best possible way, but reality has shown that this is not the case. Stricter rules could prevent some undesirable situations and provide better protection to investors. CG in Portugal has, however, been evolving to match international standards while maintaining a significant degree of pluralism.

Listed companies in Portugal are obliged to show compliance of their conduct with the CGC, including a list of recommendations they do not comply with. The annual accounts should accompany the report of the statutory auditor, a description of working processes, stock options plans, and compensation and payments of other services to auditors (Regulation 11/2003 where recommendations in 7/2001 are promoted to information duties). Referring to Regulation 1/2007, its appendix also says companies should mention recommendations adopted and those that weren't. Regulations 1/2007 and 7/2001, and changes brought about in 11/2003 and 10/2005 regarding 7/2001, can be broadly considered recommendations because companies can adopt these or not. If they don't, they have to explain; in other regulatory environments this feature is not present.

The domestic CG regulates the disclosure of the individual remuneration of each member of the management board. This dictates the publication of board compensation on an individual basis. The disclosure of each board member's compensation should facilitate the evaluation as to whether the remuneration of the concerned board member is appropriate. Also, such a disclosure should help to avoid excessive executive compensation, which is currently discussed as being incriminatory for the balance between the different participants in governance of corporations.

Nonfinancial reporting is becoming increasingly popular, especially amongst listed companies. Whereas these disclosure instruments, such as value-added statements, sustainability reports, or corporate social responsibility reports, are increasingly presented, their disclosure is still not required. But CMVM does require periodic reports on broad CG issues.

2.3 Corporate Governance and Income Management

In Portugal, financial statements have over the years been prepared on the basis of the local GAAP (PCGA), which has evolved to converge towards international practice, and occasionally defied itself, especially in what concerns the principle of specialization. Another trend is related to the tendency towards income smoothing in the reported financial statements, especially through conservative accounting, leading to low reported earnings over the years. Capital preservation has also been achieved through conservative accounting practice that has facilitated the creation of silent reserves. The restriction of profit distribution is codified in law and has served the purpose of preservation of capital. First, a specific amount of legal reserves as a percentage of equity has to be established. Furthermore, bylaws of the company can require additional reserves to be retained. The amount of distributed income is not only decided by the management of the company, but also by the shareholders in the general meeting. Further, the preservation of capital is partly achieved by several rules that are dispersed in the CSC that restrict profit distribution for specific capitalized assets. For instance, profits from recognized deferred tax assets are blocked for distribution, as long as the amount of the presented free resources is lower than the recognized tax assets.

Another aspect is the strict separation between the individual accounts and the consolidated accounts for the group. Profit distribution is still dependent on the income in the individual accounts. The introduction of IFRS has had no influence on the legal determination of payouts. However, practitioners see more relevance for disclosed income in the consolidated financial statements and try to harmonize reported income figures of the two sets of accounts within the limits of what is achievable.

The CSC determines corporate and noncorporate forms of operating business entities. In the case of limited liability companies it indicates two possible CG structures. It defines boards and committees to be created. It characterizes them and their members. It describes duties and rights, such as attendance at board meetings or compensation. It also indicates secretary and statutory auditor duties. Companies engaged in securities issuance trading in regulated markets face stricter conditions. CMVM has special concerns with independence and definition of executive and nonexecutive directors. It enforces information duties and disclosure of documents such as CG reports. Regulations are mostly recommendations and companies that do not comply are allowed to explain.

REFERENCES

Bento, J., and J. F. Machado. 2009. *Plano Oficial de Contabilidade*. Porto Editora.

Bhimani, A., M. A. Gulamhussen, and S. R. Lopes. 2009. The effectiveness of the auditor's going concern opinion as an external governance mechanism: Evidence from loan defaults. *International Journal of Accounting* 44 (3): 239–255.

Borges, A., A. Rodrigues, and R. Rodrigues. 2007. *Elementos de Contabilidade Geral. Almedina Ed*. 24th ed.

Comissão de Normalização Contabilistica. http://ww.cnc.min-financas.pt

Código do Bom Governo das Sociedades: Ante-Projecto. 2009. Lisboa: Instituto Português de Corporate Governance.

Código das Sociedades Comerciais. Lisboa: DL 262/86 and DL 76-A/2006.

D 13. Conceito de Justo Valor: CNC 07/07/1993. Lisboa: DR II 79-05/04/1994.

D 16. Reavaliação de Acivos Imobilizados Taniveis: CNC 11/01/1995. Lisboa: DR II 104-05/05/1995.

DC 25. Locações: CNC 27/02/2004. Lisboa: DR II 72-25/03/2004.

Esperança, J. P., A. P. Gama, and M. A. Gulamhussen. 2003. Corporate debt policy of small firms: An empirical (re)examination. *Journal of Small Business and Enterprise Development* 10 (1): 62–80.

Gueifão, G. 2007. *Análise do Impacto da Aplicação Obrigatória e Pela Primeira Vez das Normas do IASB nas Empresas Cotadas de Alguns Países da UE— Tese de Mestrado ISCTE*.

Portuguese Institute of Corporate Governance. 2009. *Código do Bom Governo das Sociedades—Ante-Projecto, Instituto Português de Corporate Governance, February 4, 2009*.

Vistas, F. 2007. *Análise do Resultado Extensivo numa Perspectiva Europeia— Tese de Mestrado ISCTE*.

10 Analysis of Changing Institutional Environments, New Accounting Policies, and Corporate Governance Practices in Spain

Elena de las Heras Cristobal,
Jose Luis Ucieda and Begoña Navallas

1. ACCOUNTING

1.1 International Convergence in Accounting

1.1.1 Standardization of Accounting Practices in Spain

One may argue that Spanish accounting is one of the most standardized accounting systems in the world. It has a history of highly detailed charts of accounts and standardized financial statements models that all companies must follow. Even listed companies and financial institutions must comply with specific models to prepare their financial statements. This might be seen as internal—domestic—standardization rather than international.

A quick review of Spanish accounting history[1] shows that accounting regulation started in the 1970s, when the economy under the military regime opened to international capital and markets. Standard setting has been done by a public sector entity, typically an agency related to the Ministry of Economy or Public Finances. Since 1988, the Institute of Accounting and Auditing (*Instituto de Contabilidad y Auditoría de Cuentas* [ICAC]; see www.icac.meh.es) has been in charge of drafting accounting standards, which must be passed by the Parliament (as a law) or the government (as a decree) before they are enforced.

In 1973 the first General Accounting Chart (*Plan General de Contabilidad* [PGC]) became effective with a strong influence of tax legislation. Although it was not mandatory it allowed for several fiscal benefits to those companies applying it. After Spain joined the European Economic Community in 1986, all accounting related regulation was changed to align with EU accounting directives. Thus, a new General Accounting Chart was issued in 1989 and, for the first time, mandatory consolidation rules were issued in 1990 to prepare consolidated financial statements by parent entities.

When in 2000 the European Commission (EC) announced its intention to further harmonize accounting in Europe under the International

Accounting Standards Committee (IASC) standards, the Spanish Ministry of Economy set up a 'Commission of Experts' to propose recommendations to adopt Spanish accounting to international trends. The output of this commission, known as the *White Book of Accounting*, was published in 2002, and up to date, most of its recommendations have been implemented. In particular, a new PGC became effective in 2008 with important changes in the structure and content.

At the time of writing these lines in December 2009, all listed Spanish companies must follow International Financial Reporting Standards (IFRS) as adopted by the EU in their consolidated financial statements, as required by EU Regulation 1606/2002. Their parent-only financial statements must follow the new PGC. Nonlisted companies must also apply the PGC in their parent-only financial statements, but for their consolidated accounts, they have the choice to apply (a) IFRS as adopted by the EU, or (b) consolidation rules issued in 1991.[2] Financial institutions must comply with the accounting regulations issued by the Bank of Spain. Finally, there is a small and medium-size enterprises (SMEs) PGC for those companies complying with certain size requirements.

Nowadays, Spanish accounting regulation is strongly standardized, leaving alone certain industry-specific rules (i.e., financial institutions). The system is characterized by having a General Accounting Chart with a conceptual framework similar to the IASB's, recognition and measurement rules, including fair value criteria and, detailed financial statements models: balance sheet, profit and loss statement, cash flow statement, statement of changes in equity,[3] and the notes to the financial statements. All these are mandatory for parent-only financial statements except for financial institutions and SMEs.[4]

Overall, Spanish accounting is characterized as highly standardized and has incorporated an international flavor at all levels.

1.1.2 Changes in Financial Reporting Objectives

As in other countries in Continental Europe, Spain is a code law country with a preeminent role of debt (banks and financial institutions) as the main source of funding. Capital markets, although they have a long tradition in Spain, have been a small market for a rather reduced number of companies (nearly 1 percent of Spanish companies are listed). According to the reports of the Spanish Securities and Exchange Commission (CNMV), the number of annual reports, both parent-only and consolidated financial statements filed with the CNMV by Spanish listed companies, excluding mutual and pension funds, has increased steadily in the last decade from 614 in 1999 to 875 in 2007. Another characteristic to bear in mind is the high concentration of ownership. According to Gisbert and Navallas (2009b), the average ownership concentration of Spanish listed companies is 43 percent,[5] which somewhat explains the role of capital markets in Spain.

As its predecessor, the new PGC is aimed at providing a fair view of equity, financial situation, and net income of an entity through the application of its content (principles, recognition, and measurement rules). It acknowledges that financial statements serve the goals of multiple users or stakeholders of the entities. Not only shareholders but potential investors, creditors, employees, public institutions, and of course fiscal authorities.

Financial accounting in Spain is based on principles. In particular, the previous PGC, in force from 1990 until 2007, required the application of nine accounting principles, including the principle of prudence, which had prevalence over the others. Other principles were: going concern, registry, acquisition cost, accrual basis, matching, no netting, uniformity, and relative importance. In the new PGC 2008, some of these principles have been incorporated in the conceptual framework as principles: going concern, accrual basis, uniformity, prudence, no netting, and relative importance. Acquisition cost is now a measurement criteria, matching is a hypothesis, and registry is a recognition criteria.

In the PGC 1990, the prudence principle was regarded as the key principle to comply with, so in case of conflict, prudence should prevail over all other principles. For instance, negative unrealized exchange differences (losses) were taken immediately as income, whereas unrealized positive exchange differences (gains) were deferred. In the new PGC 2008, prudence is still considered a principle, but is has somewhat lost its privileged standing. This is not to be taken as Spanish accounting is not prudent, but that the changes due to the adoption of international trends stress other characteristics, like relevance and reliability, or even the new measurement criteria, fair value, and leave prudence at a different level. Both PGCs include a set of measurement rules for transactions and assets, liabilities, revenues, and expenses.

In the past, Spanish financial accounting was strongly influenced by tax legislation. As a matter of fact, tax laws included highly detailed rules to determine taxable income in the period, identifying revenues and expenses. However, the goal of these rules was to maximize the revenue from taxes from business activities, rather than providing a true and fair view of the company performance (Gonzalo Angulo 1992).

The 19/1989 Reform Law declared accounting independent from tax influence and the Company Income Tax Law in 1995 acknowledged this situation. Nowadays, income taxes are computed according to tax rules, which take net income as shown in the profit and loss statement, and adjust it to include or exclude revenues and expenses according to the fiscal policy of the government. There is still a certain relationship between taxes and accounting. For instance, an expense must be accounted for in order to be deductible. However, not all 'accounting' expenses are deductible because the tax law gives itself, for the purposes of income taxes computation only, the right to determine what revenues and expenses apply. A good example is goodwill impairment. Under PGC 2008, goodwill is not depreciated but impaired. For tax purposes, even though goodwill is not amortized for financial reporting purposes, 5 percent may be deducted under certain requirements, including setting up a reserve for the same amount.

1.1.3 Changes in Characteristics and Constraints of Decision-Useful Financial Reporting Information

Decision usefulness of financial information is not explicitly mentioned in the new PGC. Rather, showing a true and fair view is the goal of the application of accounting standards (the PGC). Nevertheless, a significant shift in the new PGC is the consideration of the substance, economic and legal, of all transactions as the cornerstone when accounting for all transactions. In the previous PGC, this was not stated and some transactions could be accounted for considering the form rather than substance of the transaction. Accounting for leases and lease-back transactions are good examples.

The new PGC has introduced significant changes in the financial statements themselves. The largest change in the balance sheet is the new definition of equity. Whereas in the PGC 1990 equity was comprised by capital contributions of shareholders, retained earnings, and other items like currency translation (in consolidation), the new PGC 2008 has added noncontrolling interests, government and non-government grants, errors and changes in accounting policies, and changes in fair value. Thus, under the new regulation, Spanish companies have increased their equity.[6] The statement of profit and loss has also changed its format from a 'T' format to a vertical format, which makes it easy to understand (and, hence, provide more useful information). Revenues and expenses have been classified in continuing and discontinued operations, and the earnings per share (EPS)—normal and diluted—are now shown in the face of the statement. The statement of cash flows is new in Spanish accounting, although a similar statement was required for large companies in the past,[7] as so is the statement of changes in equity.[8]

There have been several classification changes in the balance sheet. The PGC 1990 classified financial assets according to its maturity (short or long term), whereas the new PGC 2008 classifies financial assets according to the way they are managed by the entity.[9] Fair value plays an important role in how some of them are measured. Certain financial instruments that were previously classified as equity (according to its legal form, rather than its substance), as is the case of preferred stocks (nonvoting stock) or redeemable shares of cooperatives, are now classified as liabilities. Finally, there are certain assets that now do not meet the definition and recognition criteria of an asset and therefore are written off against reserves (start-up costs, capital issuance expenses).

Overall, all these changes have made financial information of Spanish entities more useful for decision making as they provide more relevant and reliable information to its users.

1.2 Economic Resources and Claims on Them

1.2.1 The Usefulness of Income Measure for Valuation Purposes

One could argue that until the PGC 2008, the clean surplus concept applied to Spanish accounting information, i.e., all changes in equity went through profit and loss. However, there are a number of exceptions that question that. In the last quarter of the last century, under high inflation rates, the government issued several fiscal laws permitting the revaluation of assets with great fiscal incentives. During the 1990s, certain regulated companies going through financial difficulties due to the devaluation of the peseta, were allowed to recognize certain expenses (exchange losses) to equity. Finally, certain banks have been allowed to charge against equity pension and pre-retirement expenses.[10] However, the adoption of international standards into the PGC 2008 has brought the possibility of recognizing certain revenues and expenses in equity and in some cases recycling them through profit and loss in later years.

Comprehensive income is a rather new concept in Spain (and most European countries) that users need to learn and understand. However, whereas there is a strong debate on performance reporting in Europe (European Financial Reporting Advisory Group [EFRAG] 2006, 2009), where the concept of net income is questioned, the International Accounting Standards Board (IASB) and Financial Accounting Standards Board (FASB) are considering a new model of financial statements presentation that clearly aligns with the comprehensive income concept with some evidence that net income or operating income may not survive.[11]

Academic research has found mixed evidence on the relevance of comprehensive income over net income or operating income.[12] These results suggest that traditional income measures, i.e., operating and net income, are relevant to the market as is comprehensive income. Yet, another interpretation from a behavioral viewpoint is that investors and analysts are not familiar with the new income measure and refuse to use it, just like people reject and discard. Like all changes, investors need time to fully understand what comprehensive income is and how it impacts their everyday working routines.

See Chapter 6 of this volume, "The Impact of Mandatory Adoption of IFRS on Income Statement and Balance Sheet Properties," for the statistics on the impact of IFRS on Spanish accounts.

1.2.2 The Traditional Approach to the Company's Economic Performance Measure

Spanish accounting regulation is biased to conservatism for two main factors: taxes and fund providers. Since 1995, financial reporting and taxes have followed different rules. Taxable income is based on accounting income (net income) but fiscal policies require several adjustments resulting in definitions of revenues and expenses for tax purposes. However, accounting is not fully free of tax influence. Goodwill impairment is a good example. Before the PGC 2008, goodwill was amortized over its useful life to a maximum of twenty years for accounting purposes. Under the PGC 2008, goodwill amortization is not allowed, but must be tested for impairment. A later regulation required entities to set up a special reserve by charging to income every year a minimum of 5 percent of goodwill until it is entirely funded. For tax purposes, goodwill amortization may be deducted even if it was accounted for, if a special reserve was set up.

Because banks play a larger role in financing entities (fund providers) than capital markets do, one may expect that income determination is focused on protecting creditors more than investors. Income distribution is controlled and restricted in Spanish economic and accounting regulation. In previous PGCs, the accounting principle of prudence had a prevalent role over the others; in other words, in case of conflict, prudence should prevail (i.e., losses are recognized when suspected, whereas revenues are recognized when realized or close to realization). PGC 2008 still includes the principle of prudence but with no predominance. A good example of this conservatism was the requirement by the Spanish Central Bank that all financial institutions set up special bad debts provisions, anti-cyclic, even in good years, to be used in bad years. This treatment is not compatible with IAS 39 and a large discussion arose between the Spanish Central Bank and the IASB. However, under the current financial crisis, these provisions (along with other measures) have proved to be a good way to protect the financial system.

The adoption of IFRS by listed companies and its influence on the new PGC 2008 are strong factors facing the historically strong conservatism of Spanish financial reporting. Time will tell whether international accounting may change it.

2. CORPORATE GOVERNANCE

2.1 Regulation and the Scope of Corporate Governance

In Spain, a European country with a narrow stock market, a strong presence of banking institutions, and a high rate of cross shareholdings and a high ownership concentration, the Olivencia Report was first published in 1998 with similar objectives to the Cadbury Report in 1992. In 1997 the Spanish government created a special commission with the aim of drafting a report about the role of boards of directors in Spain. Like then, the composition of the committee included representatives from government regulatory agencies and independent experts in different economic areas.

The constitution of this committee was initially referred to a study for an ethical code for company's directors, and consequently did not address questions like the role and responsibilities of auditors, as the Cadbury Report did. As in Britain, the Spanish Securities and Exchange Commission (CNMV) issued its Circular 11/98, recommending listed companies to report the adoption of the Olivencia Report. It was a voluntary disclose requirement, and the first year for which it applied was 1998. Moreover, the CNMV itself issued a regulated model for listed companies, also based on the Olivencia Report.

On July 19, 2002, the Spanish government decided to create a new commission that should first study the complying degree and then establish criteria and guidelines for listed companies in order to increase market transparency. Then, four years after the Olivencia Report was issued, the Aldama Report was released, *Report by the Special Commission To Foster Transparency and Security in the Markets and in Listed Companies*. The reasons for the creation of this new commission could be found firstly on the scandals that occurred both in Spain (i.e., Gestcartera) and abroad (i.e., Enron) during those years. Secondly, the previous code considered that companies and the market itself would reward corporate governance (CG) compliance, whereas what really happened was that the conflicts of interest were still standing.

In this report, the committee members analyzed the level of awareness of the Olivencia Code by more than eight hundred shareholders and two hundred experts, through a survey conducted in 2000 that demonstrated the inadequacy of information provided by the companies, as both shareholders and experts believed transparency was still lacking because no enforcement mechanisms were considered in the Olivencia Report.

In order to increase information transparency, the Aldama Report goes one step further, compared to the recommendations made by the Olivencia Code, by recommending the development of an Annual Corporate Governance Report, issued by the board of directors of the company, after being studied by the Audit and Control Committee. The Aldama Report sets out the minimum content that must be incorporated in the annual report.

In an opposite direction to the voluntary nature of the recommendations by the Olivencia Code, the regulator response decided some of them should be mandatory and required by law, as established by Act 44/2002 on Measures to Reform the Financial System (hereafter Financial Act 44/2002), listed companies should have an Audit Committee. Furthermore, some of the recommendations made by the Aldama Report also became mandatory for listed companies under Act 26/2003, on Transparency Measures for Listed Companies (hereafter Transparency Act 26/2003), which requires listed companies to issue an annual report on CG (ARCG), as well as the creation of a website. Some authors considered that only mandatory regulation can be effective in Spain (del Brío, Maia Ramires, and Perote 2006), as voluntary compliance and autoregulation, which is applicable in most European countries, will not be effective in our country. Spain is a country with a high level of legal regulation due to the civil law tradition, with little experience in autoregulation measures.

As a summary, the Aldama Report follows the line defined by the Olivencia Report, deepening in some areas while maintaining the continuity of its predecessor. But the Aldama Report did not step into relevant questions like the election of board members, the separation of roles between the president and chief executive; it did not propose any anti-takeover measures or enhanced transparency in the remuneration of directors and senior executives.

Additionally, the new requirement to the "comply-or-explain" principle introduced by the Transparency Act 26/2003 added new problems as applying both the Olivencia and Aldama Reports imply different recommendations in certain areas—sometimes contradictory—and the Aldama Report did not include a list of recommendations as the previous code did. Thereby, an answer was necessary in order to achieve a better compliance with the Transparency Act 26/2003, which introduced the "comply-or-explain" principle, as companies should disclose in their annual CG report how far they have adopted CG recommendations, explaining the failure to adopt if any.

2.2 Governance Characteristics

2.2.1 Recent Regulations

A new working group was created in 2005 in order to publish a harmonized code. On January 18, 2006, the draft recommendations of the Unified Good Governance Code were released, opening a public information period ending February 28. The aim of that project was to update the existing codes, Olivencia and Aldama Reports, and to adapt the new recommendations at the international level, particularly the recent recommendations of the European Union: recommendation of December 14, 2004 (2004/913/EC), on remuneration of directors of listed companies and the recommendation of February 15, 2005 (2005/162/EC), on external committees.

Before the final report was issued, there was a big controversy between listed companies and the working group. The draft code considered the possibility of increasing mandatory measures, like the presence of women on the board, and some listed companies complained. Finally, this and other measures were finally included as new corporate recommendations.

Thus, the unified code maintained its earlier voluntary approach, with new recommendations that may apply to entities other than listed companies. The main criticisms that emerged related to the excessive interference in issues such as the presence of independent directors, as well as the necessary characteristics to be qualified as such.

Finally, a summary of the information is shown in Table 10.1 about the existing CG regulation in Spain.

Table 10.1   Corporate Governance Regulation in Spain

Year	Report	Type	Scope	Description
1998	Olivencia Report	Voluntary	Listed companies	Recommendations on CG
2002	Aldama Report	Voluntary	Listed companies	Recommendations on CG
2002	Financial Act	Mandatory	Listed companies	Audit Committee required Directors requirements about honorability and professional skills are applied to managers Disclosure of related companies operations
			Auditors	New independence requirements
				Audit and nonaudit fees disclosure in the financial statements
2003	Transparency Act	Mandatory	Listed companies	Website required
				Annual report on CG (comply-or-explain principle)
			All companies	Disclosure about directors' shares or directors' presence on the board of companies with similar objectives
2003	Orden ECO/3722/2003	Mandatory	Listed companies	CG annual report characteristics
2004	CNMV Circular 1/2004	Mandatory	Listed companies	Standard CG annual report
2005	CNMV Circular 2/2005	Mandatory	Listed saving entities	Websites and CG annual report requirements
2006	Unified Code	Voluntary	Listed companies	Recommendations on CG
2007	RD 1362/2007	Mandatory	Listed companies	Disclosure requirements for financial statements, audit report, voting rights etc.

2.2.2 Auditing

After the deep reform made in the late 1980s, Spain adapted its legal and financial system to the European Union requirements, by the adoption of Audit Law 19/1988, establishing the rules to regulate the audit activity, which also included the creation of a new public entity—Accounting and

Auditing Institute (ICAC)—run by the Ministry of Economy and Finance. The ICAC duties are not only focused on accounting regulations, but also on controlling audit activity, "proceeding ex officio when in the public interest, via review or verification of some of the auditors' work, as well as to exercise disciplinary powers in respect of auditors and audit firms" (Audit Law 19/1988). Thus, auditing in Spain became a private professional activity controlled and ruled by a public entity.

Since then, few changes were made until recent economic scandals brought new regulation that affected auditing, as those new requirements stated by the Financial Act 44/2002 in order to achieve greater transparency and to improve financial statements credibility: a new regulation for auditors. After 2002, all companies—not only listed companies—must disclose audit and nonaudit fees paid to their auditors in their annual financial statements, and a more restrictive interpretation of auditor independency meant new circumstances that determined a conflict of interests.

As explained in the Olivencia Report, a large number of the audit report opinions issued by the external auditors contained reservations or qualifications regarding the financial statements (an average of 27 percent was qualified in the three previous years). The Commission pointed out this anomalous situation without parallel in other developed markets.

The creation of the Audit Committee, which is compulsory after the Transparency Law for listed companies, would help to overcome this problem. In fact, for 2006, the proportion of unqualified audit reports was more than 95 percent, the highest level since the CNMV was created in 1989 (CNMV 2007).

2.2.3 Power and Responsibilities of Top Management

The Spanish CG regulation is focused on promoting the implementation of new committees like the audit and the nomination committees. However, in Spain, listed companies traditionally had another one known as the executive committee. This committee is often created to make management decisions and it integrates the main responsibilities given to top management: more than 80 percent of IBEX companies have an executive committee (Spenser Stuart 2008). The risk of having an executive committee may come not only from the concentration of responsibilities, but also because its composition may not match board composition. The unified report expected a decrease in the relevance of this committee: The recommendations made about smaller boards and more frequently meetings may gradually end with the presence of executive committees in Spanish listed companies. Moreover, to reduce the risk, the code considered that the executive committee should have a similar composition to the board of directors, with a similar presence of independent directors on it.

With the adoption of the Olivencia Report recommendations, listed companies should create new committees as the audit and the nomination committees. The audit committee was almost unknown by Spanish companies before the Olivencia Report release. But the creation of an audit committee in a context of voluntary compliance varies systematically across listed companies, and only 5 percent of companies created an audit committee under voluntary basis (Ruiz Barbadillo, Biedma-Lopez, and Gomez Aguilar 2007). As mentioned, the creation of an audit committee, which should be composed by a majority of independent directors, became mandatory for Spanish listed companies under the Transparency Act 26/2003.

Focusing on directors' responsibilities and duties, little attention was paid to the conflict of interest and directors duties in Spain before CG codes (CGC) were developed. The Olivencia Code, following the stream of Anglo-Saxon countries, pointed to two rules to reduce conflicts of interest: directors should avoid participating in those discussions about facts in which they have interests, and directors should reduce the number of transactions between the company and themselves.

The Aldama Report went again one step ahead by recommending that some of these matters should be required by law. Later on, the Transparency Act 26/2003 included some of the Aldama Report recommendations, not only for listed companies but also for SMEs, as the obligation to disclose, as a part of the annual report, information about the presence of the company's directors on similar or related companies, not only as shareholders but also as members of the board of directors.

2.2.4 Conflicts of Interest and the Agency Problem

As mentioned, one of the main characteristics of the Spanish Stock Exchange is the high ownership concentration, with an average value of 40 percent (Gisbert and Navallas 2009a). Due to this circumstance, the agency problem in Spain may be found not only between owners and managers, but also between controlling shareholders and minority shareholders, the so-called horizontal agency costs. Then, this may be an important difference from CG results in some other countries, like in the Anglo-Saxon countries or civil law countries like Germany.

The presence of controlling shareholders on the board of directors is consequently higher than in other countries and represents more than 40 percent of total board members (Garcia Osma and Gill de Albornoz 2007). These directors (nonexecutive, nonindependent) are also called institutional or *gray* directors, and can be considered a control mechanism in reducing the agency cost raised from the separation between ownership and control. Following LaPorta, Lopez De Silanes, and Shleifer (1999), large shareholders are usually found in a weak investor protection environment like the one existing in Spain, which is identified by Miguel, Pindado, and Torre (2005) as a civil law country characterized by having one of the weakest legal systems. This lack of legal protection explains the higher levels of ownership concentration in Spain.

Following Spencer Stuart (2008) the proportion of independent directors on the board, which is around 53 percent, is still lower than in some other countries, and far below Anglo-Saxon countries like the United Kingdom. But even though listed companies may comply with the presence of independent directors on their board and committees, controversy might come from the independence definition, as 85 percent of them were proposed by the controlling shareholder or the company president. The Aldama Report had relevant critics because of its *shy* answer to the regulation of the independent definition, whereas the unified code rounds out the Aldama Report, adding the more concise conditions stated by the UE Recommendation in 2005: Independent directors should be proposed by the nomination committee while allowing directors to be considered for no more than twelve years' service.

2.2.5 Evaluating Board Performance

Following the unified report, the board of directors must at least once a year evaluate its own performance as a collegiate body, in a formal exact manner, with special attention to: (a) the quality and efficiency of board operations, (b) based on a report issued by the nomination committee, evaluate the president and chief executive performance, and (c) the annual performance of the committees.

The board is responsible for the remuneration policy, which through practical development might be delegated to the remuneration committee. The code recommends that the board should submit a detailed report about directors' remuneration to the General Shareholders Meeting.

Another recommendation is made about the remuneration policy: External directors should not have any variable remuneration related to company performance, measured by any financial indicators or share performance, in order to avoid any conflicts of interests when making decisions that affect the company's earnings.

2.2.6 Disclosure on Corporate Governance

Since the enactment of the Transparency Act 26/2003 listed companies must publish an ARCG, which has to be approved by the board of directors and sent electronically to the CNMV. The CNMV published an ARCG model that has to be filled in. After the unified code was released in 2006, a new ARCG was published to include new disclosures recommended. Companies are obliged to disclose the recommendations applied and the reasons for not applying, under the "comply-or-explain" principle. The unified code pointed out that listed companies are free to decide whether or not to comply, but they must disclose and explain their decisions.

The CNMV *Corporate Governance Report* (2007) shows those disclosure items companies comply with more frequently, which are information about ownership structure; board of directors size, composition, and director categories; board committees; board and senior remuneration; or general shareholders meeting. On the opposite side those items for which companies must improve their explanations are conflicts of interest, related-party transactions, and risk management systems.

2.3 Evidence of Corporate Governance Practices in Spain

As previously explained, disclosing CG practices in Spain is relatively new and it is mainly focused on listed companies. Thereby, in order to identify factors influencing CG disclosure over time a total of 176 and 168 Spanish listed companies for the year 2001 and 2004 have been analyzed respectively. To identify differences between firms disclosing and not disclosing CG practices, we used a parametric (t-test) and a nonparametric (Wilconxon Z-test) univariate test. Results, which are presented in Table 10.2, show that before 2002, only a few companies adopted and disclosed voluntarily such practices. This number increased significantly after the enactment of the Financial Act 44/2002 and the Transparency Act 26/2003, which requires that Spanish listed companies should adopt and disclose the most relevant CG. However, company disclosure choices in Spain are not only influenced by the enactment of the Financial Act 44/2002 and Transparency Act 26/2003, but also by firm characteristics as those included in the index IBEX 35 and/or low ownership concentration. Consistent with previous studies related to the voluntary disclosure of CG in Spain (Babío Arcay and Muíño Vázquez 1998, 2001) it could be argued that these companies may have high incentives to increase information to reduce agency cost.

As it has been explained in the previous sections, the Spanish regulation includes high-quality CG practices: the existence of an audit committee, the separation of roles between the president and CEO, board size between five and fifteen directors, the proportion of institutional directors plus independent directors should be the majority of the board, the proportion of independent directors should be greater than one-third, and that an executive committee is not recommended but not forbidden.

Beyond these recommendations only the implementation of an audit committee became compulsory by law. Then, there are no significant changes in the disclosed CG practices over the last years. Hence, it could be affirmed that variables that represent Spanish CG practices are sticky.

In order to identify factors influencing CG practices over time a total of thirty-six and forty-eight Spanish listed companies for the year 2001 and 2004 respectively were analyzed. We used a parametric (t-test) and non-parametric (Wilconxon Z-test) univariate tests. Consistent with the findings obtained by Garcia and Suarez (2005), the results, presented in Table 10.3, show that compliance with CG recommendations in Spain is influenced by IBEX-index companies and low ownership concentration companies, which have higher incentives to reduce agency cost.

Table 10.2 Firm Determinants for Disclosure on Corporate Governance Practices in Spain

Year = 2001 Variable	Disclosure				Nondisclosure				Dif	
	obs	mean	median	std	obs	mean	median	std	T-value	Z-Value
IBEX	51	0.37	0	0,49	125	0	0	0	5.45***	7.20***
OWN	42	39.77	34.73	22.22	73	61.48	58.74	27.77	-4.33***	-3.90***
Year = 2004 Variable	**Disclosure**				**Nondisclosure**				**Dif**	
	obs	mean	median	std	obs	mean	median	std	T-value	Z-Value
IBEX	141	0.26	0	0.44	27	0	0	0	6.93***	2.95***
OWN	112	48.7	51.54	27.24	12	71.68	67.69	22.82	-3.28***	-2.83***

Notes: *, **, *** Indicates significance at p_0,1, p _ 0.05 and p _ 0.01 respectively.
Variables
IBEX = Dummy variable that equals one whether the listed company is in the IBEX and zero otherwise.
OWN = Dummy variable that equals to one whether ownership concentration, which is measured by the number of closely held shares divided by the common shares outstanding, is higher than the mean of ownership concentration (year = 2004) and zero otherwise.

Table 10.3 Firm Determinants for Corporate Governance Practices Quality in Spain

Panel A: IBEX

Year = 2001

Variable	IBEX				Non-IBEX				R	Dif	
	nobs	mean	median	std	nobs	mean	median	std		T-value	Z-Value
Audit_board	19	1.00	1	0.00	32	0.72	1	0.46	1	3.48***	2.50

Year = 2004

Variable	IBEX				Non-IBEX				R	Dif	
	nobs	mean	median	std	nobs	mean	median	std		T-value	Z-Value
Audit_board	36	1	1	0	105	1	1	0	1	-	-
Exe_board	36	0.83	1	0.38	105	0.30	0	0.46	1	6.18***	5.49***
CEO_own	36	0.64	0	0.49	105	0.46	1	0.50	1	1.89**	1.87**
N°Directors	36	14.64	14	3.92	105	8.73	9	3.51	5<x<15	8.44***	6.63***
Board_Size	36	0.39	1	0.49	105	0.13	0	0.34	1	2.88**	3.30***
Perc_gray	36	0.39	0.41	0.22	105	0.41	0.38	0.27	0.33	-0.40	-0.30
Perc_Indep	36	0.39	0.37	0.17	105	0.29	0.27	0.24	0.33	2.34**	2.49**
Perc_ext	36	0.79	0.79	0.12	105	0.71	0.75	0.22	0.75	2.68***	1.62

(continued)

Panel B: OWNERSHIP

Year = 2004	OWN_Dispersion				OWN_Concentration					Dif	
Variable	nobs	mean	median	std	nobs	mean	median	std	R	T-value	Z-Value
Audit_board	48	1	1	0	64	1	1	0	1	-	-
Exe_board	48	0.63	1	0.49	64	0.39	0	0.49	1	2.50**	2.44**
CEO_own	48	0.63	1	0.51	64	0.42	0.00	0.50	1	2.26**	2.11**
NºDirectors	48	12.06	11.00	4.11	64	10.14	9.50	4.40	5<x<15	2.35**	2.30**
Board_Size	48	0.21	0	0.41	64	0.19	0	0.39	1	0.27	0.26
Perc_gray	48	0.34	0.33	0.19	64	0.50	0.50	0.26	0.33	-3.42***	-3.14***
Perc_Indep	48	0.42	0.44	0.20	64	0.25	0.25	0.20	0.33	4.45***	4.16***
Perc_ext	48	0.76	0.78	0.15	64	0.75	0.80	0.19	0.66	0.49	0.01

*, **, *** Indicates significance at $p\_0.1$, $p\_0.05$ and $p\_0.01$ respectively.

The number of observation study for the level of ownership concentration is lower due to missing values.

Variables

IBEX = Dummy variable that equals one whether the listed company is in the IBEX and cero otherwise

OWNERSHIP_Concentration = Dummy variable that equals to one whether ownership concentration, which is measured by the number of closely held shares divided by the common shares outstanding, is higher than the mean of ownership concentration (year=2004) and cero otherwise

Audit_board = Dummy variable that equals one whether the listed company has an audit board and cero otherwise

Exe_board = Dummy variable that equals one whether the listed company has an executive board and cero otherwise

CEO_own = Dummy variable that equals cero whether the chairman office executive is the same person than the owner and one otherwise

Nº Directors= Board size is the number of board members

Board_Size = Dummy variable that equals one whether the number of directors is more than five and less than 15. The dummy equals zero otherwise

Perc_gray = Percentage of the firm's directors that are institutional directors

Perc_Indep = Percentage of the firm's directors that are independent directors

Perc_ext = The sum of the percentage of institutional and independent directors

R: Some of the recommendations on corporate governance practices included in Olivencia (1998) and Aldama (2002) reports. The main recommendations on the Olivencia and Aldama Reports include that high quality corporate governance practices imply: the existence of an audit and executive Committee (Audit_board = 1 and Exe_board =1), the separation of roles between the president and CEO (CEO_own=1), the number of directors should be between five and fifteen 5<Board_Size <15), the proportion of institutional directors plus independent directors should be the majority of the board (Perc_ext > 0.66) and the proportion of gray directors should be greater than one third (Perc_Indep > 33), hence, the proportion of gray directors should be also greater than one third (Perc_gray> 0.33).

Listed companies included in the IBEX and/or with lower ownership concentration have higher probability of having an audit committee and an executive committee, separation of roles between the president and chief executive, and more independent boards. Otherwise, only listed companies included in the IBEX have adequate boards size with a higher proportion of independent directors. Moreover, the inexistent (negative) correlation between the proportion of gray directors and IBEX-index companies (low ownership concentration companies) does not mean low-quality CG practices. It could be argued that in Spain gray directors, which are designated by institutional directors, do not mitigate the agency problem due to high alignment between institutional investors and managers interests. Previous studies found a positive relationship between the presence of gray directors and the reduction of earnings managements manipulations (García and Gill de Albornoz 2007), whereas no empirical evidence was found on the relationship between gray directors and voluntary disclosure (Gisbert and Navallas 2009a).

Additionally, it is also important to consider that the CNMV studies about the degree of compliance with CG regulations identified low levels

Table 10.4   Firm Characteristics of Companies with Low Accounting Quality

				Obs
Number of companies with Accounting irregularities:	24			
Number of companies that disclose corporate governance practices:	19			
		R	CG	
		1	Audit_board	16
		1	Exe_board	7
Number of companies that disclosure and compliance with the following recommendations:		1	CEO_own	8
		5<x<15	Board_Size	14
		0.33	Perc_gray	11
		0.33	Perc_Indep	7
		0.66	Perc_ext	13

Companies with low accounting quality have been indentify as those that have restate their accounts between years 2002-2007
CG: Variable that indicates high quality corporate governance practices
R: Some of the recommendations on corporate governance practices included in Olivencia (1998) and Aldama (2002) reports. The main recommendations on the Olivencia and Aldama Reports include that high quality corporate governance practices imply: the existence of an audit and executive Committee (Audit_board = 1 and Exe_board =1), the separation of roles between the president and CEO (CEO_own=1), the number of directors should be between five and fifteen 5<Board_Size <15), the proportion of institutional directors plus independent directors should be the majority of the board (Perc_ext > 0.66) and the proportion of independent directors should be greater than one third (Perc_Indep > 33), hence, the proportion of gray directors should be also greater than one third (Perc_gray> 0.33).

of compliance because companies do not seem to be aware of governance practices. The conclusions obtained are described as very disappointing, with a high inconsistency level on the answers received from listed companies, which explains the decision to redraft certain recommendations.

Finally, it is also considered important to evaluate the influence of the CG practices on the quality of the financial information. By doing so, we have examined the CG practices of companies that present low-quality financial reporting, which are identified as those that had to restate their accounts over the same period.[13]

Results, which are presented in Table 10.4, show that there is a low percentage of companies with low-quality financial reporting that are adopting the main Aldama and Olivencia recommendations. These companies present lower board independence, probability of having an executive committee and, separation of roles between the president and CEO. Moreover, although these companies present a considerable amount of gray directors, those could not mitigate agency problems in Spain (García Osma and Gill de Albornoz 2007). Considering the small number of our sample these affirmations should be taken with caution.

As a general conclusion, it may be highlighted that during the last ten years Spanish listed companies have been progressively incorporating CG practices led by companies included in the IBEX or with lower ownership concentration.

NOTES

1. See Cañibano and Ucieda (2005) for a more detailed review of Spanish accounting history.
2. As of December 2009, there is a draft on business combinations following IASB standards, but the final endorsement by the EU of recent changes on those standards prevents the draft from being published.
3. It includes also a statement of recognized income and expense.
4. SMEs PGC is a simplified version of the PGC in certain standards like deferred taxes, leasing, and financial instruments, and does not require a statement of cash flows.
5. Percentage of capital controlled by investors with more than a 5 percent of the voting stock of the company.
6. Certain assets that were recognized under the previous PGC that do not meet the recognition criteria under the new PGC were written off against equity (reserves); therefore, the net effect on equity varies.
7. The statement of sources and applications of funds, based on working capital changes.
8. Again, a chart with the changes of all items in equity was required in the notes, although the statement of recognized income and expenses is entirely new.
9. Loans and receivables, held to maturity, held for trading, other assets at fair value through profit and loss, investments in the entities of the group, and available for sale.
10. See Cañibano and Ucieda (2005, 46).

11 See the IASB website for further details on the project and link to the documents available at: http://www.ifrs.org/Current+Projects/IASB+Projects/Financial+Statement+Presentation/Financial+Statement+Presentation.htm (last accessed on January 25th, 2011).

12 See Ernstberger (2008), Obinata (2008), Casta and Ramond (2007), Pinto (2005).

13 The CG practices subject to study are those disclosed by the Spanish listed companies in the year 2004. We justify this choice as representative of the general company CG performance because the behavior of these variables is very sticky.

REFERENCES

Aldama Report. 2003. *Report by the Special Commission to Foster Transparency and Security in the Markets and in Listed Companies. Comisión Nacional del Mercado de Valores (CNMV).* http://www.cnmv.es (accessed December 12, 2010).

Babío Arcay, R., and M. F. Muíño Vázquez. 1998. The extent of Spanish companies disclosure on corporate governance. Its relationship with certain firm characteristics. Presented at the International Conference on Accounting and Governance, Naples.

———. 2001. Compliance with the Olivencia Code: Changes observed in Spanish companies' disclosure policy. Presented at the AECA, XI Congress.

Cañibano, L., and J. L. Ucieda. 2005. Accounting and financial reporting in Spain. In *Readings on European accounting*, ed. L. Cañibano and A. Mora, 19–55. Madrid: Ed. AECA.

Casta, J. F., and O. Ramond. 2007. *On the relevance of reporting comprehensive income under IAS/IFRS: Insight from major European capital markets.* http://www.europlace-finance.com/ief07/casta_ramond.pdf (accessed January 24, 2011).

Del Brío, E., E. Maia Ramires, and J. Perote. 2006. Corporate governance mechanisms and their impact on firm value. *Corporate Ownership and Control* 4 (1): 25–36.

EFRAG. 2006. *The performance reporting debate. What (if anything) is wrong with the good old income statement? November.* http://www.efrag.org/projects/detail.asp?id=54 (accessed January 25, 2011).

———. 2009. *Performance reporting. A European discussion paper. March.* http://www.efrag.org/projects/detail.asp?id=154.

Ernstberger, J. 2008. The value relevance of comprehensive income under IFRS and US GAAP: Empirical evidence from Germany. *International Journal of Accounting, Auditing and Performance Evaluation* 5 (1): 1–29.

Garcia Osma, B., and B. Gill de Albornoz. 2007. The effect of the board composition and its monitoring committees on earnings management: Evidence from Spain. *Corporate Governance* 15 (6): 1413–28.

Garcia, R., and E. Suarez. 2005. Informe Aldama: el Gobierno Corporativo en la Web. *Partida Doble* 167:68–75.

Gisbert, A., and B. Navallas. 2009a. Gobierno Corporativo e Información Voluntaria en las Compañías Cotizadas Españolas. *Contabilidad y Tributación* 311 (February): 135–166.

———. 2009b. The impact of independent directors on voluntary disclosure: Evidence for Spain. Presented at the European Accounting Association Annual Congress, Tampere, Finland, May.

Gonzalo Angulo, J. A. 1992. *Accounting in Spain.* Madrid: AECA.

LaPorta, R., F. Lopez De Silanes, and A. Shleifer. 1999. Corporate governance around the world. *Journal of Finance* 54:471–517.

Miguel, A., J. Pindado, and C. Torre. 2005. Ownership structure and performance: A comparison of different corporate governance systems. *Corporate Ownership and Control* 2 (4): 76–85.

Obinata, T. 2008. *Net income vs. comprehensive income. A reexamination of attributes, relevance, and price informativeness (in Japanese).* http://ideas. repec.org/p/tky/jseres/2008cj201.html (accessed January 25, 2011).

Olivencia Report. 1998. *The governance of listed companies. Comisión Nacional del Mercado de Valores (CNMV).* http://www.cnmv.es (accessed January 25, 2011).

Pinto, J. A. 2005. How comprehensive is comprehensive income? The value relevance of foreign currency translation adjustments. *Journal of International Financial Management and Accounting* 16 (2): 97–122.

Ruiz Barbadillo, E., E. Biedma-Lopez, and N. Gomez Aguilar 2007. Managerial dominance and audit committee independence in Spain corporate governance. *Journal of Management and Governance* 7:311–52.

Spanish Securities and Exchange Commission. 2007. *Corporate governance report of entities with securities admitted to trading on regulated markets on 2007.* http://www.cnmv.es (accessed January 25, 2011).

Spencer Stuart. 2008. *Annual report on corporate governance.* http://www.spencerstuart.com (accessed January 25, 2011).

Unified Good Governance Code. 2006. Comisión Nacional del Mercado de Valores (CNMV). http://www.cnmv.es (accessed January 25, 2011).

11 Analysis of Changing Institutional Environments, New Accounting Policies, and Corporate Governance Practices in Sweden

Niclas Hellman

1. ACCOUNTING AND CORPORATE GOVERNANCE IN SWEDEN

With a population of about nine million people, Sweden is a relatively small country. However, Swedish business life during the twentieth century has been characterized by the development and growth of many multinational companies, such as Ericsson, Electrolux, Volvo, Tetra Pak, and IKEA. In 1997, Sweden had 282 listed companies with a weight in the world index of about 2.1 percent (Dahlquist and Robertsson 2001). Sweden's multinationals grew strong in an institutional environment where CEOs were given strong positions in which they were able to balance the requirements of different stakeholders, i.e., the government, the banks, the shareholders, and the employees. Accounting and company legislation supported this strong position for top management, by dividend restrictions and encouraged creation of (hidden) reserves. In turn, the appointments of CEOs in the multinationals were to a large extent governed by the ownership spheres that controlled most of the multinationals in Sweden.

The survival and advances of the Swedish model of corporate governance (CG) are interesting from an international perspective. This chapter will evaluate the development of CG in Sweden and the role that changes in the financial reporting area have played in this context.

2. THE RELATIONSHIP BETWEEN ACCOUNTING AND CORPORATE GOVERNANCE IN SWEDEN

2.1 Swedish Accounting and Long-Term Survival of the Firm

The accounting tradition that emerged in Sweden during the first half of the 1900s was subject to strong influences from Germany. Sweden's first accounting professors in academia came from Germany, all with some connection to the famous Professor Schmalenbach (Engwall 1995). In turn, academia had much impact on the development of financial accounting, primarily via Oskar Sillén who was a student of Schmalenbach's. Sillén was appointed professor at the Stockholm School of Economics during 1915–1951, the certified auditor of many large corporations, and initiator to the founding of *Föreningen Auktoriserade Revisorer* (FAR), the Swedish professional body of certified accountants (Wallerstedt 1988).

In one of the early classifications of accounting systems, Swedish accounting was found to fit the Continental European model (Nair and Frank 1980). Originating from Germany, this model is characterized by its emphasis on conservatism and creditor protection (see Mueller, Gernon, and Meek 1991). Prominent representatives of Swedish accounting, such as Sillén and Västhagen (1962, 69–70), argued that managers have a responsibility to be conservative by creating reserves in order to protect their companies against downturns in the business cycle and against short-term-oriented shareholders who might threaten the long-term survival of the company:[1]

> The reserves that are created for the above mentioned reasons are primarily meant to prevent that too high or even fictitious earnings are presented, giving rise to large payments of dividends, and thus endangering the survival of the company . . . Shareholders do not always understand what is beneficial and necessary from the company's point of view, they sometimes have a short-sighted speculative interest in withdrawing as large a dividend as possible, or in an increasing stock price.

The prevailing view was that a single good year should not result in dividends, but profits should be retained as "reserves for the future" (Artsberg and Nilsson 1993, 37). Dividend restrictions were prescribed in the company legislation and accordingly the measurement of nonrestricted shareholders' equity became an important function of financial accounting.

A few years after the Nair and Frank (1980) classification, Nobes (1983) provided a different classification of international financial reporting practices in which Swedish accounting was characterized as government-driven and tax-oriented. Sweden is a country with a comprehensive tax–accounting link, which means that expenses must be recognized in the individual company accounts in order to become tax deductible. A strong link between accounting and taxation tends to work in favor of conservatism because more prudent valuations of assets and liabilities will also lead to lower taxable income. In Sweden, the government encouraged such conservative valuation by providing tax incentives related to investments in assets such as machinery, equipment, and inventory. Firm investments in such assets were expected to benefit the economy. In the mid-1960s, a Swedish accountant described the calculation of profits, as follows (Davidson and Kohlmeier 1966, 208):

> In Sweden we start at the top and bottom of the income statement and work toward the middle, minimizing taxes along the way. Sales are determined by outside forces, the directors decide the size of the dividend, and then we determine expenses and income to fit. The larger the reported income, the more income tax, so we maximize reported expenses within the provisions of the law.

The quotation illustrates that the conservative accounting significantly affected the interpretation of the income statement. During the 1970s, the impact of the link between accounting and taxation increased even more due the introduction of a number of new tax incentives (Blake et al. 1997). The political climate at this time favored high taxation of companies, and, in response, the government increased the statutory tax rate, but compensated the companies by letting them create even bigger untaxed reserves. In recent years, the statutory tax rate has been lowered and the corporate tax incentives have been reduced.

In sum, the strong adherence to conservatism and dividend restrictions, supported by leading academics and the government, and prescribed by legislation, turned into a tool for ensuring the survival and growth of Swedish (large) companies. This tool was handed to the managers of the companies who were supposed to create reserves in order to lower the room for dividends and thereby secure the financing of growth also in bad times. Why would shareholders accept such a system? The reason can be found in the Swedish CG model, where ownership spheres with their own banks collaborated with the Swedish government and trade unions.

2.2 The Swedish Corporate Governance Model

As described in Section 2.1, the long-term growth and survival of the firm was supported by the conservative accounting practice and the shareholders' right to dividends was delimited. The Swedish Company Act in force during a large part of the twentieth century included rules on dividend restriction and compulsory retention of profits in order to protect the company from shareholders that could threaten the existence of the company (Jönsson 1991, 529). Instead, industrial owners who wanted to reinvest profits for future growth were cherished. A negative aspect of this model was that capital was locked in the already existing companies, leading to insufficient reallocation of capital in the economy (see Henrekson and Jacobsson 2003). Furthermore, it was difficult for investors to estimate the fair value of companies' shares due to the lack of transparency in the financial reporting, referred to in the preceding section. However, under this Swedish model of CG many companies grew to become large multinational enterprises, such as Ericsson, Electrolux, Volvo, Tetra Pak, and IKEA.

One may wonder why shareholders would want to accept a system where managers applied arbitrary and often tax-driven conservative accounting, leading to low levels of transparency (hidden reserves), understated profits during good years, and overstated profits during bad years. The main answer is to be found in what Collin (1993) refers to as "the brotherhood of the Swedish spheres." The term "sphere" was coined by the Swedish journalist Sven-Ivan Sundqvist, who analyzed the ownership of Swedish listed companies by going beyond formal ownership in order to capture the complete networks of ownership. Since 1985, Sundqvist has annually published a book in which the spheres are carefully described (see, for example, Fristedt and Sundqvist 2008). In 2008, there were sixteen spheres (ibid.) and the two largest, the Wallenberg and the Handelsbanken spheres, were created during the 1920s and 1930s. The Wallenberg and the Handelsbanken spheres each centers on an "ownership company" (Investor AB and Industrivärden AB, respectively) that owns control positions in the industrial companies and the "sphere bank" (SEB and Handelsbanken, respectively). In addition to the ownership companies, there are also various related family foundations, pension funds, and mutual funds that contribute to the power base of the spheres.[2] The spheres use, for example, cross-ownership to maintain power within the sphere, but shares with different voting rights stand out as the most important vehicle for controlling many companies with a limited amount of capital. For example, in the end of 2008, 48 percent of votes in Investor AB were controlled by three Wallenberg family foundations. The 48 percent voting power corresponded to 22.3 of the share capital with a market value of about 20 billion SEK. In turn, Investor AB was a large shareholder in eight listed companies (see Table 11.1).[3]

Table 11.1 illustrates how the Wallenberg sphere gains considerable influence over many large corporations via relatively small equity stakes. For example, Investor AB has a voting share of 19.4 percent in Ericsson,

Table 11.1 Investor AB's Holdings of Listed Shares in Core Companies per December 31, 2008

Company	Voting Share	Capital Share	Investor AB's Holding (bn SEK)	Total Market Cap. (bn SEK)
ABB	7.3%	7.3%	19.2	264.2
AstraZeneca	3.6%	3.6%	15.8	444.2
Atlas Copco	22.3%	16.6%	13.6	78.4
Ericsson	19.4%	5.1%	9.6	191.0
SEB	21.1%	20.7%	8.6	41.7
Electrolux	28.8%	12.7%	2.6	20.7
Husqvarna	28.7%	15.4%	2.3	15.8
SAAB	38.0%	19.8%	1.5	7.8

Source: Investor AB's annual report 2008.

although its capital share is only 5.1 percent. However, the table also shows that this system is threatened when the shares with different voting rights disappear, as in the two companies with parent companies outside Sweden (ABB and AstraZeneca).

The Swedish spheres gained *financial control* over many large corporations by using their banks and votes with different voting power. However, they also gained *management control* over the companies by developing networks of loyal CEOs and board members, referred to by Collin (1993) as the "brotherhood." As referred to earlier, top management had a key role in balancing different stakeholder interests. Carlsson (2003, 6) summarized the Wallenberg sphere's way of working as follows:

> The family works through two key structures: Investor AB—an investment company which has a board of non-executive directors and two executive vice chairmen most of whom are experienced CEOs from industry and commerce; and independent company boards, with strong CEOs—which they change as necessary to ensure that they have the competencies required to deliver the agreed strategies.

This way of working would not have been possible without support from the political sector and the trade unions. Since the end of World War II, Sweden has been ruled almost continuously by Social Democrats and Sweden has a strong focus on employee rights (Randøy and Nielsen 2002). The spheres' long-term interest in industrial development and growth combined with the stability of the spheres over time corresponded well with the interests of the Social Democrats and the unions (see Henrekson and Jacobson 2003).

A potential drawback of the Swedish model of governance is the risk of unfair treatment of minority shareholders. From the preceding description, it appears as if the spheres would be able to use their power in order to expropriate minorities and LaPorta, Lopez-de-Silanes, and Shleifer (1999) classifies Sweden as one of the countries in Europe with the weakest minority protection. Agnblad et al. (2002, 252) analyzed this issue and concluded that the social costs in Swedish society are too high for unfair treatment of minorities:

> The focus on formal rules of minority protection . . . is a very narrow—and essentially static—perspective . . . The one-sided focus on minority protection misses what we believe to be the crucial problem with the Swedish corporate governance model—the lock-in effects when ownership and control are strongly separated . . . Minority protection is a minor problem because of the disciplining effect of social benefits of control.

The spheres grew strong in a system with weak financial markets and low demands on accounting transparency. The two largest spheres were actually created in the aftermath of the financial market failure beginning in 1929. With more international capital markets, a much larger share of institutional investors and more transparent accounting, the conditions for the Swedish CG model has changed dramatically. Already in 1993, Collin (1993, 85) speculated, "Unless there is political or governmental interest in the survival of the spheres, they must walk down the road to past history." To what extent this has actually happened is discussed in Section 4.

3. DECISION MAKING AND CONTROL ACCORDING TO THE SWEDISH MODEL OF CORPORATE GOVERNANCE

3.1 Four Key Bodies

The Swedish Companies Act (Aktiebolagslag 2005, 551) provides the framework for CG of Swedish listed companies. The law prescribes that there must be three decision-making bodies (the annual general meeting, the board of directors, and the chief executive officer) in a hierarchical structure (see Figure 11.1) and one controlling body (auditors) appointed by the annual general meeting (AGM).

Figure 11.1 is from the *Swedish Code of Corporate Governance* (Swedish Corporate Governance Board 2008) and illustrates the hierarchical relationship between the three decision-making bodies and the basic idea that the AGM appoints auditors that monitor the board of directors and the CEO. The roles of these bodies are presented in the following.

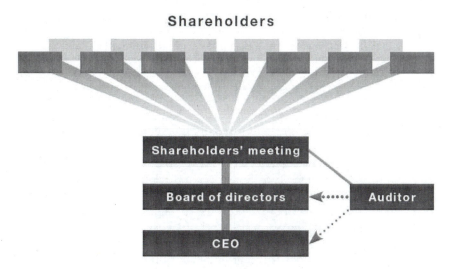

Figure 11.1 An illustration of the key bodies in the Swedish corporate governance model. Source: The Swedish Code of Corporate Governance (2008).

3.1.1 The Annual General Meeting

The AGM is the highest decision-making body in Swedish limited companies and all shareholders can exercise their influence directly at the AGM. Under Swedish legislation, one share is sufficient in order to be entitled to debate the board's and the CEO's responsibilities for actions and decisions at the AGM (Nilsson and Hassel 2003). Auditors typically attend AGMs and should be prepared to answer questions from shareholders regarding the audit process, according to the guidelines issued by FAR (2003).

AGMs are sometimes referred to as ritual, lacking connection to other forms of CG (Hodges, Macniven, and Mellet 2004). However, AGMs in Swedish listed companies are often quite lively events because the Swedish Shareholders' Association, representing some 77,000 members (December 2007), has long been attending AGMs and has debated issues concerning, for example, remuneration and dividend/buy-back policies. Carrington and Johed (2007) conducted a study based on participant observation of thirty-six AGMs in Swedish listed companies. They report that rules and legislation give the meeting an important role in the evaluation of stewardship of public companies. To some extent this pertains to the Swedish (and Finnish) legal rules regarding the AGM decision of whether or not to discharge responsibility on the part of the CEO and the board of directors.[4] Furthermore, Carrington and Johed (2007, 722) conclude that "accounting guides and triggers action at such meetings by providing arguments for debating or promoting stewardship." They support this statement by various examples from the AGMs where debates originate from accounting information, for example, shareholder questions concerning the treatment of goodwill or the levels of growth and profitability related to corporate strategy. The results suggest that shareholders' use of accounting information at the AGM improve their ability to evaluate stewardship.

3.1.2 The Board of Directors

Sweden has a system of unitary boards and CEO duality is not allowed in public companies. The board of directors is responsible for the company's organization and management of the company's business and it has extensive decision-making authority according to the Swedish Companies Act. The board may delegate tasks, but may not disclaim liability for organization, management, or control of the company's financial position (Swedish Corporate Governance Board 2008, 11). As described in Section 2.2, one important feature of the Swedish model of CG is the significant influence of ownership spheres and the board of directors plays an important role for ownership spheres when executing ownership power. Kärreman (1999) studied the work of directors in boards of listed companies and found three categories of board members: independent directors, labor representatives, and owner representatives. The independent directors were elected by the AGM on the basis of specific competencies and they generally perceived their role as ensuring that the industrial perspective was being properly taken into account in connection with decision making. The labor representatives tended to be passive with regard to issues other than the ones pertaining to the employees, and used the board meeting as an information source.[5] Finally, the owner representatives were perceived by the other board members to be of a higher rank in the sense that they were viewed as interpreters of the owner's intentions and principles. In sum, this system generally provides a strong connection between the large owners and the board of directors and, according to Jonnergård and Kärreman (2004, 238), this represents a difference compared to the typical relationship between owners and boards in the US.

3.1.3 The Chief Executive Officer

The CEO is subordinate to the board of directors and is responsible for the company's day-to-day management. The CEO must prepare and present issues that are outside the scope of day-to-day management to the board, in accordance with the written instructions provided by the board (Swedish Corporate Governance Board 2008, 12). However, in terms of firm involvement and information access, the CEO typically has a stronger position compared to the members of the board. The CEO is usually the only director on the board with a management position in the company and the chairmanship is seldom a full-time position (Jonnergård and Kärreman 2004).

The CG literature commonly assumes that agency problems related to CEO behavior may be mitigated by carefully designed compensation packages. At the same time, the national setting appears to have substantial impact on the use of incentive compensation practices (Jansen, Merchant, and Van der Stede 2009). On the basis of an empirical study of Swedish and Norwegian companies, Randøy and Nielsen (2002, 75–76) report:

> We did not find a significant relationship between company accounting performance or stock performance and CEO compensation in either Norway or Sweden . . . On the other hand, the empirical evidence from both Norway and Sweden reveals significant positive relationships between board size and CEO compensation, foreign board membership and CEO compensation, and market capitalization and CEO compensation. A significant negative relationship was also found between CEO ownership and CEO compensation.

The authors explain these results by referring to the "success" of the Social Democratic party in breaking the link between CEO pay and performance, by measures such as putting union members on the board (the employee representatives), very high taxation of stock options, and the nonallowance of CEO/chairman duality in public companies. Randøy and Nielsen (2002) use data from 1996–1998 and some changes have taken place in recent years. For example, the results of Jonnergård, Kärreman, and Svensson (2004) suggest that the boards of directors have increased their emphasis on CEO and top management incentives. However, the level of CEO remuneration in Sweden is still in the lower bound within Europe and considerably below the remuneration level in US (Söderström et al. 2003).

3.1.4 Auditors

Auditors are appointed at the AGM and the audit report serves as a key basis for the owners at the AGM when they decide on the adoption of the income statement and balance sheet and whether the company's profit or loss should be appropriated in accordance with proposals made by the board of directors (Swedish Corporate Governance Board 2008). The Swedish audit legislation does not provide detailed guidance, but has left the evolvement of auditing standards to practice by referring to the concept of *god revisionssed*, e.g., good auditing practice. FAR issues standards that prescribe what is considered good auditing practice.[6] In 2004, International Standards on Auditing (ISAs) were implemented via a new standard issued by FAR. According to examinations made during the 1990s, Swedish GAAS is well in line with the ISAs (see FAR 2002). The remaining differences compared to ISAs are due to the requirements of Swedish legislation. One important difference compared to ISAs concerns the management audit (*förvaltningsrevision*) that must be conducted in addition to the financial audit. The management audit concerns the management performed by members of the board of directors and the CEO. The audit report includes a separate statement referring to the management audit, which serves as a basis for the AGM when it decides on the responsibility discharge issues (see Section 3.1.1). Although the auditor's assignment includes monitoring the board of directors, there is also a case of reverse monitoring in the sense that one of the audit committee's duties is to "evaluate the auditing work and inform the company's nomination committee of the results of this evaluation" (Swedish Corporate Governance Board 2008, 22).

From a historical perspective, there have been strong elements of self-regulation in Sweden in the area(s) of auditing (and accounting), e.g., the profession (via FAR) has had considerable influence on development (see Wallerstedt 2005). The state has sometimes intervened, as in the 1980s, when auditors became obliged by law to check their clients' payments of taxes and public sector fees (ibid.). A governmental body, *Revisorsnämnden* (Supervisory Board of Public Accountants), is responsible for authorization and surveillance of auditors. As described by Diamant (2004, 55), this supervisory board has the right of interpretational precedence. However, in practice, the profession has considerable influence over the development of good audit practice in Sweden (Diamant 2004, 58–71).

3.2 The Swedish Code of Corporate Governance

Since 2005, the Swedish Companies Act has been supported by a code of CG. The first version, in force during the period July 1, 2005, to June 30, 2008, was required by the Stockholm Stock Exchange (SSE) for listed companies whose market capitalization exceeded 3 billion SEK. The revised version of the code, in force since July 1, 2008, represents good stock exchange practice for all Swedish companies whose shares are traded on a regulated market (Swedish Corporate Governance Board 2008). Both versions of the code include supplementary rules concerning issues related to the four key bodies described earlier (AGM, board of directors, CEO, and auditors). In particular, these codes include prescriptions regarding a nomination committee established by the AGM, and remuneration and audit committees in the board of directors.

4. UNDERSTANDING THE TRANSITION PERIOD: DEREGULATED MARKETS AND IAS-BASED ACCOUNTING

4.1 Adoption of IAS/IFRS

In the late 1980s, a new standard-setting body for public companies was formed in Sweden named *Redovisningsrådet* (the Swedish Financial Accounting Standards Council [SFASC]).[7] This marked a new era in Swedish accounting in that the SFASC set out to issue recommendations on the basis of the body of rules and regulations of the International Accounting Standards Committee (IASC, later the International Accounting Standards Board [IASB]). Swedish accounting was to become more oriented towards equity investor interests and accordingly the Swedish companies listed on the SSE became obliged to comply with the SFASC recommendations (or explain deviations from these recommendations).[8]

Although Swedish accounting had been subject to influence from the US and has gradually become more transparent since the 1960s, the forming of the SFASC marked the beginning of an era where the explicit purpose of the consolidated accounts was to serve the needs of capital market participants. As noted by Cooke (1989), Sweden has a "disproportionate number of multinational enterprises," and these companies advocated the need for Swedish accounting to become more capital markets–oriented. Two issues were particularly urgent to deal with. First, the strong relationship between taxation and accounting created problems for foreign readers of Swedish consolidated accounts. Large amounts under headings such as "untaxed reserves" and "appropriations to untaxed reserves" were hard to communicate and various adjustments were necessary in order to make equity and profit numbers usable from an investor perspective. The SFASC issued its first recommendation in 1991 concerning business combinations (RR 1:00), which introduced deferred tax accounting that put an end to the use of Swedish tax-related concepts in the consolidated accounts.

Second, Swedish accounting pre-SFASC was a system where practice led regulation. The accounting legislation provided general rules and then referred to the concept of *god redovisningssed*, e.g., "good accounting practice." There were three different bodies providing guidance regarding the interpretation of "good accounting practice,"[9] but this guidance, to varying extent, reflected already existing practice. Hanner (1980) described this as follows:[10]

[The Companies Act (ABL 1975) and the Accounting Act (BFL 1976)] introduced many changes regarding the annual report. New requirements included: complete and public consolidated statements, for larger companies: open disclosure of hidden reserves related to inventory valuation, cash flow statements and interim reports. These new requirements, however, merely reflected the development that had already taken place during the 10–20 years preceding 1975.

This way of letting practice lead regulation meant that accounting practice could vary much between the leading companies and the ones that were reluctant to change. During the 1980s, this problem of variation in accounting practice became worse as the multinational companies leading the development of Swedish accounting practice disagreed on how to account for goodwill. In a study of the Swedish companies providing US GAAP reconciliations during 1982–1990, Hellman (1993, 509) reports that 54 percent of the eighty-four observations of net profit measured according to Swedish GAAP were either materially higher (> 10 percent) *or* materially lower (> 10 percent) compared to net profit measured according to US GAAP. Using goodwill accounting as an example, many different treatments were used during this period: direct write-off against equity, direct write-off over the income statement, progressive amortization, and linear amortization for a varying number of years.[11] The first SFASC recommendation, which was based on IAS 22, prescribed more restrictive rules for applying the pooling method and prescribed straight-line amortization of goodwill for a maximum period of twenty years.

During the period 1991–2004, the SFASC voluntarily adopted nearly all the International Accounting Standards (IASs) in the form of recommendations (see Rundfelt 1993, for a description of the early work). In 1995, Sweden joined the EU, which led to changes a few years later in the format of income statements and balance sheets and an introduction of the concept of "true and fair view." However, with regard to accounting measurement and disclosure, the most important changes were caused by the stepwise adoption of IASs via recommendations issued by the SFASC. In 2005, Sweden adopted International Financial Reporting Standards (IFRS) and at this point in time, only three IASs (39, 40, and 41) had not yet been adopted by the SFASC. This incremental approach to the adoption of IAS/IFRS has also been taken by countries such as Australia and South Africa (Godfrey and Chalmers 2007), but differs from the strategy in, for example, Switzerland and Germany, where listed companies were given the opportunity of adopting nonnational standards in full (US GAAP or IAS/IFRS) instead of converging the national standards to IAS/IFRS. The better comparability across the listed companies within a country is an advantage of the incremental approach compared to the Swiss/German approach, but the risks of deficient local versions of IASs and insufficient enforcement institutions represent potential drawbacks. The SFASC recommendations were not always identical to its IAS counterparts in that the SFASC sometimes made adjustments because of Swedish legislation or for other strong reasons. Furthermore, although compliance with the recommendations was required by the SSE and monitored by auditors, this was not an environment of strong enforcement. Some reports have been published that indicate a lack of compliance (Grundvall et al. 2004; Fagerström, Hassel, and Cunningham 2007).[12] Even after the establishment of a Swedish Panel for Monitoring Financial Reporting in 2003, there were deviations from the SFASC recommendations in accounting practice (Panelen för övervakning av finansiell rapportering 2005). Although most of the deviations discovered by the panel concerned the lack of disclosure, recent research suggest that Swedish listed companies utilized the soft adoption of IAS/IFRS under the SFASC regime in order to act in accordance with their reporting incentives (Hellman 2011).

4.2 Some Economic Consequences of the Transition

Runsten (1998) performed an empirical evaluation of the association between accounting information and stock prices in Sweden under different accounting regimes. For the purpose of the current text, the movement from hidden reserves to open disclosure of such reserves is interesting. Runsten's data series begins in 1967, when approximately only 10 percent of the companies openly disclosed their hidden reserves related to depreciable assets, and ends in 1981 when almost all Swedish listed companies disclosed this information (1998, 164–65). The change in accounting practice took place gradually and when performing pooled regressions of early periods compared to late periods in value-level tests, using the market-to-book value premium as the dependent variable, the R^2s were between two and three times higher for "open disclosure firms" compared to the "nondisclosure firms."[13] Runsten (1998, 232) concludes, "The more informative, open accounting procedure, thus appears to be associated with a better mapping to the stock price." Similar results were reported with regard to the regressions explaining value changes (276–77).[14] More recently, Skogsvik (2008) examined the predictive ability of financial statements information on the Swedish stock market, using tests conducted in the spirit of Ou and Penman (1989). First, a large set of accounting ratios were analyzed and incorporated into models for predicting future return on equity. Second, trading strategies based on predictions of the estimated prediction models were evaluated for three different time periods (1983–1985; 1986–1988; and 1989–1991), using abnormal return metrics. Skogsvik (2008, 816) concludes that "stock prices in the Swedish stock market seem to have reflected available accounting information better in the second and the third subperiod (i.e. 1986–1994)." In sum, the results of Runsten (1998) and Skogvik (2008) suggest that the increased transparency and lowered emphasis on conservatism following from IAS influence, was beneficiary for a more well-functioning stock market in Sweden. Unfortunately, there are no comparable studies covering the period from which the Swedish IAS adoption began (1991).

4.3 Increased Institutional Ownership and Questioning of Brotherhood Model

Swedish financial markets were deregulated during the 1980s, which led to the development of well-functioning short-term and long-term money markets (see, for example, Henrekson 1988). Both foreign and Swedish institutional investors were gradually given greater degrees of freedom, especially during the late 1980s (Jonnergård and Kärreman 2004, 237). The Swedish stock market trading volumes increased from USD 4 billion in 1980 to USD 16 billion in 1989, but a far greater increase occurred during the 1990s and in 1999 the stock market trading volume was USD 314 billion (Hellman 2000, 1). Jonnergård and Kärreman (2004, 237) describe this as follows:

> The stock market attracted new actors, and the previous stable pattern of financial groups [e.g., ownership spheres] underwent changes. Among the new actors were various institutional and foreign investors.

Ownership changed dramatically during the 1990s. First, the shift from individual to institutional ownership was intensified during this period as households began to use financial intermediaries (e.g., funds) to a much greater extent than before (Hellman 2000, 3). Second, foreign ownership increased from 12 percent in 1992 to 39 percent in 1999 (Jonnergård and Kärreman 2004, 237–38). This meant that both Swedish and foreign institutional investors grew stronger during this period and the Swedish model of CG was challenged. The first case of institutional shareholder activism was in 1993 when institutional owners used their joint power to prevent the Volvo-Renault merger (Hellman 2000, 15). At this point in time, Volvo was a conglomerate and, inspired by the development in Anglo-Saxon countries, institutional investors argued that companies like Volvo should focus on their core businesses and divest or spin-off noncore business. Accordingly, this actually took place in many companies during the 1990s, including Volvo. This also led to a lower degree of cross-ownership.

Although the institutional investors used their increased ownership influence with regard to salient issues such as increased focus on core business, CEO remuneration, and optimized capital structure, they were very seldom prepared to assume board positions in the companies where they were large owners. This is logical because these institutional investor organizations are not designed for taking on such responsibilities in the CG processes of listed companies (Hellman 2005). Thus, although the Swedish model of CG was challenged during the 1990s, the boards of directors continued to be governed by the ownership spheres. Material changes certainly took place in terms of externally observable things such as increased dividend levels and disbandment of conglomerates and cross-ownerships, but there seemed to be a tacit understanding between the institutional investors and the ownership spheres, which meant that the ownership spheres still controlled "their" companies. Jonnergård, Kärreman, and Svensson (2004, 113–14) compared the behavior of boards in Swedish listed companies in 1994 and 1999 and reported: "we find no significant changes concerning directors' attitudes toward the role of the stock market or other governance mechanisms between 1994 and 1999." This indicates that the boards were able to continue to base their decisions on industrial aspects (2004, 136), although their results also show some tendency of increased consideration of external and financial factors in 1999 compared to 1994.

5. THE SWEDISH MODEL OF CORPORATE GOVERNANCE REVISITED

During the 2000s, the trend with increased Anglo-Saxon influence has continued in the public domain. In 2000, share buybacks became permitted by law and the first Swedish code of CG came in force in 2005. With regard to CEO remuneration, Sweden is still a highly egalitarian country and in a few cases, where previously praised company leaders have received remunerations at American levels, the criticism has been massive from practically all parties.[15] Still, institutional and foreign ownership has remained on a high level (see Fristedt and Sundqvist 2008) and the listed companies have generally become more transparent and shareholder-oriented during the 2000s in terms of more detailed and frequent reporting; more developed investor relations services; and high awareness with regard to dividend, buyback, and capital structure policies. However, beyond the public domain, it seems like the Swedish model of CG is still alive and kicking. Jonnergård and Larsson (2007) examined the submitted formal responses to the draft version of the first Swedish code of CG in 2004. Their investigation showed that the Swedish institutional investors chose to join forces with the group referred to by the authors as the *Swedish business insiders*, which includes the representatives of the ownership spheres. The foreign investors became marginalized. Jonnergård and Larsson (2007, 476) state:

> we presumed that power had shifted from owners of the owner-dominated companies to the institutional investors, that the institutional investors and dominant owners had different interests . . . However, for most issues discussed during the referral process, national culture trumped agency.

Although foreign influence played an indirect role in adopting a code of CG in the first place, Jonnergård and Larsson (2007, 484) conclude that "we have not detected salient changes in the position of power or in the relations among actors involved in the corporate governance system in Sweden as a result of the formation of a new code."

As described in Section 1, conservative accounting was historically a tool given to top management in order to protect the company during downturns in the business cycle and from short-term-oriented shareholders. Many of these CEOs belonged to the brotherhoods inside the Swedish ownership spheres. How have the CEOs and the ownership spheres reacted to the more capital-market-oriented financial reporting that has been adopted in Sweden since the early 1990s?

One example is the president's statement in the annual report of 2004 from Petter Stillström, CEO of the Swedish listed investment company Traction:[16]

Year	1999	2000	2001	2002	2003	2004
Reported result, MSEK	60	351	23	−19	−38	83
Corrected result, MSEK	275	54	47	−111	85	192*

* According to IFRS pro forma.

Figure 11.2   Presentation of annual results for a listed investment company according to Swedish GAAP and IFRS, respectively.
Source: Traction's annual report 2004.

Historically, Traction has reported profit only after it has been truly earned and realized, thus refraining from including future, not yet realized gains . . . Now the so-called modern reporting forces us to confuse the issues. Our group of subsidiaries will report based on fairly historical/ realized transactions . . . The part that consists of holdings in other companies, smaller stakes as well as associated companies, will be subject to market valuation. This means that for listed companies the market share price will be applied and for other companies the Board of Directors will have to decide on a valuation. This means that future profits will be included based on assessments of profit before it has been earned. This is not something that we like. We just don't think it is true and fair. Reasonable theoretical underpinnings are also lacking . . . As can be seen [see Figure 11.2], the sequence of results changes significantly. Year 1999 stands out as our record year rather than 2000, when we realized large portions of 1999's appreciation. 2003 was actually a pretty good year instead of a year of major losses. 2004 was more than twice as good using the new reporting, compared to traditional accounting.

The example illustrates a preference for more conservative accounting than IFRS represents, but this is only one anecdotal observation and there has not been any systematic criticism against, for example, fair value accounting. One might perhaps speculate that the few instances of criticism are because IFRS meets the need of accounting flexibility. The forward orientation of many IASB standards, in terms of probability judgments and estimates of inflows and outflows of future economic benefits, provides managers with a tool that can potentially be used for both conservative and aggressive purposes (Hellman 2008).

In sum, the Swedish model of CG has been affected by the movement towards the shareholder model and capital markets influence, but important parts of the core, in terms of maintaining long-term industrial perspectives, have also survived due to what appears to be tacit agreements between the ownership spheres and the domestic institutional investors. From a financial reporting point of view, the traditional conservative and historical cost-based accounting was strongly supported in Sweden and gave power to the CEOs to balance different stakeholder interests. However, beginning in the 1980s, the accounting gradually became more transparent and less influenced by the creation of reserves, as reflected in the improved correspondence between accounting information and stock prices (see Section 4.2). This reduced the accounting flexibility of top executives, but the ownership spheres and their brotherhoods of CEOs and board members of the ownership spheres survived this change. They seem to have adapted to an environment where demands for transparency from other investors must be taken into account to a high extent and the forward orientation of IFRS still leaves top management with a certain level of discretion that can be used to manage different stakeholder interests.

NOTES

1. This quotation is from the 1965 edition of Sillén and Västhagen (1962), as translated from Swedish in Runsten (1998, 99).
2. Spheres of this kind are also common in Germany and Japan (Berglöf 1990).
3. Please note that the Wallenberg sphere also owns shares in some of the companies in Table 11.1 via other sphere entities.
4. According to Carrington and Johed (2007, 704), this AGM decision regarding discharge of responsibility is a distinctive feature of the Swedish and Finnish systems of CG. Note that the term *discharge* has a stronger significance in Sweden and Finland compared to the UK and the US.
5. Under Swedish legislation for large companies, a minimum of two board positions are reserved for the employees.
6. In 2006, FAR merged with another organization of accountants, whereafter the name changed to FAR SRS. In 2010, the name FAR was readopted.
7. SFASC was founded by FAR, *Bokföringsnämnden* (BFN, the Swedish Accounting Standards Board; a governmental body), and *Sveriges Industriförbund* (the Federation of Swedish Industries).
8. For convenience, the denotation SSE is used throughout the chapter although the name has changed several times due to acquisitions. Currently, the Stockholm stock exchange is part of Nasdaq OMX Nordic.
9. The three bodies were FAR, BFN, and *Näringslivets Börskommitté* (the Industry and Commerce Stock Exchange Committee).
10. The translation from Swedish was made by Runsten (1998, 97).
11. In addition to goodwill there was flexibility with regard to the accounting treatment of associated companies, capitalization of R&D expenditure, writedowns of tangible fixed assets, revaluations of tangible fixed assets, foreign currency translation, and liabilities (see Heurlin and Peterssohn 1991).
12. Note that the SFASC recommendations used the format of "comply or explain."
13. For the whole transition period, 1967–1980, the R^2 was 47.3 percent for the "open disclosure firms" and 24.9 percent for the "nondisclosure firms."
14. Runsten (1998, 277) states: "the open disclosure firms showed an R^2 that was twice as high (for the period 1968–1981), and finally eight times as high (for the period 1976 to 1977). These results indicate that the open disclosure practice regarding depreciation and valuation of depreciable assets has indeed provided a more informative description of the value creation."
15. For example, the case of ABB, where very high pensions to the former CEOs Percy Barnevik and Göran Lindahl were unveiled in 2002 (Carlsson and Nachemson-Ekwall 2003), and the case of Skandia, unveiled in 2003 and 2004, where very high amounts had been paid out to top executives such as the CEO Lars-Eric Pettersson (Nachemson-Ekwall and Carlsson 2004).
16. Traction is the investment company in the Stillström ownership sphere (see Fristedt and Sundqvist 2008).

REFERENCES

Agnblad, J., E. Berglöf, P. Högfeldt, and H. Svancar. 2002. Ownership and control in Sweden: Strong owners, weak minorities, and social control. In *The control of corporate Europe*, ed. F. Barca and M. Becht, 228–58. Oxford: Oxford University Press.

Artsberg, K., and C. Nilsson. 1993. Accounting and taxation: Examining the difference between state and market claims on accounting. In *Accounting research in Lund*, ed. K. Artsberg, A. Loft, and S. Yard, 25–41. Lund: Lund University Press.

Berglöf, E. 1990. Corporate control and capital structure. PhD thesis, Institute of International Business at Stockholm School of Economics.

Blake, J., K. Åkerfeldt, H. J. Fortes, and C. Gowthorpe. 1997. The relationship between tax and accounting rules—the Swedish case. *European Business Review* 97 (2): 85–91.

Carlsson, B., and S. Nachemson-Ekwall. 2003. *Livsfarlig ledning—Historien om kraschen i ABB* [Dangerous management—the story of the ABB failure]. Stockholm: Ekerlids Förlag.

Carlsson, R. H. 2003. The benefits of active ownership. *Corporate Governance* 3 (2): 6–31.

Carrington, T., and G. Johed. 2007. The construction of top management as a good steward—a study of Swedish annual general meetings. *Accounting, Auditability and Accountability Journal* 20 (5): 702–28.

Collin, S-O. 1993. The brotherhood of the Swedish sphere. *International Studies of Management and Organization* 23:69–86.

Cooke, T. E. 1989. Disclosure in the corporate annual reports of Swedish companies. *Accounting and Business Research* 19 (74): 113–24.

Dahlquist, M., and G. Robertsson. 2001. Direct foreign ownership, institutional investors, and firm characteristics. *Journal of Financial Economics* 59 (3): 413–40.

Davidson, S., and J. M. Kohlmeier. 1966. A measure of the impact of some foreign accounting principles. *Journal of Accounting Research* 4 (2): 183–212.

Diamant, A. 2004. Revisors oberoende—Om den svenska oberoenderegleringens utveckling, dess funktion och konstruktion [Auditor's independence—the legislative development, function, and construction of the Swedish regulations on independence]. PhD thesis, Uppsala, Iustus Förlag.

Engwall, L., ed. 1995. *Föregångare inom företagsekonomin* [Forerunners in business administration]. Stockholm: SNS Förlag.

Fagerström, A., L. G. Hassel, and G. M. Cunningham. 2007. Compliance with Consolidation (group) Accounting Standards—The Vertical Adjustment Issue: A Survey of Swedish Multinationals. *Journal of Global Business Advancement* 1(1): 37–48.

Föreningen Auktoriserade Revisorer. 2002. *RS Revisionsstandard i Sverige 2002* [RS—Auditing standards in Sweden 2002]. Stockholm: FAR Förlag AB.

———. 2003. *Frågor på bolagsstämman* [Questions at the AGM]. Stockholm: FAR Förlag AB.

Fristedt, D., and S-I. Sundqvist. 2008. *Ägarna och makten i Sveriges börsföretag* [Owners and power in Sweden's listed companies]. Stockholm: SIS Ägarservice AB.

Godfrey, J. M., and K. Chalmers. 2007. Globalisation of accounting standards: An introduction. In *Globalisation of accounting standards: Monash studies in global movements*, ed. J. M. Godfrey, and K. Chalmers, 1–14. Cheltenham, UK: Edward Elgar.

Grundvall, B., S. Heurlin, B. Magnusson, and R. Rundfelt. 2004. *Börsbolagens årsredovisningar 2003* [Listed companies' annual reports 2003]. Stockholm: Stockholmsbörsen AB.

Hanner, P. V. A. 1980. Några milstolpar i redovisningens utveckling i Sverige under 1900-talet [Some milestones in the development of accounting in Sweden during the 1900s]. Unpublished Working Paper, Stockholm School of Economics.

Hellman, N. 1993. A comparative analysis of the impact of accounting differences on profits and return on equity: Differences between Swedish practice and US GAAP. *European Accounting Review* 2 (3): 495–530.

————. 2000. Investor behaviour—an empirical study of how large Swedish institutional investors make equity investment decisions. PhD thesis, Stockholm School of Economics.

————. 2005. Can we expect institutional investors to improve corporate governance? *Scandinavian Journal of Management* 21:293–327.

————. 2008. Accounting conservatism under IFRS. *Accounting in Europe* 5 (2): 71–100.

————. 2011. Soft adoption and reporting incentives: A study of the impact of IFRS on financial statements in Sweden. *Journal of International Accounting Research*, forthcoming.

Henrekson, M. 1988. *Räntebildningen i Sverige* [The forming of interest rates in Sweden]. Stockholm: SNS Förlag.

Henrekson, M., and U. Jacobsson. 2003. The Swedish model of corporate ownership and control in transition. IUI Working Paper Series No. 593, Stockholm, The Research Institute of Industrial Economics.

Heurlin, S., and E. Peterssohn. 1991. Sweden. In *The European accounting guide*, ed. D. Alexander and S. Archer, 767–824. London: Academic Press.

Hodges, R., L. Macniven, and H. Mellet. 2004. Governance of UK NHS trusts: The annual general meeting. *Corporate Governance: An International Review* 12 (3): 343–52.

Jansen, E. P., K. .A., Merchant, and W. A. Van der Stede. 2009. National differences in incentive compensation practices: The differing roles of financial performance measurement in the United States and the Netherlands. *Accounting, Organizations and Society* 34:58–84.

Jonnergård, K., and M. Kärreman. 2004. Board activities and the denationalization of ownership—the case of Sweden. *Journal of Management and Governance* 8:229–54.

Jonnergård, K., M. Kärreman, and C. Svensson. 2004. The impact of changes in the corporate governance system on the boards of directors—experiences from Swedish listed companies. *International Studies of Management and Organizations* 34 (2): 113–51.

Jonnergård, K., and U. Larsson. 2007. Developing codes of conduct: Regulatory conversations as means for detecting institutional change. *Law and Policy* 29 (4): 460–92.

Jönsson, S. 1991. Role making for accounting while the state is watching. *Accounting, Organizations and Society* 16 (5–6): 521–46.

Kärreman, M. 1999. *Styrelseledamöters mandat—en ansats till teori om styrelsearbete I börsnoterade företag. Lund Studies in Economics and Management 54* [Board members' mandate—an emerging theory of board work in listed companies]. Lund: Lund University.

LaPorta, R., F. Lopez-de-Silanes, and A. Shleifer. 1999. Corporate ownership around the world. *Journal of Finance* 54 (2): 471–517.

Mueller, G., H. Gernon, and G. Meek. 1991. *Accounting: An international perspective*. Burr Ridge, IL: Irwin.

Nachemson-Ekwall, S., and B. Carlsson. 2004. *Guldregn—Sagan om Skandia* [Rain of gold—the tale of Skandia]. Stockholm: Bonnier Fakta.

Nair, R. D., and W. G. Frank. 1980. The impact of disclosure and measurement practices on international accounting classifications. *Accounting Review* 55 (3): 426–50.

Nilsson, S., and G. L. Hassel. 2003. Attendance at the annual general meeting in large Swedish companies. *International Journal of Vestnik Corporate Governance* 4:128–33.

Nobes, C. W. 1983. A judgmental international classification of financial reporting practices. *Journal of Business Finance and Accounting* 10 (1): 1–19.

Ou, J. A., and S. H. Penman. 1989. Financial statement analysis and the prediction of stock returns. *Journal of Accounting and Economics* 11:295–329.

Panelen för övervakning av finansiell rapportering. 2005. *Rapport för 2005* [The 2005 Report from the Swedish Panel for Monitoring Financial Reporting]. http://www.overvakningspanelen.se/files/arsrapport2005.pdf (accessed March 30, 2009).

Randøy, T., and J. Nielsen. 2002. Company performance, corporate governance, and CEO compensation in Norway and Sweden. *Journal of Management and Governance* 6:57–81.

Rundfelt, R. 1993. Standard setting in Sweden—a new regime. *European Accounting Review* 2 (3): 585–91.

Runsten, M. 1998. The association between accounting information and stock prices—model development and empirical tests based on Swedish data. PhD thesis, EFI at Stockholm School of Economics.

Sillén, O., and N. Västhagen. 1962. *Balansvärderingsprinciper* [Balance sheet valuation principles], 7th ed. Stockholm: P. A. Norstedt and Söners Förlag.

Skogsvik, S. 2008. Financial statement information, the prediction of book return on owners' equity and market efficiency: The Swedish case. *Journal of Business Finance and Accounting* 35 (7–8): 795–817.

Söderström, H. T., E. Berglöf, B. Holmström, P. Högfeldt, and E. M. Meyersson Milgrom, eds. 2003. *Corporate governance and structural change—European challenges. Summary in English. SNS Economic Policy Group Report 2003.* Stockholm: SNS Förlag.

Swedish Corporate Governance Board. 2008. *Swedish code of corporate governance.* http://www.corporategovernanceboard.se/files/docs/SweCodeofCorpGov_2008_publicerad.pdf (accessed March 30, 2009).

Wallerstedt, E. 1988. *Oskar Sillén—professor och praktiker. Några drag i företagsekonomiämnets tidiga utveckling vid Handelshögskolan i Stockholm* [Oskar Sillén—professor and practitioner. Some aspects of the early developments of business administration at the Stockholm School of Economics]. Stockholm: Almqvist and Wiksell International.

———. 2005. Kriser och konsolidering: revisionsbranschen i Sverige under hundra år [Crises and consolidation in the Swedish accounting industry during 100 years]. In *Uppdrag revision* [Audit mission], ed. S-E. Johansson, E. Häckner, and E. Wallerstedt, 24–44. Stockholm: SNS Förlag.

12 Analysis of Changing Institutional Environments, New Accounting Policies, and Corporate Governance Practices in Italy

Roberto Di Pietra

1. ACCOUNTING

1.1 International Convergence in Accounting

1.1.1 Accounting in Italy: Old Continental Roots and Recent Changes towards Accounting Standardization

The first official mention of financial reporting in Italian law can be traced back to the Commercial Code of 1865 (which was broadly based on the Napoleonic Code).[1] The Italian Commercial Code has required Italian companies to prepare financial statements (FS) since its amendment in 1882. During the twentieth century, financial reporting was regulated by the Civil Code of 1942, whose rules were supplemented and strongly influenced by fiscal regulations. The establishment of the Italian Stock Exchange and the Companies and Stock Exchange Commission (*Commissione Nazionale per le Società e la Borsa* [CONSOB]) in 1974 marked a fundamental change in the regulatory process. This regulatory authority was based on the US Securities and Exchange Commission (SEC). CONSOB was empowered from the outset to demand audited FS from companies quoted on the stock exchange. However, the number of companies affected was not large at the outset and is currently still limited (Riccaboni and Ghirri 1995). Notwithstanding the enactment of different regulations and reforms related to the enactment of European Union Directives over the years, the auditing market is still restricted to a limited number of companies and large part of this activity is performed by the statutory auditors (see Cameran 2008).

Until the European accounting directives were enacted in Italy in 1991, the FS (*Bilancio*) of most Italian companies consisted of only a balance sheet (*Stato patrimoniale*) and a profit and loss account (*Conto dei profitti e delle perdite*), in accordance with the Italian Civil Code of 1942. Enactment of the EU Company Law Directives brought about wide-reaching change in the accounting regulations, through extensive revision of the Civil Code.

At the same time, a joint board of representatives of the professional accounting bodies set about revising its earlier recommendations in order to achieve conformity with the new provisions of the Civil Code. The principles of the CSPC (*Commissione per la Statuizione dei Principi Contabili*—Commission for the Establishment of Accounting Principles) have never been officially recognized as law, although some limited acknowledgment has been forthcoming from CONSOB, along with default recognition of the international accounting standards. (Through resolution no. 1079 of April 8, 1982, CONSOB recommended the application of 'correct accounting principles' and thereby gave some recognition to the accounting profession principles, whose guidelines were the only valid source in Italy. Moreover, CONSOB stated that, in cases in which such principles were found to be inadequate, reference should be made to international accounting standards, on the condition that these did not conflict with national legal provisions).

In general, the regulation of accounting in Italy continues to live up to its traditional image of rigid legal prescription by the state, combined with a certain flexibility of interpretation.

In Italy, the state exercises its authority through a number of regulatory instruments comprising not only laws (*Legge*) made by Parliament, but also legislative decrees (*Decreto Legislativo*) and decree laws (*Decreto Legge*) prepared by the government. Law-decrees are also issued by the president of the republic, in the form of presidential decrees (*Decreto del Presidente della Repubblica*).

Because of the rigidity of the law-making process, there are a number of ways in which official interpretations of the law can be given. These include circulars (*Circolare*) and ministerial decrees (*Decreto Ministeriale*), which provide legal clarification. Rulings resulting from court hearings are issued by the *Corte di Cassazione* (Court of Cassation), the Constitutional Court, and regional tribunals.

CONSOB regulates the activities of the capital markets and ensures the functioning of a market in stocks and shares. CONSOB has a high level of operational autonomy, but submits annual reports on its activities to the Ministry of the Economy, which forwards them to Parliament. The regulatory power of CONSOB is particularly relevant to the preparation of FS, as it oversees the listing of securities issued by companies. The Bank of Italy has a similar set of functions in the specific sphere of financial institutions.

CONSOB releases circulars and formal resolutions (*Delibera*) as well as other announcements (*Comunicazione*) that tend to be in the form of responses to particular queries. These are published in the CONSOB bulletin.

The change in accounting strategy desired by the European Union in favor of IFRS, which has meant a shift towards accounting standardization, has also influenced the choice of European capital market regulators. In Italy, CONSOB has been called upon by the national legislator to require International Financial Reporting Standards (IFRS) to be adopted in the preparation of consolidated FS by security-issuing companies.[2]

Article 117 of Legislative Decree no. 58/1998, also known as the Consolidated Law on Financial Intermediation (*Testo Unico della Finanza* [TUF]), deals with accounting, as well as specifying the responsibility of the executive charged with preparing a company's accounting documents (Article 154-bis). The TUF has been amended several times over the years in order to offer capital market operators increasingly clearer regulations in response to the financial and accounting scandals that occurred in 2001 (above all the Parmalat case) and 2005 (when the real estate market bubble burst and the Ricucci market rigging case—or "Bancopoli"—exploded). The TUF has been amended by Law 262/2005, Legislative Decree 303/2006, and Law 69 of 2009 to provide, amongst other things, harsher rules and sanctions concerning both FS and auditing, as well as the corporate governance (CG) of companies that are listed and issue shares on the capital market.

The transition to accounting standardization—chosen by the EU as a way of pursuing what was initially referred to as accounting harmonization—has also influenced the work of national law-making bodies charged with issuing professional accounting principles. In this sense Italy's experience can be seen as resulting from around twenty-five years of work of the Commission for the Establishment of Accounting Principles (CSPC).

Prior to the CSPC, the process of developing and updating this body of accounting rules was in the hands of the *Dottori Commercialisti* and *Ragionieri* (professional accountants), whose respective national administrative bodies are the *Consiglio Nazionale dei Dottori Commercialisti* (CNDC) and the *Consiglio Nazionale dei Ragionieri* (CNR). When it was established in 1975, the CSPC was only nominated by the CNDC, although the CNR was subsequently provided with half of the seats. Between 1975 and 2002, the CSPC issued a total of thirty accounting principles. Following the creation of the Italian Standard Setter (*Organismo Italiano di Contabilità* [OIC]) in 2001, the CSPC continued to operate as a permanent commission but left the task of establishing Italian accounting principles to the OIC. The OIC was established with the legal status of a foundation in order to become the national standard setter and be capable of representing the majority of public and private institutions operating in the field of accounting and FS.[3] General acceptance of the accounting principles established by the OIC was facilitated by the broad representativeness of its founding members.

The main duties of the OIC involve: (a) issuing accounting principles for the preparation of private, nonprofit, and public companies' FS; (b) assisting the legislator in issuing accounting rules; (c) supporting the adoption of international accounting standards in Italy; (d) collaborating with and stimulating the work of the International Accounting Standards Board (IASB); (e) working in close contact with the European Financial Reporting Advisory Group (EFRAG); (f) promoting an accounting culture.

To date the OIC has adopted the accounting principles of the CSPC (approved on May 30, 2005) and issued specific interpretations and five new accounting principles (see Table 12.1). Over the years the OIC has systematically provided detailed comment letters in response to the

IASB's various Exposure Drafts (EDs) (22), or regarding the working documents of the International Financial Reporting Interpretations Committee (IFRIC) (11). Similarly, the OIC has provided its observations concerning the plans to reform Italian corporate law and tax regulations, as well as carrying out an important interpretative function regarding legal provisions on accounting.

Table 12.1 Accounting Principles and Interpretations Issued by OIC (June 2009)

Documents	Year of Approval	Title
Accounting principle 11	2005	Financial statements, purpose, and contents
Accounting principle 12	2005	Content and layout of financial statements
Accounting principle 13	2005	Inventories
Accounting principle 14	2005	Liquid assets
Accounting principle 15	2005	Credits
Accounting principle 16	2005	Tangible fixed assets
Accounting principle 17	2005	Consolidated financial statements
Accounting principle 18	2005	Accruals and deferrals
Accounting principle 19	2005	Provision for liabilities and charges, severance pay, debts
Accounting principle 20	2005	Securities and investments
Accounting principle 21	2005	Equity method
Accounting principle 22	2005	Memorandum accounts
Accounting principle 23	2005	Contract work in progress
Accounting principle 24	2005	Intangible assets
Accounting principle 25	2005	Accounting treatment of income tax
Accounting principle 26	2005	Foreign currency transactions and items
Accounting principle 28	2005	Net equity
Accounting principle 29	2005	Changes in accounting principles, estimates, error correction, etc.
Accounting principle 30	2006	Interim reports
OIC 1	2004	The main effects of the corporate law reform on the preparation of financial statements
OIC 2	2005	Assets and funds for special purpose entities
OIC 3	2006	Information on financial instruments to be included in the notes to the accounts and the management report (Articles 2427-bis and 2428, para. 2, no. 6-bis of the Civil Code)
OIC 4	2007	Mergers and spin-offs
OIC 5	2008	Statement of liquidation
Interpretation 1	2005	Accounting principle 12
Interpretation 2	2006	Accounting principle 25—Accounting of consolidated statements and fiscal transparency
Appendix	2005	Amendment to OIC 1

After a long wait, the accounting professions in Italy were finally unified in 2005. On the basis of this reform, introduced by Legislative Decree 139/2005, the legislator established that a single professional body would replace the two existing ones in 2008. Thus the *Consiglio Nazionale dei Dottori Commercialisti e degli Esperti Contabili* (CNDCEC) is now the competent authority and the only professional accountancy body in Italy.

This law distinguished between two new professional levels (Section A and Section B), which differ in the scope and level of professional activities performed. To be admitted into Section B (*Esperti contabili*) applicants must possess at least a first-cycle degree in economics and business administration (three-year course). For admission into Section A (*Dottori Commercialisti*) applicants must possess at least a master's degree in economics and business administration (two-year postgraduate course). In both cases applicants are required to have undergone a three-year training period and passed a state examination. The latter consists of three written examinations and one oral examination.

The CNDCEC currently plays a key role in the work of the OIC, making a significant contribution to its activity of issuing national and international accounting rules, as well as encouraging their general acceptance by facilitating their translation into effective accounting behavior in the preparation of the FS of the most numerous sector of Italian companies (i.e., the small and medium-size enterprises [SMEs]).

It should be pointed out that other organizations representing regulators and the world of auditors, preparers, and users are also involved in the activities and structure of the OIC. Thus the OIC's working groups include representatives of CONSOB, the Association of Italian Joint-stock Companies (*Associazione fra le Società Italiane per Azioni* [ASSONIME]), the Italian Association of Auditors (*Associazione Italiana Revisori Contabili* [ASSIREVI]), the Italian Banking Association (*Associazione Bancaria Italiana* [ABI]), and various other interested parties.

1.1.2 Issuing Accounting Rules in Italy: National Political Forces and the Impact of EU Strategy

When rules are set down by the legislature, the normal processes of law making are involved. Thus, when the Italian Ministry of Justice created a working group to draft the law to enact the Fourth and Seventh Directives, it was quickly transformed into a full ministerial commission, composed mainly of jurists (the "D'Alessandro Commission," named after its chairman, a professor of corporate law). To begin with, the twenty-member commission comprised eight judges, nine professors of law, one certified accountant, one professor of accounting, and one official from the Ministry of the Economy.

A similar approach to enacting European Commission (EC) directives was replicated in Italy over the years in order to introduce the various changes and integrations of the Fourth and Seventh Directives. Although the Ministry of the Economy has started to involve the OIC in its work by requesting its comment letters, in such a technical area the commission is still dominated by the presence of jurists rather than accountants. More details on the enactment process of the EC directives and on the recent strategies that the EU has decided to pursue are available on the specific chapter devoted to the European Union context.

Enactment of the directives involved complex legal drafting issues. For instance, within the implementing decree (Legislative Decree no. 127 of April 9, 1991) Articles 1–20 amended the Civil Code with respect to the provisions of the Fourth Directive, whereas Articles 21–46 set out a new law concerning groups of companies without reference to the Civil Code.

The revision of the Civil Code involved changes in the preparation of FS, balance sheet layout, income statement layout, valuation criteria, notes to the accounts, and management reports.

Similar profound changes took place with the implementation of the directives amending the Fourth and Seventh Directives. Legislative Decree 394/2003 (concerning the implementation of Directive 65/2001) already amended some articles of the Civil Code by introducing, for example, the detailed disclosure of information on the use of fair value in the valuation of financial instruments. Legislative Decree 32/2007 (concerning the implementation of Directive 46/2006), on the other hand, made significant changes to the content of management reports. Further changes were introduced by Legislative Decree 173/2008 (concerning the implementation of Directive 46/2006), both affecting the content of notes to the accounts and further modifying the criteria for the preparation of abridged FS.

Plans to amend the rules of the Civil Code regarding FS in order to complete the implementation of the aforementioned directives are still being finalized. These drafts, drawn up by the OIC upon the request of the Ministry of the Economy and with the input of the CNDCEC, delineate changes that on the one hand will bring the content and form of FS closer to the requirements for IFRS-compliant statements and, on the other hand, will help expand the use of abridged FS to an ever-greater number of companies. However, the risk emerging is that of having a specific set of rules for the FS of each different category of firm:

1. IFRS regulations standardized by the European Union for the FS of listed companies (or other companies to which their adoption has been extended, such as under the provisions of Legislative Decree 38/2005 in Italy)
2. the rules of the Civil Code updated according to the amending directives for the FS of unlisted firms (with a series of provisions that render the code more complex and comprehensive than it was prior to 2003)
3. the rules of the Civil Code that define the contents of the abridged FS for SMEs, who benefit from this legislative advantage (in view of the EU strategy of modernizing its accounting directives to reduce the costs of preparing annual accounts)[4]

As we will better clarify on the specific section devoted to the EU, Italy was the first EU member state to take advantage of the opportunity to extend both the optional and mandatory adoption of IFRS to other types of FS and other categories of firms (Article 5 of Regulation [EC] 1606/2002). Following the EU provisions of Regulation 1606/2002, the Italian Community Law of 2003 and Italian Legislative Decree 38/2005 extended the scope of the EC regulations to:

- listed companies, concerning the preparation of their FS
- companies issuing financial instruments to the public, regarding the preparation of their FS and consolidated FS (Article 116 of the Consolidated Law on Financial Intermediation)
- banks and financial institutions that are subject to the supervision of the Bank of Italy, regarding the preparation of annual and consolidated FS
- insurance companies, regarding the preparation of consolidated FS and FS, but the latter only if they are listed and do not prepare a consolidated FS

The opportunity (rather than the obligation) to use IFRS was offered to unlisted companies that prepare a full (unabridged) FS. Legislative Decree 38/2005 essentially only excludes from the use of IFRS companies that can prepare an abridged FS under Article 2435-bis of the Civil Code.

The segmentation of the rules for the preparation of FS mentioned earlier entails some obvious risks from the point of view of the comparability of FS prepared at a national level, as the balance sheets and income statements of different categories of firms have distinct purposes, contents, and layouts. In particular, whereas an IFRS-based FS is oriented towards investors, and especially towards shareholders, FS that adhere to the provisions of the Civil Code have a different purpose. In the latter case, the administrators take on the responsibility of preparing the FS (which they submit for the approval of the shareholders' meeting) with the aim of protecting the interests of third-party creditors. In brief, it seems evident that the IFRS reference framework presupposes large companies listed on the stock market that the Civil Code, on the other hand, seems to exclude, preferring unlisted companies largely financed by third parties (banks and other financial institutions).

These different approaches are perfectly in line with the characteristics of the Italian economic and entrepreneurial scenario (see the statistics in Table 12.2). Moreover, the diversity described in the preceding makes it perfectly clear how it is easier to assign to IFRS-based FS the function of a useful communication tool for economic decision making in the market or markets in which the firm in question operates. Civil Code–based FS are not characterized by this emphasis on decision making, as they are prevalently concerned with protecting the interests of the weakest parties—first creditors and then minority shareholders—in relation to the behavior of administrators who are entirely or almost entirely appointed by majority shareholders.

Table 12.2 Firms, Undertakings, Companies, and Listed Companies and their Capitalization in Italy (2008)

Enterprises by legal status				
Sole proprietorships	3,391,051			
Partnerships	929,045			
Joint-stock companies	878,005			
Other types of company	118,003			
Total	5,316,104			
	2008	2000	1990	1980
Listed companies	336	297	266	169
Capitalization	374,702 million EUR	818,384 million EUR	94,333 million EUR	18,228 million EUR
% GDP	23.6%	70.2%	13.8%	9.2%

Sources: Movimprese–Infocamere, 2008; Borsa Italiana SpA–Bit Stat, market statistics, 2008.

In many areas of policy making, the traditional forms of regulation have comprised either corporatist self-regulatory arrangements or the assignment of regulatory functions to government departments under the direct control of the political executive. In other countries, these approaches are being replaced to varying extents by statutory regulation administered by expert agencies (Majone 1996). In Italy, however, control of the regulatory process in accounting remains firmly in the hands of the lawmakers and their political superiors, in spite of the existence of public agencies and professional institutes with specific competence in the accounting domain.

Three different modes of regulation can be identified in the literature (see Table 12.3). The first—regulation through Parliament and government—ties the risk of regulatory failure to political accountability, eventually in the form of accountability to the electorate. However, as the Italian context shows, a complex legislative framework is necessary in order to manage the regulatory details, and this is prone to short-term political interference. Statutory agencies, on the other hand, are likely to be independent of direct political control, particularly as the delegation of significant policy-making powers is consistent with a perceived need on behalf of governments to commit themselves to longer-term regulatory strategies whilst maintaining political credibility in the shorter term.

By implication, such agencies are not accountable to the electorate, and control therefore tends to rely on the strictness of procedural requirements and the transparency of decision making. Although the third approach—that of self-regulation—can imply a lower number of rules, their design for

Table 12.3 Modes of Regulation

Form	Characteristics of Different Modes of Regulation
Regulatory Bureaucracy	Hierarchical control with direct oversight by the legislature. Laws, decrees, and orders subject to democratic accountability. Political interference creates a risk of regulatory failure.
Delegated Regulation	Powers exercised by a public agency on the basis of a legislative mandate. Statutory regulations issued by expert and independent agencies. Prone to lobbying by the regulated parties, bargaining over compliance.
Self-Regulation	Affirmation of neo-corporatist collaboration. Less formalized rules with more flexible enforcement. Operated for the benefit of the regulated parties, with a risk of market failure.

Source: Di Pietra, McLeay, and Riccaboni (2001, 75).

the benefit of the regulated parties themselves and the tendency towards more flexible enforcement means that it runs the risk of market failure.

Aside from the political accountability issues that differentiate the alternative modes of regulation, some of the changes in regulatory structure appear to be driven by two other factors, which have also been observed elsewhere, i.e., cost considerations and the effect of globalization. In the first case, the administrative costs of self-regulation are normally internalized in the activity that is subject to regulation, whereas the cost of a public agency or bureaucracy would typically be borne by government. The growing economic interdependence inherent in globalization has the effect of weakening the domestic impact of regulations while strengthening their impact externally, thus reducing the need for national coercion and increasing the need for international credibility. In the field of accounting, the US Financial Accounting Standards Board (FASB) provides a model of delegated regulation with minimal legislative oversight (Young 1994). In Europe, the UK's Accounting Standards Board (ASB), France's *Comité de la Réglementation Comptable* (CRC), and Germany's *Deutsche Standardisierungsrat* (DSR) represent a move in the same direction as the FASB, although the ASB maintains more of the characteristics of a self-regulating professional standard-setting body, whereas the CRC and DSR are shaped by the dirigism and bureaucratic centralization that preceded them. In each of these cases, however, the regulatory strategy is to internalize political control. This is not the case in Italy, where political activity is highly visible and the traditional regulatory model is still adopted across much of society. In the realm of accounting, neither the transition towards self-regulation through an authorized professional standard-setting body nor the delegation of regulation to a specialized public agency has occurred.

1.1.3 Changes in Financial Reporting Objectives

As it is in large part of the continental European countries, in order to understand the objectives pursued with FS in Italy it is useful to provide an overview on the characteristics of the Italian financial system. This system was traditionally based on the predominating role played by the bank industry. On the contrary, the stock market played a marginal role. Only in 1974 was a modern legislation issued in order to regulate the development of the stock market and the establishment of the supervisory authority (the CONSOB).

In the Italian stock market a relatively small number of companies are listed. These companies are characterized by a high degree of ownership concentration.

On this basis, the legislature and the accounting literature have assigned a consistent objective to the FS. In Italy the main objective of the FS is to focus on the concept of the shareholders' perspective (instead of the stakeholders' perspective) and to protect their interests. Together this protection assumes a priority the need to protect the creditors' interests (mainly banks) and the tax authorities.

The creditors' interests' protection implies the preservation of capital in order to ensure the interest payments and the debt reimbursements. Due to the traditional role played by the Italian banking industry, the Civil Code has clearly regulated and limited the distribution of profits to shareholders. Following this approach the fundamental accounting principles defined by the Italian legislation are the principle of prudence and the historical cost valuation.

A consistent conservative accounting rule could be found on the asset revaluation approach traditionally followed in Italy. The Italian legislation does not allow the business entities to revaluate their assets freely. The revaluation of assets is permitted only in extraordinary cases. Due to the fact that inflation cannot be considered an extraordinary event, revaluations due to this phenomenon are allowed only under specific conditions regulated by law (these rules define: which specific categories of assets could be revaluated, the procedures to adopt, the changes to be made to the FS, and the fiscal effects). Over the years, a long list of laws allowing the revaluation of assets has been issued in many cases with an evident fiscal effect (any distribution from the revaluation surplus was subject to taxation).

The aforementioned case of the assets revaluation confirm that the objective of FS in Italy is also strongly influenced by the fiscal regulation. The tax authorities try to protect their own interest with a set of interferences on the profits calculation and their distribution. This is the case of the tax treatment of depreciation where business entities have tended to report fiscal depreciation in their FS. This was the case with the introduction, and subsequent abolition, of the so-called fiscal appendix as a part of the income statement. This appendix was an attempt to distinguish from the total which part of profits was influenced by the fiscal rules. Due to this abolition, two specific items were introduced within the income statement ("value adjustments made exclusively as a consequence of tax policies" or "provisions relating to tax benefits"). Unfortunately, after only one year of application the Italian government has abolished the fiscal appendix, confirming the traditional impact that the tax authorities want to have on the objective of the FS prepared by the Italian business entities.

The Italian legislation on the FS, the accounting literature, and the accounting praxis were for four decades anchored in the interests' protection of the shareholders, the creditors, and the tax authorities. Notwithstanding the enactment of the EU Fourth Directive (introducing the true and fair value principle), this change had no impact on recognition and measurement methods. The Fourth Directive enacted in Italy in 1991 has changed deeply the disclosure level of the balance sheet and the income statement, and the contents of the notes to the accounts.

Even if the modernization process of the EU accounting directives has recently reinforced the usefulness principle as the main objective of the FS it is not possible to affirm that this has already modified the traditional stewardship approach traditionally stated in the Italian Civil Code.

1.1.4 Economic Resources and Claims on Them

The final sentence of the previous section allows us to highlight a dual system operating in Italy on the objective and characteristics of the FS.

From one side, the large majority of the Italian business entities are still preparing their FS on the basis of the conservatism principle, trying to preserve the interest of the shareholders, the creditors, and the tax authorities. This implies that these entities are disclosing a low level of reported profit and a high rate of resources internally generated, or creating hidden resources through a process of undervaluation. This process is usually considered as a favorable instrument of self-financing.

The modernization of the EU accounting directive has not yet produced any effect on the Italian legislation on these entities. Even if the enactment process of the new directive was started two years ago, the Italian government has not yet issued a revision of the Civil Code on this issue. From the accounting profession perspective and from the juridical point of view the changes required by this modernized directive are not considered favorably. The adoption of the fair value accounting recalls the fear that the Italian business entities could generate more profits than they could. This behavior was considered particularly "dangerous" in a situation of financial crisis. The fair value approach has some potential pro-cyclical effect and this is perceived with a negative meaning by the Italian accountants and scholars.

As it was mentioned before, the endorsement of the EU accounting regulation has made compulsory the adoption of IAS/IFRS for the preparation of consolidated FS of the listed companies. This legal requirement was extended in Italy to a larger group of companies and also for the preparation of the individual FS. Out of the total of business entities operating in Italy this group of companies represents a small number. From the 2005 financial year these companies have to prepare their FS adopting the international accounting standards. This has meant the preparation of FS in which the stakeholders' protection coincides with the protection of the investors interests (as clearly stated by the IASB's framework). The IAS/IFRS transition has also determined the broad adoption of the fair value accounting, with all the fears that this change has determined.

In sum, the situation described in this section put in evidence that in Italy there are two sets of rules driving the business entities to prepare two different kinds of FS, based on two different objectives to pursue. The large majority of the Italian business entities have to apply the Civil Code rules, whereas the listed companies have to adopt the IAS/IFRS recently endorsed in Italy. This second group of entities seems to be forced to prepare FS in which the different objective could determine a greater amount of profits. As it will be pointed out in the next section this perception was not confirmed after four years of IAS/IFRS adoption in Italy.

1.2 The Impact of IAS Compliant Consolidated Financial Statements on the Performance of Italian Listed Companies

Before we assess the impact that the transition to IFRS has had on the consolidated FS of Italian listed companies, we will take a look at some characteristics that have made this transition particularly profound.

Due to the traditional approaches of the national lawmaker and the provisions of the European accounting directives, the measurement of economic results in Italy has always been oriented towards highlighting net income rather than operative income. Net income is the measure of economic performance most commonly used by Italian firms in their economic and financial communications, as well as being used by financial analysts as a basis for their (more frequently used) financial ratios. Therefore, the use of comprehensive income, as required by IFRS, clearly constitutes a profound change for firms to deal with.

In addition to the orientation of income statements towards the determination of net income, it is also important to point out that they are influenced by the close relationship between the rules of the Civil Code and the provisions of the Consolidated Law on Income Tax (*Testo Unico delle Imposte sui Redditi* [TUIR]). Although the latter are formally subordinate to the rules of the Civil Code, the financial rules end up having a profound influence on the system of measurement and valuation of the items included in income statements. The main conflict between tax regulations and accounting law concerns the relationship between the valuation criteria provided by the Civil Code and those included in the TUIR. Because the Civil Code states that the valuation criteria to be applied in drawing up an income statement are those laid down in the Civil Code, whereas Article

75 of TUIR states that costs, in order to be deductible, must be charged to the income statement, there is an inherent conflict of laws. Despite various attempts to overcome this conflict, we are currently still dealing with a marked interference of the tax rules on valuation criteria in the preparation of FS based on the rules of the Civil Code.[5]

It should also be pointed out that the rules of the Civil Code are strongly oriented towards respect for the principle of prudence, the application of which implies strict reference to valuation according to the historical cost principle.

Reference to the principle of prudence has a significant impact on both the rules on accounting recognition and the methods of valuation. Adopting the principle of prudence and historical cost valuation significantly limits the possibility of distributing net profits among the investors, especially minority investors, instead protecting stakeholders who are strongly oriented towards the long term, as well as creditors and especially banks (Caponera et al. 2006).

The connection between valuation methods, size of distributable income, and reference to companies' main stakeholders illustrated in the preceding is perfectly comprehensible if we consider that the entire body of Italian accounting legislation, although based on EU directives, seeks to protect the interests of the principal investors and lenders in Italian firms, i.e., financial institutions.

As mentioned earlier, the Italian economic environment is still characterized by a clear prevalence of firms financed with resources deriving from the credit system, which are essentially closed to the capital market. It is important for firms to demonstrate as great a capacity for solvency as possible to the banks, i.e., their ability to repay loans secured by the value of the resources among their assets. Thus, whereas the principles behind the preparation of FS and valuation methods contribute to reducing the net profit and the consequent possibility of its distribution, outside investors and lenders can effectively count on greater total assets because a significant portion of the value created by management is maintained within the company or not effectively represented in the values of statements of assets and liabilities: Whereas assets are underestimated, liabilities are overestimated.

Outside investors and lenders see more security in the FS of firms that are strongly based on historical cost valuation and oriented towards the principle of prudence. To them, this is of far more worth than the message conveyed by FS oriented towards the disclosure of the value (including potential value) that a company is capable of creating and therefore the ability to generate income that it can demonstrate to outside investors and lenders.

The approach to the preparation of FS found in the Civil Code is consistent with the characteristics of the economic scenario in the same way as the framework of rules that define the mechanisms of CG, identify prevailing interests, and specify the forms of interest protection.

Considering this concept of FS, it becomes clear that IFRS are based on a fundamentally different viewpoint, as they refer to a different type of firm operating in a different economic environment. This explains why the transition to IFRS has been experienced as a radical change—and even an "accounting revolution"—in Italy and elsewhere. The transition to new rules has been seen as a change to be wary, or even fearful, precisely because it was believed that the new approach would entail a marked change in the items included in FS.

When adopting IFRS approved by the EU, Italian firms were obviously obliged to deal with a set of rules inspired by a new approach to the preparation of FS, but they nonetheless continued to refer to the national and European accounting tradition. The result may be met with surprise, as the feared complete transformation of net income or net capital values did not materialize. The impact of the transition was also surprising in that a remarkable variety of behaviors and consequences have been observed. In short, the idea that applying IFRS in Italy would lead to FS with a high level of potential income disclosure and distribution has been proved wrong by the rather conservative behavior observed in relation to the value created within firms.

This sort of conclusion can be reached by referring to the following review of studies conducted in Italy to assess the effects of adopting IFRS, starting from the preparation of the consolidated FS for the 2005 financial year. In 2005 Branciari, Gioia, and Ricci examined the quarterly reports of twelve Italian listed groups. From this analysis it has emerged that the impact of international accounting standards caused an average equity decrease of -4.30 percent and an income decrease of -1.64 percent.

One year later Nigro et al. conducted an analysis on the first forty Italian banking groups and their FS. In their study they highlighted that total assets increased by 10 percent and the impact of adopting IAS 32 and 39 meant a ROE variation of 0.8 percent. In 2006 Nigro et al. published another study on the FS of the first nine Italian banking groups (seven of which have adopted the fair value option). The impact on equity was negative (with a rate decreasing between 10 and 16 percent).

In 2007 we conducted research on the first thirty Italian listed groups (Di Pietra 2006). From this research we have determined the impact of IFRS adoption on the consolidated income statement and on the consolidated balance sheet. In both cases this impact was not so relevant and not always with the same direction (on the income statement the adoption of IAS/IFRS has determined an increased profit in twenty cases—30.72 percent—and an increased loss in nine cases -17.90 percent—in one case there was no variation, whereas on the balance sheet the adoption has determined in five cases the variation was less than 1 percent; on equities the IAS First Time Adoption (FTA) caused an average variation of 5.51 percent). The same year Azzali (2007) published the outcome of a large study on the Italian listed group (181). The impacts on the profits were various (increased in 75.70 percent; decreased in

24.31 percent; for minority shareholders 42.46 percent increased, and 38.35 percent decreased). The same situation was observed on the equity (increased in 66.30 percent; decreased in 33.70 percent; for minority shareholders 43.15 percent increased; 37.67 percent decreased). In conclusion this study highlighted a very heterogeneous impact (larger on profits than on equity; less favorable for minority shareholders).

A similar analysis was replicated one year after by Cordazzo (2008). On the FS of 194 Italian listed groups it has emerged that, on average, profits and equity have increased after the transition (with a larger impact on profits 25.34 percent than on equity 4.78 percent).

In 2008 Dunne et al. published a comparative study between the UK, Italy, and Ireland in order to understand pre-and post-IFRS implementation—sample of a total of 175 pre-IFRS annual reports and 175 post-IFRS annual reports (138 in the UK; twenty-seven in Italy; and ten in Ireland). The impact of IFRS implementation on profit was significant; on average, profit calculated under national GAAP increased by a sizeable percentage (48.51 percent) once figures were translated to IFRS. The results show that the introduction of IFRS reduced the equity calculated under national GAAP by 14.39 percent, although this effect was not common across all three countries; Italian companies experienced a slight increase in equity whereas the UK and Irish companies in the sample recorded a decrease (2008, 93).

Whereas we are aware that numerous other studies have been published over the last four to five years with the aim of determining the impact of transition to IFRS, Table 12.4 offers a sufficiently broad view for us to propose some general comments on the process.

The review presented in Table 12.4 shows that the various analyses did not come to the same conclusions. In general terms, however, we can affirm that the impact of IFRS has shown the following tendencies:

- the greatest effects of the transition to IFRS were only experienced following FTA, after which they have gradually diminished over the years
- the most significant consequences regarded the amount of net income rather than the net equity value
- these effects were, however, less favorable from the point of view of minority shareholders

The changes recorded by the aforementioned analyses confirm the hypothesis of largely conservative behavior that, following the introduction of the changes in accounting practice required by IFRS adoption, effectively led Italian companies to minimize the effects on both net income and net equity, thus perpetuating the traditional approach aimed at maintaining economic value within the company. As we shall see in the following, the general philosophy behind this accounting behavior is perfectly coherent with the characteristics of CG in Italian firms.

2. CORPORATE GOVERNANCE

2.1 The Italian Corporate Governance Model: Soft Rules Complementing a Legislative Corpus

Italian CG has characteristics that differentiate it from CG in many other countries and has its origins in Italy's political and economic history. Italy itself is a relatively new nation, if we compare its 150 years of national unity to the centuries of history of other countries. The relatively recent creation of a unified Italian state has influenced the characteristics of both the national legal system and the establishment of suitable legal institutions. From an economic viewpoint, the necessity to make up for Italy's economic backwardness in comparison to the first industrialized countries meant that it needed to put in place a comprehensive system of tried-and-tested rules, institutes, and institutions that in other states developed gradually over the centuries.

As can be seen from the economic literature, Italy is a latecomer characterized by a significant number of SMEs. The majority of Italy's firms, including the larger ones, seem to be run following a "family business" approach, to the extent that Italian capitalism can be called family capitalism. Italian economic development has taken place in parallel with the development of family firms, which have created family groups or holdings that have afforded them easier access to the sources of finance available on the credit and capital markets.

The need to make up for the delay in industrialization led to the prevalence of an indirect system of finance through banks, which in turn defined the role of the capital market. This characteristic constitutes the fundamental premise behind the Italian financial system, approach to financing business growth, and rules that govern the functioning of joint-stock companies.

Despite attempts to develop the capital market, the banking system continues to be the main route of access to financial resources for Italian firms. Some changes have obviously taken place following the legislative innovations introduced between 1974 and the present day. However, the structure of the listed companies in Italy as a whole has maintained a series of characteristics, such as: (a) the prevalent role of shareholders or majority shareholders (blockholders), which on average is still quantifiable at 40 percent or more of the share capital; (b) the fact that the two largest shareholders of Italian listed companies generally own over 50 percent of the shares; (c) over 50 percent of the shares are held by a single shareholder in half of all listed companies; (d) percentage ownership of the share capital below 10 percent only occurs in a limited number of Italian listed companies (approximately 5 percent). In addition to this, a series of mechanisms and behaviors (such as the frequent use of shareholder agreements) significantly reduce the contestability of ownership.

As can be seen from the literature, the structure of the CG system is determined by the characteristics of the capitalistic system. In economies characterized by high capital concentration, issues related to the separation of ownership and control are not particularly important. This is particularly true in Italy, as capital ownership is highly concentrated in the Italian family capitalism-oriented system.

On the basis of these fundamental characteristics, we can offer an overview of CG in Italy by reconstructing the applicable regulatory framework, which comprises both *de jure* and *de facto* regulation. Whereas the former includes all law in force on the subject of governance, the latter includes all mechanisms of voluntary regulation.

Among the *de jure* rules on CG in Italy, those that have had the greatest impact are:

- Legislative Decree 58/1998 (TUF)
- Legislative Decrees 5–6/2003 (Corporate Law Reform)
- Law 262/2005 (Law on the Protection of Savings)

The aim of the TUF was to direct savings towards the share capital of listed companies. In order to pursue this objective, rules were introduced to: (a) protect minority shareholders (by promoting greater participation in decision-making processes); and (b) regulate shareholder agreements (by rendering information about their existence mandatory; see Melis 1999, 128–39; Zanigni 2004, 73–116; Zattoni 2006).

Through a specific statutory provision, the corporate law reform introduced the possibility of choosing a model of CG other than the traditional one (Di Pietra 2005a, 145–78). In this context, in addition to the rules related to the traditional model of governance, rules for the dualistic (or German) and monistic (or Anglo-Saxon) models were also introduced. In the traditional model, CG is entrusted to: (a) a board of directors or a sole director; (b) a board of statutory auditors (*Collegio Sindacale*); (c) an auditor or auditing company; (d) a shareholder's meeting. The board of directors is the management body invested with exclusive responsibility for corporate management—i.e., the task of defining strategic and organizational objectives, with the aim of maximizing shareholder value. The dualistic model is characterized by an organizational solution in which CG is entrusted to: (a) a management board; (b) a supervisory board; (c) an auditor or auditing company; (d) a shareholder's meeting. The management board is the administrative body charged with exclusive responsibility for corporate management and performs all the operations necessary to attain the corporate objectives. Lastly, the monistic model is characterized by an organizational solution in which CG is entrusted to (a) a board of directors; (b) a committee for management control; (c) an auditor or auditing company; (d) a shareholder's meeting. The board of directors is the body charged with exclusive responsibility for corporate management and the power to appoint the committee for management control.

The law on the protection of savings has made a significant difference to the forms of protection for minority shareholders, with reference to the administrative body (mode of appointment and introduction of list voting, as well as the composition of the board), the control body (with new rules regarding the composition, duties and obligations of the board of statutory auditors), disclosure, and reporting on governance.

Among the *de facto* rules on CG in Italy, we shall essentially refer to rules that are not binding for those to whom they are addressed. These rules are issued by CONSOB and the stock market management company (Borsa Italiana 2006, 2007; Zanigni 2004, 92–95; Di Pietra 2005a, 178–83; Mazzotta 2007, 67–70); they originate from British sources and have the form of a code of best practice.

In Italy, the need for a code of best practice became a priority towards the end of the 1990s, when Borsa Italiana launched a study focusing on the structure of Italian firms and their criticalities. Based on the results of this investigation, in 1999 a committee set up by Borsa Italiana drew up a code of best practice on CG, calling it a code of self-regulation. This code was introduced in order to reassure international investors of the existence in Italian listed companies of an organizational model involving an appropriate distribution of responsibilities and powers and a just balance between management and control. The code contains recommendations on:

- the composition of the board of directors
- procedures for appointment
- the remuneration of directors
- the rights of and relations with shareholders
- the establishment by the board of various committees (for internal control, for the remuneration of directors, for appointment offers)
- relations with institutional investors and other shareholders

Following the issue of the code of best practice (self-regulation), Borsa Italiana revised its own regulations with explicit reference to the code. The code itself was revised in 2002 to take into account the remarks put forward by CONSOB, adding, for example, a principle dedicated entirely to operations with related parties. In 2006 the code was revised again, defining the role of the board of directors in greater detail, consolidating its responsibilities with respect to its competences, introducing the principle of limiting the plurality of offices, and imposing the obligation of transparency regarding the board of director's activities and the rate of members' participation, also in internal committees. Particular attention was paid to defining independent directors and the role assigned to them. All the various versions of the code have affirmed the voluntary nature of compliance with its provisions, with the aim of allowing firms to enhance their "reputation on the market."

Respect for *de jure* rules and voluntary compliance with the provisions of the self-regulation code have contributed to defining the current model of governance of Italian firms over the last decade. Research has revealed that Italian boards of directors are composed of five to eleven directors on average and have committees for remuneration and internal control, whereas committees for appointments are generally lacking. There is a sufficient number of independent directors but there are generally no minority directors or minority auditors. Italian boards of directors have slightly more members than their counterparts in other countries, leading to difficulties in coordination within corporate groups and possibly less effective and efficient decision-making processes. Although there are some independent directors, they are appointed by the majority shareholder and depend on him for the renewal of their appointment and as such are not in a position to fulfill their role correctly or set an errant board of directors back on the right path. Concerning the protection of minorities, although some changes appear to have taken place, there are still few directors elected by minorities.

2.2 Corporate Governance and Performance: A Survey of a Work in Progress

The choice of CG must be disclosed to the public. Improved disclosure makes the quality of governance and management visible and enhances companies' reputations on the market. Entrepreneurs convince investors of the goodness of their firms by informing them of the firms' CG choices and performance; investors then decide whether and in what to invest, with reference to the choice of governance made and the performance achieved.

CG and performance therefore appear to be closely related. Given that the choice of governance affects firms' results and the way in which stakeholders' expectations are met, it can be said that good governance leads to good performance.[6]

Although less numerous than the studies conducted in the US and UK, the studies on CG in Italian companies can be divided into several areas. Whereas a first group has described the size and composition of boards of directors, a second has sought to identify correlations between firms' governance and performance.

As to the studies belonging to the first group, among many others, we could mention the following five.

Crisci and Tarizzo (1994) conducted an analysis on five hundred Italian firms, carrying out three main conclusions: (a) the limited number of independent directors and the superficial role of many of them; (b) the limited number of firms that set up committees within the board of directors; (c) the mediocre performance of the board of directors. In 1996 Corbetta and

Tomaselli published a study on the role of boards of directors in one thousand large firms and found that they tend to ratify decisions already made by managing directors or shareholders.

Molteni (1997) highlighted that in Italy there was a reluctance to accept rules that favor the presence of outside directors or an executive committee.

Andrea Melis (1999) concluded that in Italy there is the presence of separate leadership structures and a substantial lack of nonexecutive directors.

Fiori and Tiscini (2005) finally emphasized that firms in Italy take particular care regarding the appointment procedure and the composition of the board of directors and do not intend to change their model of organization and control.

As to the researches focused on the correlation between governance and performance in Italy we could recall the outcomes emerging from the following seven studies.

Bianco and Casavola (1997) showed the ambivalent effect of and unclear relationship between ownership structure and performance.

Brunello, Graziano, and Parigi (2003) focused their attention on board turnover, highlighting a significant negative relationship between performance and turnover of managing directors, and that this relationship depends on the firm's ownership structure. Turnover is lower in family-controlled firms and higher in companies controlled by shareholders. The same team of authors in 2003 has published an analysis of the relationship between the remuneration of managers and performance. The results show that a relationship does exist and that it is stronger when profits decrease than when they increase. Managers are penalized when profits fall more than they are rewarded when profits grow.

In 2001 Volpin published a study on the factors determining the turnover of top executives and firm valuation. The results of the study show that firms in which the main shareholders are also the firms' top executives are less sensitive to turnover and have lower corporate valuation. In 2002 Barontini and Caprio examined the relationship between turnover of directors and performance. In their study, on average, directors remain in their positions for shorter periods than in other countries. The frequency of turnover increases with the percentage of capital held by the main shareholder. There is no clear hierarchy between the various executive roles (chairman, vice chairman, managing director). The relationship between turnover and performance estimated for directors with executive roles is the same as that for nonexecutive directors.

In 2007 Mazzotta contributed with research focused on the results obtained supporting the hypothesis of a positive correlation between governance and performance. In fact, diverse, interesting, and significant results are obtained when different market-based measures of performance are used (Market Value Added). In any case, the results confirm the hypothesis that good governance is a variable that can lead to improved company performance.

And, finally, Di Pietra et al. (2008, 73–91) analyzed the system of listed companies in Italy. This system is characterized by the large size of boards of directors, which, in contrast to international literature, is not a significant variable in relation to stock market performance. The attribution of a high number of directorships within the same corporate group is a phenomenon known in the international literature as "busy directors." The investigation carried out on Italian listed companies confirmed that this practice has a significant negative impact on share performance.

This review of the literature confirms a series of characteristics of the Italian CG. However, whereas the studies conducted on the relationship between governance and company performance suggest a positive relationship, this relationship is found to be subject to a series of conditions. In the presence of these conditions, good governance can become the basis for good company performance.

The general results confirmed by the many studies conducted show an essentially closed approach to CG in the larger Italian firms. Listed companies do not appear to be particularly motivated to achieve the advantages

Table 12.4   Main Outcomes of the Analysis Performed in 2006 and 2008

	31 December, 2005	31 December, 2007
Listed companies	278	287
Companies with nodes	201	204
Tot. board member positions	2,778	2,904
Tot. board members	2,251	2,413
Average no. of positions	1.234	1.203
Board size (max-min)	24.3	33.3
Average board size	10	10
Tot. executive board members (independent)	687 (1)	858 (13)
Tot. nonexecutive board members (independent)	1,950 (1,119)	2,039 (1,094)
Board members with one position	1,915	2,095
Board members with two, three, four positions	316	304
Board members with five positions	20	14
Board members with more than five positions	Carlo De Benedetti (7)	Giovanni Tamburi (7)
Company with most links	Pirelli (37)	Pirelli (32)
Average distance between two nodes	3,506	3,848
% of companies with ≤ four positions	81.8%	70%
% of financial institutions with ≤ four positions	62.5%	90.2%

in terms of improved performance promised by good governance. In fact, it is precisely the characteristics of CG in Italian firms that lead to limited disclosure of company results through their FS. In this context, we report in the following the main results of a study that we carried out in 2006 and repeated in 2008 on the social network relations that characterize the "small world" of boards of directors in Italian listed companies (similar analyses have been conducted using the same methodology in the French context by Chabi and Maati 2006; Maati 2006; Demaria and Dufour 2007).

Using the Social Network Analysis (SNA) method, we were able to reconstruct the full cluster of existing relations, identify specific subclusters, and count the degrees of separation between Italian companies listed on the stock market. The overall picture that emerged from the reconstruction of these relationships is that of a dense group of listed companies in a small market.[7]

Our research was based on the composition of the boards of directors of companies listed as of December 31, 2005, and was repeated with reference to the companies listed as of December 31, 2007. The year 2005 was chosen to coincide with the first-time adoption of IFRS in Italy and the entry into force of the savings protection law, whereas 2007 coincided with the expansion of IFRS to FS.

The results of this analysis reveal an extremely closed situation in which the majority of board members in the entire network of Italian listed companies are only contactable by a few people, through a closed network of relationships.

The ownership of Italian listed companies has the power to appoint a small number of board members who are capable of forming a dense network of social relations, as clearly suggested in the representation of the whole network proposed in Figure 12.1.

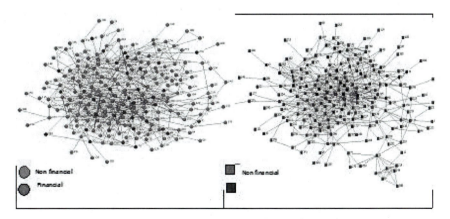

Figure 12.1 Cloud clusters of social relations between boards of directors of Italian listed companies in 2005 and 2007.

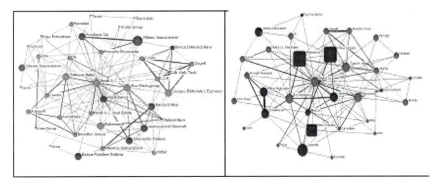

Figure 12.2   Main node of the cloud: Pirelli (with thirty-seven companies reported in 2005 and thirty-two in 2007).

Among the approximately three hundred Italian listed companies, the network of relations connected to the Pirelli node is particularly remarkable (in this respect, see Figure 12.2 regarding the situation in 2005 and 2007).

SNA is a useful method to show that Italian listed companies are part of a fairly stable, relatively closed, and still strongly integrated network of social relations. Over the last few years this network has remained essentially unchanged, despite the reforms introduced in the form of *de jure* rules and notwithstanding the adoption of self-regulation codes. This allows us to conclude that the network of social relations between members of boards of directors is a symptom of a sort of "old-world syndrome" in which managers seem to be interested in limiting the impact of changes (above all to reduce the effectiveness of CG reforms).

The strong influence of ownership in the formation of boards of directors tends to limit firms' interest in demonstrating their economic value, or the economic value of their group. The interest of the ownership is nonetheless focused on the long term, which reduces the need to demonstrate a firm's potential income and economic richness through FS. The current network of social relations therefore restricts the efficiency of the link between good governance and good performance.

At the same time, the "old-world syndrome" makes the capital market even less efficient, as it is often based on the existence of clear conflicts of interest, which have a strong negative influence on competition in the market, and especially within specific economic sectors. Clear evidence of conflicts of interest can be seen when one, two, or more board members are stable members of the boards of directors of companies operating in the same industry (this is the case in some Italian financial institutions, as clearly highlighted by the annual analysis of the Italian Antitrust Authority published on December 23, 2008).

3. PRELIMINARY CONCLUSIONS FOR THE
CONSTRUCTION OF A RESEARCH AREA

Whereas the occurrence of several events connected to the life of a firm need not necessarily be interpreted as the result of a common trend, the changes that have taken place in the economic sector cannot be considered as entirely fortuitous. We can, however, affirm that the reforms that have affected the rules of CG and the preparation of FS have fulfilled a need to respond more effectively to the pressing integration of economies and social systems. This is even truer with reference to the drive towards integration, including political integration, within the EU.

In order to deal with the ongoing changes, the European lawmaker has launched a series of reform processes regarding the world of accounting regulation, and individual EU countries have begun to revise their models of CG. In both cases the reforms are intended to provide an appropriate response to the economic situation of the twenty-first century. Unfortunately, the possibility of effectively achieving this result is limited by resistance to change on the part of the systems to which the reforms are addressed.

This is certainly the case in Italy, which is characterized by resistance and even imperviousness to change in the rules of CG and those concerning financial reporting. The introduction of CG reforms has met with opposition that has hindered the launch of processes favoring the disclosure of best performance through FS, and the transition to IFRS has been limited to mere compliance and limited application.

Judging by the results in terms of net income and effect on FS items, the fears initially expressed regarding the transition to IFRS were completely unjustified. The supposed disclosure of potential income values essentially translated into very cautious management of first-time adoption. The impact of IFRS on the consolidated FS of Italian listed companies was lower than expected for 2005, whereas a greater impact concerning some specific items was seen in the consolidated FS for 2007 (larger impact on profit than equity; lower impact on minority shareholders). Thus adoption of IAS/IFRS has had an impact on consolidated FS, which reflect the increasing capacity of boards of directors to deal with these standards (greater impact on profits for the majority shareholders, lower impact on equity).

These results are perfectly consistent with the characteristics of Italian CG, and are a clear manifestation of the choices that corporate management has made in the preparation of FS, in response to the need of the ownership of Italian listed companies to put mechanisms into place to protect their own interests. In their adoption of IFRS, Italian preparers of consolidated FS have followed an evaluation perspective characterized by the intent to preserve existing ownership. This is perfectly consistent with the outcomes of the SNA illustrated earlier, which clearly emphasize that the Italian capital market is controlled by a specific group of listed companies, that "conflicts of interest" persist, and that the *status quo ante* has been preserved. Notwithstanding all the reforms, a small and old world is trying to resist.

NOTES

1. Regarding the characteristics of the Italian Accounting Regulation Model and the political and legal powers that continue to determine its development, we have made frequent reference to the comments proposed in a previous contribution of ours with S. McLeay and A. Riccaboni and debated during previous editions of the Workshop on Accounting and Regulation (Di Pietra, McLeay, and Riccaboni 2001, 59–78). See also Riccaboni and Di Pietra (1996); Di Pietra (1997); Nobes and Parker (1998); and Riccaboni (1999).

2. Note that with the adoption of accounting directives during the 1970s, the EU launched a process based on an approach of accounting harmonization. Starting from the variety of the different accounting cultures, the EU sought to begin a process aimed at identifying common features shared by EU member states. In this perspective, the target of accounting harmonization was based on the recognition of common principles. The decision to make the IASB standards mandatory for the preparation of annual accounts of listed companies within the EU modified this approach because it shifted attention to rules that by nature propose specific solutions to be adopted in the process of preparing annual accounts. On the concepts of accounting harmonization and standardization, see the following contributions: Samuels and Piper (1985, 56); Tay and Parker (1990, 73); van der Tas (1992, 28); Raffournier, Haller, and Walton (1997); McLeay (1999, 1–23); Di Pietra (2005b, 75–86).

3. There were fifteen founding members of the OIC. The Board of Founders included institutions and organizations representing the accounting and auditing professions (two), preparers (eight), and users (five). The constitution of the OIC was approved by the Ministry of the Economy and stock market regulator (CONSOB), the financial institutions (Bank of Italy), and the insurance company sector (ISVAP). In addition to the Board of Founders, the OIC's governance structure includes a supervisory board (seventeen members), a management board (nine members), a technical committee (nine members), and a board of auditors (three members).

4. COM(2008)/195—Proposal for a directive amending the Fourth and Seventh Directives as regards certain disclosure requirements for medium-size companies and the obligation to draw up consolidated FS. COM(2009)/83—Proposal for a directive amending the Fourth Directive on the FS of certain types of companies as regards micro-entities. For more details on the amending process of the European accounting directives please see the specific section devoted to the European Union legislative environment.

5. The Civil Code reform of 2003 introduced changes intended to resolve the conflict with the provisions of the Consolidated Law on Income Tax. However, this attempt did not succeed in clearly separating the two regulatory systems, which remain so closely interrelated as to cause what in Italian accounting literature we continue to call the "fiscal pollution" of FS.

6. The literature includes numerous empirical studies investigating the relationship between CG and performance, which can be divided into two main areas. Some studies seek to analyze the relationships between individual aspects of governance (size and composition of the board of directors, leadership and internal structure, the functioning of the board of directors) and performance (Forbes and Milliken 1999; Zhara and Pearce 1989; Rosenstein

and Wyatt 1997; Rechner and Dalton 1989; Weisbach 1988; Yermack 1996), whereas others analyze the relationship between governance as a whole and performance (Gompers, Ishii, and Metrick 2003).

7. On the use of SNA in relation to the composition of boards of directors, see Watts and Strogatz (2006). On its application in relation to Italian data, see Casaleggio et al. (2004) and Boroli (2007). The former conducted a study of 223 listed companies in 2003: with an average of 4.2 appointments, every board member could contact every other board member; 15 percent of board members had at least two appointments (3 percent had at least four to seven appointments); eighteen listed companies constituted the core of an integrated network, within which there were subnets (or clusters); the most important cluster was Pirelli (with forty-two listed companies). The latter highlighted the trend to accumulate appointments (inside and outside the capital market).

REFERENCES

Azzali, S., ed. 2007. *Trasparenza dei Bilanci e tutela del risparmio nei gruppi aziendali*. Milan: McGraw-Hill.

Barontini, R., and L. Caprio. 2002. *Il Consiglio di amministrazione, la rotazione degli amministratori e la performance dell'impresa: l'esperienza italiana in una prospettiva comparata*. CONSOB, Quaderni di Finanza, Studi e ricerche, no. 51, Rome: Consob.

Bianco, M., and P. Casavola. 1997. Italian corporate governance: Effect on financial structure and firm performance. *European Economic Review* 43(4), 1057–69.

Boroli, P. 2007. *Composizione Consiglio di Amministrazione, Il Sole 24 Ore, 11 maggio 2007*, Milan: Il Sole 24ORE.

Borsa Italiana. 2006. *Regolamento dei mercati organizzati e gestiti da Borsa Italiana SpA*, Milan: Borsa Italiana.

———. 2007. *Istituzioni al regolamento dei mercati organizzati e gestiti da Borsa Italiana SpA*, Milan: Borsa Italiana.

Branciari, S., A. Gioia, and G. Ricci. 2005. L'impatto degli IAS sulle quotate: prime evidenze empiriche dalle relazioni trimestrali. *Revisione Contabile* 65.

Brunello, G., C. Graziano, and B. M. Parigi. 2003. CEO turnover in insider-dominated boards: The Italian case. *Journal of Banking and Finance* 27.

Cameran, M. 2008. Auditing in Italy. The development of a highly-regulated setting before and after the Parmalat case. In *Auditing, trust and governance. Developing regulation in Europe*, ed. R. Quick, S. Turley, and M. Willekens, 144–67. London: Routledge.

Caponera, A., M. L. Giacchetti, F. Orlando, and G. Giordano. 2006. I riflessi degli IAS sui bilanci consolidati al 31 dicembre 2005. *Bancaria* 7–8 (July–August): 28–37.

Casaleggio et al. 2004. *Rapporto 2004*, Maffa del Potere. www.casaleggio.it.

Chabi, S., and J. Maati. 2006. The small world of the CAC 40. *Banque & Marchés* 82 (May–June): 41–53.

Corbetta, G., and S. Tomasselli. 1996. I consigli di amministrazione nelle imprese familiari. Una ricerca sul loro ruolo e sul loro funzionamento. *Economia & Management* 3: 403–21.

Cordazzo, M. 2008. *Principi contabili internazionali e risultati economici delle quotate italiane, L'impatto della transizione*. Milan: F. Angeli.

Crisci, G., and D. Tarizzo. 1994. *Il governo dell'impresa. Il ruolo dei consigli di amministrazione e dei consiglieri non esecutivi nelle aziende italiane*. Milan: Egon Zehnder Int., Executive Interim Management Italia.

Demaria, S., and D. Dufour. 2007. Les choix d'options comptables lors de la transition aux norms IAS/IFRS: quel role pour la prudence? *Comptabilité—Contrôle—Audit/Numéro thématique* (December): 195–218.

Di Pietra, R. 1997. Accounting regulation models in Italy, France and Spain. In *Comparative studies in accounting regulation in Europe*, ed. J. Flower and C. Lefebvre, 249–86. Leuven: ACCO.

———. 2005a. *Governo aziendale e standards contabili internazionali*. Padua: Cedam.

———. 2005b. *La comunicazione dei comportamenti aziendali mediante i dati contabili, Il ruolo della ragioneria internazionale*. Padua: Cedam.

———. 2006. Italian listed companies and IFRS consolidated financial statements: A "little and ancient world" is trying to resist. Paper presented at the EAA, Lisbon.

Di Pietra, R., C. A. Grambovas, I. Raonic, and A. Riccaboni. 2008. The effects of board size and 'busy' directors on the market value of Italian companies. *Journal of Management and Governance* 12 (1): 73–91.

Di Pietra, R., S. McLeay, and A. Riccaboni. 2001. Regulating accounting within the political and legal system. In *Contemporary issues in accounting regulation*, ed. S. McLeay and A. Riccaboni, 59–78. Boston: Kluwer Academic Publishers.

Dunne, T., G. Finningham, G. Hannah, D. Power, S. Fifield, A. Fox, C. Haller, and M. Veneziani. 2008. *The implementation of IFRS in the UK, Italy, and Ireland*. Edinburgh: The Institute of Chartered Accountants of Scotland.

Fiori, G., and R. Tiscini. 2005. *Corporate governance, regolamentazione contabile e trasparenza dell'informativa contabile*. Milan: Franco Angeli.

Forbes, D. P., and F. Millikan. 1999. Cognition and corporate governance. Understanding boards of directors and strategic decision making groups. *Academy of Management Review* 3:489–505.

Gompers, P., J. Ishii, and A. Metrick. 2003. Corporate governance and equity prices. *Quarterly Journal of Economics* 118:107–55.

Maati, J. 2006. *Les administrateurs européens du FTSEurofirst 100 constituent-t-ils un petit monde?* Paris: Reseau FTSE.

Majone, G. 1996. *Regulating Europe*. London: Routledge.

Mazzotta, R. 2007. *La corporate Governance e le performance aziendali, Una analisi sulle società italiane quotate in borsa*. Milan: F. Angeli.

McLeay, S. 1999. *Accounting regulation in Europe*. London: Kluwer.

Melis, A. 1999. *Corporate governance, Un'analisi empirica della realtà italiana in un'ottica europea*. Turin: Giappichelli.

Molteni, M., ed. 1997. *I sistemi di corporate governance nelle grandi imprese italiane*. Milan: Egea.

Nigro, R., E. Aiolfi, E. De Blasio, and I. F. Mattei. 2006. L'adozione degli IAS 32 e 39: modalità e impatti sul bilancio consolidato dei principali gruppi bancari italiani dell'S&P MIB. Milan: *Quaderni AIAF* 129.

Nobes, C., and R. Parker. 1998. *Comparative international accounting*. Englewood Cliffs, NJ: Prentice Hall.

Raffournier, B., A. Haller, and P. Walton. 1997. *Comptabilité internationale*. Paris: Vuibert.

Rechner, P. L., and D. R. Dalton. 1989. The impact of CEO as board chairperson on corporate performance: Evidence vs. rhetoric. *Academy of Management Executive* 32:141–43.

Riccaboni, A. 1999. Italy. In *Accounting regulation in Europe*, ed. S. McLeay, 204–36. London: Macmillan.

Riccaboni, A., and R. Di Pietra. 1996. Il processo di armonizzazione contabile in Italia dopo il recepimento della IV Direttiva CEE. *Rivista dei Dottori Commercialisti* 4: 615–52.

Riccaboni, A., and R. Ghirri. 1995. *European financial reporting in Italy*. London: Routledge.

Rosenstein, S., and J. Wyatt. 1997. Outside directors, board independence and shareholder wealth. *Journal of Financial Economics* 44: 175–92.

Samuels, J., and A. Piper. 1985. *International accounting: A survey*. Sydeny: Croom Helm.

Tay, J., and R. Parker. 1990. Measuring international harmonization and standardization. *Abacus* 1: 71–88.

van der Tas, L. 1992. *Harmonization of financial reporting: With a special focus on the European Community*. Rotterdam: Datawyse.

Volpin, P. F. 2001. *Governance with poor investor protection: Evidence from top executive turnover in Italy*. London: London Business School.

Watts, D. J., and S. H. Strogatz. 2006. Collective dynamics of 'small world' networks. In *The structure and dynamics of networks*, ed. M. E. J. Newman, A. L. Barabási, and D. J. Watts, 1–582. Princeton, NJ: Princeton University Press.

Weisbach, M. S. 1988. Outside directors and CEO turnover. *Journal of Financial Economics* 20: 431–60.

Yermack, D. 1996. Higher market valuation of companies with a small board of directors. *Journal of Financial Economics* 40: 185–212.

Young, J. J. 1994. Outlining regulatory space: Agenda issue and the FASB. *Accounting, Organizations and Society* 19 (19): 83–109.

Zanigni, M. 2004. *Assetti di governance ed implicazioni sul sistema di controllo interno*. Padua: CEDAM.

Zattoni, A. 2006. *Assetti proprietari e corporate governance*. Milan: Egea.

Zhara, S., and J. Pearce. 1989. Boards of directors and corporate financial performance: A review and integrative model. *Journal of Management* 15:291–334.

13 Analysis of Changing Institutional Environments, New Accounting Policies, and Corporate Governance Practices in the UK

George Iatridis

1. ACCOUNTING

1.1 International Convergence in Accounting

1.1.1 Standardization of Accounting Practices in the UK

The main accounting regulatory authority in the UK is the Financial Reporting Council (FRC). The FRC is independent and sets standards for financial reporting and auditing. It is responsible for the monitoring and enforcement of those standards and works closely with the professional bodies to enhance the quality of accounting practice and reporting. The primary aim of the FRC is to reinforce the efficiency and credibility of the UK financial reporting and auditing system and to strengthen national and international investors' and other market participants' confidence.

The operating bodies of the FRC and their activities, as illustrated by the FRC, consist of the Accounting Standards Board, which issues accounting standards for financial reporting purposes; the Auditing Practices Board, which issues standards for auditing and guidance for ensuring auditors' independence; the Professional Oversight Board, which provides independent oversight of the accounting and auditing regulation; the Board for Actuarial Standards, which sets standards for actuarial practice; the Financial Reporting Review Panel, which examines company compliance with the law and accounting regulation; and the Accountancy and Actuarial Discipline Board, which is an independent accounting disciplinary body.

The objectives of the Accounting Standards Board include the development of new accounting standards, or reformation of existing accounting standards, and the development of principles for the accounting standard setting process. The Urgent Issues Task Force (UITF) deals with situations of inadequacy or inconsistency in the interpretation of accounting standards that may cause problems in the correct implementation of accounting regulation. The Committee on Accounting for Smaller Entities aids the Accounting Standards Board in the planning and reformation of accounting standards that relate to small companies. The Financial Sector and Other

Special Industries Committee and the Committee on Accounting for Public-Benefit Entities aid the Accounting Standards Board in the preparation of statements of recommended practice for the financial sector and other industries of the private sector and for public sector companies respectively. The Advisory Panel on With-Profits Life Assurance specializes in the actuarial sector and life assurance. The Advisory Panel on Pensions studies the accounting for insurance and pensions, the accounting method that should be applied, and the arising disclosure and implementation issues.

The Auditing Practices Board focuses on the information content of financial statements and its main objective is the publication of accounting reports that reflect the true and accurate picture of companies and help in this way investors in making reliable predictions and efficient decisions. The Auditing Practices Board also prepares a code of ethics and inspects the process, objectivity, and independence of audit that is carried out by auditing firms. The Small- and Medium-Size Enterprises Audit Sub-Committee focuses on the auditing of companies of small and medium size. The Investment Circulars Sub-Committee assesses the financial behavior of companies and whether the latter meet the stock market regulations, e.g., listing requirements. The Public Sector Sub-Committee gives guidelines to audit firms with regard to the auditing of companies that belong to the public sector, and it also advises the FRC on public sector issues. The Technical Advisory Group seeks to examine the technical precision and applicability of auditing regulations before their official publication.

The Professional Oversight Board seeks to reinforce the confidence of investors, stock market, and other interested parties in the effectiveness and usefulness of auditing regulations and in the accuracy of the information content of published financial statements. The objectives of the Professional Oversight Board include the independent inspection of the rules and processes of auditing as well as of the accounting standards, the examination of the activities of the accounting bodies that are responsible for the inspection of the work of audit firms, and for the provision of professional certifications, dealing with staff training, discipline issues, and imposition of penalties.

The mandatory generally accepted accounting principles (GAAP) in the UK comprise the Companies Acts 1985 and 1989; the Financial Reporting Standards (FRSs); the Statements of Standard Accounting Practice (SSAPs); the UITF Abstracts; and the listing rules issued by the London Stock Exchange. The advisory GAAP include the Statements of Recommended Practice (SORP); the Financial Reporting Exposure Drafts (FREDs); the Technical Releases; and the Combined Code.

Based on the European Commission (EC) Regulation 1606/2002/EC, the implementation of IFRS for all UK listed groups and for some unlisted groups and companies commenced on January 1, 2005. In particular, for all UK listed companies, group accounts must be prepared based on International Financial Reporting Standards (IFRS). Other UK companies and groups may choose between IFRS and UK GAAP. It is noted that this choice must be applied with consistency for all group companies. Companies that use IFRS (UK GAAP) in their consolidated accounts may use the UK GAAP (IFRS) in their individual accounts. This would not hold for listed companies, which must report their consolidated accounts under IFRS. The Alternative Investment Market (AIM) has adopted a rule that will require AIM companies to submit IFRS financial statements starting in 2007. Unlisted companies other than small and medium-size enterprises (SMEs) must follow FRSs, SSAPs, and UITF Abstracts issued by the Accounting Standards Board. The Accounting Standards Board has issued a consultation paper "Policy Proposal: The Future of UK GAAP," whereby it proposes all non-publicly-accountable entities, except those that elect to apply the Financial Reporting Standard for Smaller Entities (FRSSE), would apply the IFRS for SMEs, but would have the option of using EU-adopted IFRS if they wished. Small entities may choose to continue to apply the FRSSE if their turnover and balance sheet total do not exceed £6,500,000 and £3,260,000, respectively, and their average number of employees does not go above fifty. The latter set of firms would have the option of using the IFRS for SMEs. The use of IFRS by the UK government while preparing the budget and the accounts should be mentioned here starting with the financial year that begins April 1, 2008. The UK Government Resources and Accounts Act 2000 requires that "Whole-of-Government" accounts should be prepared to present a "true and fair view" and to "conform to generally accepted accounting practice."

1.1.1 Changes in Financial Reporting Objectives

Major Institutional Differences between IFRS and UK GAAP

The major differences between IFRS and the equivalent UK accounting standards, as depicted by Ormrod and Taylor (2004), PricewaterhouseCoopers (2007), and Deloitte and Touche (2008), relate to the following issues.

ACCOUNTING FRAMEWORK

The UK Statement of Principles is consistent with IFRS, but also deals with issues, such as presentation of accounting information, derecognition of assets and liabilities, etc. According to the IFRS framework, the balance sheet recognition of assets and liabilities is feasible when it is probable that economic benefits will flow in or out of the firm. In contrast, under the UK Statement of Principles, there should be sufficient evidence that economic benefits will flow in or out of the firm. This difference might entail certain assets and liabilities being recognized under IFRS, whereas not under the UK GAAP.

Whereas under IFRS they must be revalued, derivatives should generally not be reported at fair values under the UK GAAP. Also, investment property may be recognized at fair values under the UK GAAP, whereas it must under IFRS.

With respect to the presentation of the balance sheet and income statement, IAS 1 "Presentation of Financial Statements" appears to be less prescriptive than the UK Company Act. For example, it requires assets and liabilities to be presented following a current/noncurrent distinction. Under IAS 1, the statement of total recognized gains and losses may be presented as a statement of performance, which is similar to its former form. Alternatively, it may be presented as a subset within the statement of changes in equity, although under FRS 3 "Reporting Financial Performance" these two statements are distinctive. Under the Company Act, shareholders' funds should be distinguished between equity and nonequity components, whereas fixed and current assets should be presented separately. Similarly, for the income statement, two alternative presentations are generally used, i.e., (a) disclosure of gross profit as the residual of turnover minus cost of sales, and (b) disclosure per type of expense.

Unlike UK GAAP, IFRS do not use the term 'exceptional' items. Instead, they require disclosure of items, whose size and occurrence call for a separate disclosure in order to describe company performance. Under the UK GAAP, exceptional items must be disclosed under the appropriate heading on the main face of the income statement.

For the presentation of the cash flow statement, the UK GAAP appears to implement a more standardized format and headings than IFRS. In contrast to IFRS, the UK GAAP–based cash flow statement excludes cash equivalents from cash.

Whereas under IFRS there are no exemptions, the UK GAAP allows some exemptions for certain parent companies that prepare consolidated statements and subsidiaries that are owned at least by 90 percent, or meet other prescribed conditions.

Under IAS 8 "Accounting Policies, Changes in Accounting Estimates and Errors," there is no distinction between fundamental errors and other material errors. Under FRS 3, a restatement of financial statements is required only for fundamental errors. All other errors should be dealt with through the income statement and be accompanied by appropriate disclosures.

With regard to special purpose entities, IFRS indicate that they must be consolidated when control is identified. The UK GAAP uses the term 'quasi subsidiaries' and requires them to be consolidated. Under IFRS, all subsidiaries should be consolidated.

Upon consolidation, subsidiaries that are held for sale should be presented separately, e.g., separate presentation of assets and liabilities held with a view to be sold. Under the UK Company Law, subsidiaries may not be consolidated when severe long-term restrictions exist, when they are held with a view for resale, or when information cannot be collected without significant cost or delay.

With respect to the presentation of the financial accounts of associates, IFRS require use of the equity method, whereas the UK GAAP requires use of the expanded equity method, whereby more related information is disclosed separately. Under IAS 28 "Accounting for Investments in Associates," where an associate makes losses, the investing firm shall recognize a liability if payments or obligations have been recorded on behalf of the associate. Under FRS 9, a liability should be recognized, unless the investing firm is going to terminate the business relationship with the investee as its associate.

For the disclosure of joint ventures, IFRS require use of the equity method or proportional consolidation, whereas the UK GAAP requires use of the gross equity method.

BUSINESS COMBINATIONS

When the company issues shares as consideration and the acquisition is completed in phases, IFRS suggest that fair values prevailing on each phase-day of the transaction are used. Under the UK GAAP, if the market price on one phase-day is not reliable, market prices relating to the pre-acquisition period should be used.

IFRS require firms to capitalize goodwill and not amortize it. Goodwill should be subject to annual impairment review. Under the UK GAAP, firms are required to capitalize and amortize goodwill over a maximum period of twenty years. Indefinite life may in certain cases be used, in which case no amortization would be required, although an annual impairment review would be essential. In case negative goodwill arises, IFRS require the acquiring firm to reassess the acquired firm's assets and liabilities and record any resulting differences in the income statement. Under the UK GAAP, the negative goodwill that is up to the fair value of the acquired assets should be recorded in the income statement and set against the respective depreciation figure. The residual should be taken to the income statement over the expected useful period. The UK GAAP requires firms to disclose negative goodwill together with positive goodwill.

The disclosure requirements of the UK GAAP are similar to those of IFRS, with the addition that under the UK GAAP companies must also disclose information on book values, fair value adjustments, and fair values of balance sheet items that have been acquired. IFRS suggest the use of either the pooling-of-interests (merger) method or the purchase method. The UK GAAP permits the use of the merger method when certain conditions are met. Although IFRS do not permit the use of the uniting-of-interests method, the UK GAAP allows the application of that method under certain criteria.

IFRS require use of the projected unit credit actuarial method to identify the benefit-related obligation. Any actuarial gains and losses that might arise should be taken immediately to the income statement or be amortized over the expected useful working life of the employees that are concerned. Alternatively, firms may record actuarial gains and losses in a statement of recognized income and expense. The UK GAAP requires the difference described in the preceding to be included in the statement of total recognized gains and losses.

ASSETS

The capitalization criteria for development costs are similar for IFRS and UK GAAP, although under the UK GAAP, firms may choose not to capitalize but to expense development costs. The capitalization criteria under the UK GAAP appear to be less stringent than under IFRS, as they refer to a *reasonable expectation* of future benefits compared to the IFRS expression of a *demonstration* of future benefits. With respect to the amortization of intangible assets, IFRS provide no maximum useful life, whereas under the UK GAAP there is a limit of twenty years from the acquisition date.

IFRS call for regular revaluations to ensure that the carrying amount of tangible assets does not exceed the fair value. The UK GAAP is more specific and requires firms to undertake a full valuation every five years at minimum and interim valuations at year three.

With regard to gains and losses on disposal of fixed assets, IAS 16 "Property, Plant and Equipment" requires the cost of the asset given up to be measured at fair value, unless the transaction lacks commercial substance or cannot be reliably measured, in which case the carrying amount of the asset given up should apply. Under FRS 15, there is no equivalent requirement. When it comes to the review of residual values, IAS 16 requires increases in an asset's residual value to be carried out using current prices, whereas FRS 15 generally uses prices at the date of acquisition or latest valuation.

With regard to finance leases, IFRS use the pretax net investment method for the allocation of gross earnings, whereas the UK GAAP requires use of the post-tax net cash investment method. IFRS require recognition of the leased asset at an amount that is the lower of the fair value of the leased asset and the present value of minimum lease payments. The requirements of the UK GAAP are similar, although they allow the use of the fair value of the leased asset, if the fair value is close to the present value of the minimum lease payments. For a finance lease, IFRS require deferment and amortization of profit resulting from sale and leaseback transactions over the period of the lease agreement. According to the UK GAAP, no profit should be recorded. For an operating lease, where the sale is at more than fair value, IFRS require deferment of the difference between sale revenues and asset's fair value over the expected useful life of the asset. The UK

GAAP requires deferment and amortization of the difference over a period that is the shorter of the lease term and the useful life of the asset.

Under IAS 40 "Investment Property" investment property may be measured using fair values or depreciated cost. If fair value is used, any gains and losses that may arise should be recognized in the income statement. Under SSAP 19, investment property should be measured using open market values and any arising gains and losses should be recognized in the statement of total recognized gains and losses.

Under IFRS, biological assets are measured at fair value less selling costs prevailing at the date of sale. Following the UK practice, historical costs are used for the measurement of biological assets.

IFRS require financial assets to be derecognized upon transfer of risks and rewards or expiration of the right to an asset's cash flows, or alternatively, when the control of the assets is transferred. The UK GAAP uses similar risk and reward transfer criteria and pays particular attention to the substance of the transaction over its legal form.

LIABILITIES

With regard to deferred taxation, both IFRS and UK GAAP require use of the full provision method. However, IFRS give emphasis on balance sheet temporary differences, i.e., differences between carrying amount and tax base. The UK GAAP emphasizes timing differences, i.e., differences between accounting and taxable profit. With regard to the measurement of deferred tax, IFRS do not permit discounting, whereas the UK GAAP allows discounting. Under IFRS, deferred tax assets and liabilities must be presented as noncurrent. Under the UK GAAP, deferred tax liabilities must be presented as noncurrent, whereas deferred tax assets must be presented as current.

Both IFRS and UK GAAP allow the recognition of government grants as deferred income and their subsequent amortization, although the UK Company Law does not allow the offset of capital grants against the value of the corresponding asset.

EQUITY

Under IFRS, a firm that repurchases its own shares should treat the shares deductively from shareholders' equity. Under the UK GAAP, employee benefit shares and/or own shares that are repurchased by the firm, and that are held as treasury shares, are treated in line with IFRS. Following the UK Company Law, other shares that are repurchased are cancelled and a capital redemption reserve is subsequently formed.

MISCELLANEOUS TOPICS

With regard to segment reporting, IFRS require reporting of business segments as primary format and reporting of geographical segments as secondary format. This distinction depends on the related impact on risks and returns. The UK GAAP does not make such distinction between primary and secondary formats in business and geographical segment reporting. The disclosure requirements for primary segment reporting under IFRS are more demanding compared to those for secondary segment reporting. The UK GAAP places equal importance on the disclosure requirements for business and geographical segment reporting.

According to IFRS, operations can be regarded as discontinued when they have been disposed of or held for sale. The UK GAAP attributes a more permanent character to the classification of operations as discontinued and requires that they must be terminated permanently. IFRS require discontinued operations to be measured at the lower of the carrying value and the fair value net of selling costs. The UK GAAP requires use of the recoverable amount for the measurement of discontinued operations, which is the higher between the net realizable value and the value in use. Under IFRS, firms must present the post-tax profit figure of discontinued operations in the income statement together with an accompanying description in the notes to the accounts for current and prior periods. The UK GAAP requires that in their income statement firms must provide detailed information about their turnover and operating profits and also show which parts come from continuing, acquired, and discontinued operationsIFRS do not require preparation of interim financial statements, although interim reporting is encouraged, whereas in the UK, listed firms must provide interim financial reports on a half-yearly basis.

Both IAS 10 "Events after the Balance Sheet Date" and the SSAP 17 distinguish between adjusting events and nonadjusting events. IAS 10, however, appears to place greater emphasis on the distinction making reference to specific items, such as dividends to holders of equity instruments and dividends from subsidiaries declared after the balance sheet date, etc.

Major Regulatory Changes

NEW STANDARDS

The Accounting Standards Board sought to structure the convergence between the UK GAAP and IFRS in a way so as to reduce the burden for companies that choose to report under the UK GAAP. The convergence of UK accounting standards with IFRS has been intended to be prompt, so as to avoid prolonged periods of change and adjustment. In 2002, the Accounting Standards Board published the following FREDs to align UK accounting standards with IFRS: FRED 23 "Financial Instruments: Hedge Accounting"; FRED 24 "The Effects of Changes in Foreign Exchange Rates; Financial Reporting in Hyperinflationary Economies"; FRED 25 "Related Parties Disclosures"; FRED 26 "Earnings per Share"; FRED 27 "Events after the Balance Sheet Date"; FRED 28 "Inventories; Construction and Service Contracts"; FRED 29 "Property, Plant and Equipment; Borrowing Costs."

The UK convergence process would involve the issue of new accounting standards in 2005 and 2006, in order to reinforce the UK financial reporting requirements, and subsequently a series of changes replacing existing UK accounting standards where appropriate. The new accounting standards would include FRS 20 on share options, based on IFRS 2 "Share-Based Payment"; FRS 17 on retirement benefits to replace SSAP 24 and be consistent with IAS 19 "Employee Benefits"; replacement of SSAP 17 to be in line with IAS 10 "Events after the Balance Sheet Date"; replacement of FRS 14 to be consistent with IAS 33 "Earnings per Share"; replacement of FRS 8 to be in line with IAS 24 "Related Party Disclosures"; amendment to FRS 23 to implement the changes made to IAS 21 "The Effects of Changes in Foreign Exchange Rates"; and modifications to FRS 26 to implement amendments to IAS 39 "Financial Instruments: Recognition and Measurement," relating to cash flow hedge accounting of forecast intragroup transactions, fair values, and financial guarantee contracts and credit insurance.

COMPANIES ACT CHANGES

The government published a White Paper Modernising Company Law in July 2002. The proposals included significant changes to the way in which companies are constituted and governed in law. For example, for large public and very large private companies, the directors' report would be replaced by a new style mandatory operating and financial review (OFR), which should include a statement of the company's business, a review of performance, and a presentation of the future prospects of the business. For companies not required to prepare an OFR, the directors' report would be replaced with a short supplementary statement. The Companies Act would be amended to permit measurement of financial assets and liabilities at fair value with an immediate recognition of all changes in fair value in the profit and loss account.

It is essential to identify the changes that were required to UK regulations as part of the convergence project. In Section 50, the Finance Act 2004 revises the GAAP in order to encompass both international accounting standards adopted by the European Union and the UK GAAP for periods commencing on or after the official period of adoption, i.e., January 1, 2005. Section 50 made IFRS acceptable for tax purposes in the same manner as the UK GAAP, making a reference to IFRS for each UK GAAP provision. The Finance Act 2005 has amended Section 50 in order to account for companies that are subjected to the law of a non-EU member country that allows the use of the full version of IFRS instead of the EC version. This amendment also takes into consideration the possibility that some UK companies may be using the full version of IFRS. The Finance Act 2005 accepts both versions for tax purposes. This issue may now be of lesser importance where the EC has adopted the full version like in the case of IAS 39.

To reflect the adoption of IFRS, a number of provisions in tax and other acts are amended by the Finance Act 2005. For example, paragraphs 32 and 33 Schedule 4 in the Finance Act 2005 have respectively amended paragraph 30 (1) Schedule 12 of the Finance Act 1997 and Section 219 of the Capital Allowances Act 2001. Paragraph 6 Schedule 6 of the Finance Act 2006 introduces Sections 774A to 774G, referring to consolidated group accounts. Accordingly, Sections 43A to 43F ICTA have been replaced. Paragraph 38 of Schedule 4 introduces amendments to paragraph 6 Schedule 29 of the Finance Act 2002 relating to intangible fixed assets. The new paragraph 6 (3) Schedule 29, which has replaced paragraph 38 (3) of Schedule 4, prevents resort to consolidated accounts if they follow an accounting framework that differs from that used in the individual accounts. Section 51 of the Finance Act 2004 deals with the case where a company is allowed to use IFRS and has entered into a transaction with another company that uses the UK GAAP. If the transaction leads to granting a tax advantage as a consequence of the different accounting settings, the company that uses IFRS will have to apply the UK GAAP to account for the transaction for tax purposes.

In agreement with the Financial Services Authority and Inland Revenue, the Financial Reporting Review Panel (FRRP) has adopted new operating procedures aiming at the enforcement of financial reporting standards in the UK. These procedures are in line with the changes to the Companies Act to give the FRRP statutory power to require companies, directors, and auditors to provide documentation and explanations relevant to whether financial statements comply with reporting requirements.

CONCEPTUAL FRAMEWORK CHANGES

The UK Conceptual Framework is the Statement of Principles, published by the Accounting Standards Board in 1999. The Statement of Principles is based on the Framework for the Preparation and Presentation of Financial Statements, published by the International Accounting Standards Committee (IASC) in 1989. The main differences between the Statement of Principles and the IASC Conceptual Framework as discussed by Lawrence (2002) are as follows. The IASC Conceptual Framework does not refer to the 'stewardship function.' The Statement of Principles sets the boundaries of a reporting entity. In the Statement of Principles, there are seven elements, whereas in the IASC Conceptual Framework there are five elements, whose definitions vary in certain cases. The Statement of Principles provides more detailed descriptions of measurement bases, and also deals with issues, such as discounting and subsequent remeasurement, which are not dealt with by the IASC Conceptual Framework. The IASC Conceptual Framework does not present particular requirements about the presentation of financial information. In contrast, the Statement of Principles provides a separate chapter with details on the structure of primary financial statements as well as on the provision of supplementary financial information. In contrast to the IASC Conceptual Framework, the Statement of Principles presents information on 'accounting for interests in other entities.'

ACCOUNTING POLICIES, FINANCIAL REPORTING, AND SUBSTANCE

With regard to accounting policies, financial reporting, and substance, the convergence project identifies respectively the following three main sets of accounting standards: FRS 18 "Accounting Policies" and IAS 8 "Net Profit or Loss for the Period, Fundamental Errors and Changes in Accounting Policies"; FRS 3 "Reporting Financial Performance" and IAS 1 "Presentation of Financial Statements"; and FRS 5 "Reporting the Substance of Transactions" and IAS 1.

Removing the option given in IAS 8 to treat adjustments that follow from accounting policy changes and those that relate to fundamental errors as current period items would align IAS 8 with FRS 18. In addition, removing the provision of the UK GAAP that only realized profits should be included in the profit and loss account would bring the profit and loss figures reported in the income statement and the statement of total recognized gains and losses in a single statement. Although IAS 1 requires that the financial statements should provide information that "reflect the economic substance of events and transactions and not merely their form," FRS 5 better describes and presents the substance over form requirements, especially with regard to items and transactions of complex nature, whose substance may not be easily determinable. Although in the international accounting regulation there is IAS 18 "Revenue" that deals with revenue recognition, in the UK, it is the legislation that requires that revenue must be realized before recognition in the income statement.

1.1.2 Changes in Characteristics and Constraints of Decision-Useful Financial Reporting Information

There are no significant differences in the characteristics of decision-useful financial reporting information. The attributes of financial information under the UK GAAP are similar to those identified under IFRS. The Statement of Principles focuses on information that is useful for assessing the stewardship of management. Although this is not clear in the IASC Conceptual Framework, both statements explain that the objective of financial information is to aid users in making correct economic decisions. The Statement of Principles talks about users in a clear manner and distinguishes investors among other groups of users as the defining class of user. Both documents value relevance, reliability, understandability, and comparability as some of the main characteristics of high-quality financial information. However, the IASC Conceptual Framework treats materiality as a subcategory of relevance, whereas the Statement of Principles treats it as separately.

Moreover, both documents state that information is expected to influence users' decision making. The IASC Conceptual Framework identifies the accrual basis and the going concern as underlying assumptions. The Statement of Principles does not describe them as such, but their role as presented in the statement is the same. With regard to the constraints of decision-useful financial reporting information, the financial statements do not meet all the information needs of users. They both are principle-based and information-oriented, but still provide conventionalized representations of company transactions and events. They focus less on the effects of nonfinancial information and they reflect information that is mainly historical. Practically, the differences are minor and of no significant implications for accounting practice.

IFRS have required extensive risk management disclosures and have substantially contributed to the reporting of informed and value-relevant financial information. Information systems must be flexible in order to capture new information on a consistent and timely basis. Hence, IFRS implementation should be approached from a long-term perspective, suggesting that companies that treat the IFRS switch as a short-term task, relying on ad hoc adjustments and parallel systems, may increase the risk of error and the amount of effort needed in the future. These considerations may be more crucial for companies that have US cross-listings and are subject to the Sarbanes-Oxley Act. In terms of decision-useful financial reporting information, large private companies consider switching to IFRS in order to make themselves competitive relative to their listed counterparts. Firms that plan to carry out acquisitions should consider the impact of IFRS on the transaction. Also, any company that considers an initial public offering must produce IFRS-based accounts as well as comparative figures for previous years.

Changes in the attributes of the financial reporting information include the annual impairment tests on goodwill, the disclosure of key management assumptions, the recognition of pensions, the valuations of financial instruments and intangible assets, such as brands and licenses, and accounting for deferred tax. Also, the recognition of share-based payment expenses in the income statement and the need to use sophisticated option valuation models that are needed to calculate the expense have resulted, on a number of occasions, in the restructuring of executive remuneration schemes. Factors that might have restrained or delayed groups from converting their subsidiary accounts to IFRS include the recognition of pension deficits, the higher provisions for deferred taxation, the deduction of dividends paid from subsidiaries' pre-acquisition profits from the cost of investment, and the demanding disclosure requirements, especially for cash flow statements and related parties, which might potentially affect distributable reserves in a negative manner.

1.2 Economic Resources and Claims on Them

The financial statements are prepared under the historical cost convention, except for derivative financial instruments and available-for-sale financial assets that are measured at fair value. The preparation of financial statements requires the use of judgments, estimates, and assumptions that affect the reported assets and liabilities at the year-end date and the revenues and expenses during the accounting period. The estimates and the assumptions are based on historical experience and on expectations of future events.

The comprehensive income is the change in equity during a period except those items resulting from investments by owners and distributions to owners. It reflects a broader view of financial performance instead of a single performance measure, e.g., bottom-line earnings. The other comprehensive income consists of accounting items that are directly taken to shareholders' equity and are not included in the income statement. Ramond (2007) has found that aggregate other comprehensive income is value-relevant. He also reports that higher transparency on reporting other comprehensive income as required by FRS 3 may explain the significant association between company stock returns and comprehensive income.

In the UK, SSAP 2 "Disclosure of Accounting Policies" describes conservatism as "revenue and profits are not anticipated, but are recognized by inclusion in the profit and loss account only when realized in the form either of cash or of other assets the ultimate cash realization of which can be assessed with reasonable certainty; provision is made for all known liabilities (expenses and losses) whether the amount of these is known with certainty or is a best estimate in the light of the information available."

Dargenidou, McLeay, and Raonic (2007) note that the investor base is more widespread in the UK and argue that conservative accounting may be driven by the demand created by shareholders. Stronger investor protection mechanisms would tend to lead to a timely and more reliable recognition of bad news in earnings. It is noteworthy that stricter corporate governance (CG) mechanisms could control for weaknesses in investor protection (Dargenidou, McLeay, and Raonic 2007). Watts (2003a, 2003b) provides evidence of conservative reporting in the UK. Similarly, Ball, Kothari, and Robin (2000) have found that financial reporting in the UK is significantly more conservative than reporting in code law countries. Beekes, Pope, and Young (2004) have shown that conservative accounting is associated with the presence of independent directors on the boards of UK companies, which reflects effective governance mechanisms and investor protection mechanisms.

2. CORPORATE GOVERNANCE

2.1 Regulation and the Scope of Corporate Governance

The *Combined Code on Corporate Governance* sets the grounds for good CG in the UK. Effective CG seeks to assist management in performing their duties in the best interest of shareholders. The provisions of the Combined Code should provide shareholders with a clear picture of a company's governance setting. Noncompliance with the Combined Code should be communicated and explained to shareholders, but may be justified if effective governance is achieved by alternative means. In such a case, the noncomplying company should show that it does meet the minimum requirements presented in the Combined Code. Firms listed on the Main Market of the London Stock Exchange should state in their annual report whether they abide by the primary principles of the Combined Code and also the extent to which they may have not shown compliance with the Combined Code. A company may describe in the annual report the actions that it has taken to improve the governance arrangements. On the other hand, shareholders should take into consideration the companies' environment and characteristics as well as size and organizational structure, complexity, and risks. It is vital to note that a departure from the provision of the Combined Code should not be seen as a violation. An effective communication between companies and investors is essential for the reinforcement of CG. To this end, companies can contribute by enabling and supporting discussion with shareholders and by providing comprehensive explanations of noncompliance.

2.2 Governance Characteristics

The main characteristics of CG in the UK are presented in the following as described in the *Combined Code on Corporate Governance* issued by the Financial Reporting Council (2008).

2.2.1 Auditing

The Auditing Practices Board requires companies subject to the IAS regulation to state, in a footnote, compliance with IFRS as adopted by the IASB. Auditing in the UK is carried out based on the International Standards on Auditing (ISAs), from January 1, 2005. This applies for all UK companies, except for companies whose turnover and gross assets do not exceed £5.6 million and £2.8 million respectively. The Auditing Practices Board has issued final guidance for auditors on first-time application of IFRS in APB Bulletin 2005/03, *Guidance for Auditors on First-time Application of IFRSs in the United Kingdom and the Republic of Ireland*. The auditors are appointed for one year. The UK practice suggests that audit partners of listed companies should rotate at least every five years, and other key audit members should rotate at least every seven years. If rotation is not possible due to size, nature of activities, etc., appropriate settings, such as external consultation, should be in place to ensure auditor independence and objectivity (see Code of Ethics, Association of Chartered Certified Accountants [ACCA]).

The accountancy bodies that are recognized as supervisory bodies may issue audit licenses and dictate the conduct of audit, in accordance with the Companies Act 1989. They may provide generally accepted guidelines on issues that are not covered by standards and include the ACCA; the Institute of Chartered Accountants in England and Wales (ICAEW); the Institute of Chartered Accountants in Ireland (ICAI); and the Institute of Chartered Accountants in Scotland (ICAS).

In order to perform statutory audits, auditing firms need to be registered by the recognized supervisory bodies and must comply with the audit framework and requirements that the latter set. The Audit Inspection Unit monitors the audit process of listed and other companies. The recognized supervisory bodies follow and assess the audit inspection process and outcome and may impose disciplinary penalties to registered auditing firms, if necessary. They should monitor compliance of their registered auditing firms with accounting and auditing regulation regularly. The ACCA together with the ICAEW, the Chartered Institute of Management Accountants (CIMA), and the Chartered Institute of Public Finance and Accountancy (CIPFA) are members of the Accountancy Investigation and Discipline Board, which is concerned with public-interest issues.

2.2.2 Power and Responsibilities of Top Management

The board should formulate the company's corporate strategy and safeguard shareholders' assets and wealth. All directors must make decisions objectively in the interests of the company. The board's role is to lead the company within a framework of effective controls that enables risk to be assessed and managed. It should be supplied in a timely manner with sufficient information. Nonexecutive directors should help develop proposals on strategy. They should scrutinize the performance of management in meeting agreed goals and objectives and monitor the company's financial reporting. The annual report should describe the type of decisions that are taken by the board and those that are taken by the management. It should also identify the chairman, the chief executive, the senior independent director, and the chairmen and members of the nomination, audit, and remuneration committees. The nonexecutive directors should meet without the presence of the chairman in order to be able to assess his/her performance.

There should be a clear division of responsibilities at the head of the company between the running of the board and the executive responsibility for the running of the company's business. Independence is vital and it should be clear that board directors are independent. The chairman of the board should ensure that directors, especially nonexecutive directors, have access to independent professional advice at the company's expense. The chairman should reinforce the relations between executive and nonexecutive directors. The chairman should ensure that the directors continually update their skills and also that they are provided with adequate resources and means to fulfill their role. The responsibilities of the chairman and the chief executive should be explicitly identified and agreed. The roles of chairman and chief executive should not be exercised by the same person.

If under exceptional circumstances a board agrees that chairman and chief executive should be the same person, major shareholders should be consulted in advance.

A nomination committee should be responsible for board appointments. The majority of members of the nomination committee should be independent nonexecutive directors. The nomination committee should be chaired by the chairman or an independent nonexecutive director. The nomination committee should disclose its role and how it operates. It should evaluate the skills, expertise, and experience of board members. Subsequently, the nomination committee should describe the job specification required for each appointment. The directors should be subject to reelection by shareholders at regular intervals of no more than three years, based on their performance. In the light of reelection, the chairman should confirm to shareholders that the director's performance has been evaluated and has been found to be satisfactory and effective. Nonexecutive directors may serve longer than three three-year terms, subject to annual reelection.

2.2.3 Conflict of Interests

The board should comprise executive and independent nonexecutive directors so as no individual or small group of individuals can influence the board's decision-making process. The annual report should identify the independent nonexecutive directors. The board should verify whether the director is truly independent and whether there are issues or circumstances that could possibly influence his/her judgment. For large firms, at least half the board should consist of independent nonexecutive directors. For small firms, at least two nonexecutive directors should be independent.

An appropriate relationship should be maintained between directors and the company's auditors. The directors should explain their responsibility for preparing the accounts, and there should be a statement by the auditors about their reporting responsibilities. The directors should conduct a review of the effectiveness of the group's system of internal control. The review should take place at least annually and should cover all controls, including financial, operational, and compliance controls and risk management. The board should establish an audit committee of at least three directors, all nonexecutive, with explicit guidelines on its authority and duties. The audit committee should monitor the integrity of the financial statements of the company and review significant financial reporting judgments contained in them, monitor the external auditor's independence and the effectiveness of the audit process, and review the company's internal financial controls and risk management systems. Where there is no internal audit function, the annual report should explain why such a function is not in place. The audit committee should also make recommendations with regard to the appointment or removal of the external auditors. If the board does not agree with the audit committee's recommendation, the reasons of disagreement should be included in the annual report.

2.2.4 Evaluating Board Performance

The board should annually evaluate its own performance. The evaluation would reflect on the quality of the work of each board member and would also indicate how they perform with respect to their role and responsibilities. The chairman should make use of the evaluation and reward board members for their performance and take action when performance is poor, for example, by seeking to replace poor performers with new members. The nonexecutive directors should be responsible for the evaluation of the chairman. The performance evaluation should be disclosed.

Directors' remuneration should be sufficient to motivate them to deliver high-quality work and run the company effectively. A significant proportion of executive directors' remuneration should be structured so as to link rewards to corporate and individual performance. The performance-related part of a director's remuneration should comprise a significant proportion of the total remuneration of executive directors. Their remuneration should reflect their responsibilities and role in the company.

Remuneration committees should consist exclusively of nonexecutive directors who are independent of management and free from any business relationship, which could materially interfere with the exercise of their independent judgment. The remuneration committee should be able to determine the remuneration for all executive directors and the chairman. It should also take care of the remuneration of senior management, i.e., the first level of management below the board. The board should determine the remuneration of the nonexecutive directors. No director should be involved in deciding his or her own remuneration.

Remuneration for nonexecutive directors should not include share options. Otherwise, shareholders' approval would be required. Normally, share options should not be exercisable in less than three years. Any shares that have been bought after exercising the share options should be held until at least one year after the nonexecutive director leaves the board. All new long-term incentive schemes as well as any significant changes to existing schemes should be approved by shareholders. The remuneration committee should judge whether the directors are eligible for annual bonuses and other benefits. The company's annual report should contain a statement of remuneration policy and details of the remuneration of each director.

2.2.5 Disclosure on Corporate Governance

Directors should use the annual general meeting to communicate with private investors and encourage their participation. The chairman, chief executive officer, the members of the remuneration committee, the members of the audit committee, and the nonexecutive directors considered by the board to be independent should be identified in the annual report. The annual report should also include information on the work of the nomination committee and indicate whether an executive director serves as a nonexecutive director elsewhere, and what his/her remuneration will be if s/he retains such earnings. Additional information that is needed includes a statement from the directors that the business is a going concern, a report stating that the board has reviewed the company's internal controls, a separate section describing the work of the audit committee, an explanation of how auditor independence and objectivity are maintained, of whether the auditor provides nonaudit services, etc. The chairman should ensure that the views and concerns of shareholders are communicated to the board. The chairman should discuss governance and strategy with major shareholders.

2.3 Corporate Governance and Income Management

Income management can be seen as the managers' intervention in the financial reporting process in order to rip private gains (Schipper 1989). Such gains could, for example, relate to higher compensation levels and benefits for managers (Holthausen, Larcker, and Sloan 1995). Income management may arise because of flexibility in financial reporting (Evans and Sridhar 1996). Good CG, e.g., presence of outside directors on the board, could ensure that managers' actions and decisions made are in line with the best interests of shareholders (Fama and Jensen 1983; Weisbach 1988). Beasley (1996) has found that financial statement fraud tends to be lower when there is significant representation of outside directors on the board and effective CG.

With respect to the UK, Peasnell, Pope, and Young (2005) have similarly found that income-increasing abnormal accruals tend to be lower when the proportion of outside directors on the board is higher. In other words, abnormal accruals would be lower when earnings are negative or below the earnings target if good CG mechanisms exist. This appears to be the case especially for firms where there is a greater distinction between ownership and control. Peasnell, Pope, and Young (2005) obtain little evidence that the presence of outside directors impacts on income-decreasing abnormal accruals when earnings are higher. The contribution of outside directors towards reducing income management can be further enhanced when an audit committee is in place. This implies that audit committees support the monitoring process significantly as they enable outside directors to perform their duties more successfully. Effective CG would increase investors' confidence in companies' reported numbers and would lead to the timely reporting of losses and earnings declines.

3. EPILOGUE: IFRS ADOPTION AND IMPLICATIONS

According to the ICAEW (2007), the areas where IFRS adoption has led to most changes in accounting policies refer to deferred tax, employee pensions, and impairments. The areas where most restatements have taken place refer to deferred tax, employee pensions, financial instruments, impairments, revenue recognition, goodwill, consolidation, intangible assets, derivatives, employee share options, debt/equity, leases, etc.

The ICAEW (2007) shows that the adoption of IFRS has resulted in higher-quality financial reporting and has improved the quality of accounting disclosure. It indicates that IFRS-based financial statements facilitate more effective comparisons across countries, competitors and industry sectors. The ICAEW (2007) argues that IFRS adoption has enabled regulatory and supervisory authorities and has improved the efficiency of European Union capital markets. Armstrong et al. (2007) show that IFRS implementation has led to lower cost of capital. Likewise, Hail and Leuz (2007) report that first-time IFRS adopters display a significant reduction in cost of capital.

The FRRP has found that UK firms have complied well with IFRS. The UK is a common-law country and the UK GAAP exhibits significant similarities with IFRS, and as a result no significant transition problems were identified. Cuijpers and Buijink (2005) and the ICAEW (2007) note that larger companies as well as companies with significant needs of external financing had familiarized themselves with IFRS requirements early and had invested significant resources in training their staff. Similar considerations applied for companies with more foreign exposure and reliance on equity financing. However, the FRRP has identified that on a number of occasions firms may provide 'boilerplate' disclosures of accounting policies in their financial statements. It appears that disclosures of judgments and assumptions relating to company accounting policies exhibit significant variation. The FRRP has expressed specific concerns regarding business combinations, goodwill impairment, and income statement presentation.

The costs of adopting IFRS involve costs of transition from domestic GAAP to IFRS and costs of compliance for firms and enforcement for regulatory authorities (Carnachan 2003). In the report *EU Implementation of IFRS and the Fair Value Directive*, the ICAEW (2007) shows that the costs of preparing the first IFRS consolidated financial statements relate mainly to internal audit, training of staff, external technical and tax advice, information system changes, additional external audit costs, costs arising from contractual changes, etc. The ICAEW reports that the costs of implementing IFRS are as follows (2007, 8):

> Companies with turnover below €500m: 0.31 percent of turnover.
> Companies with turnover from €500m to €5,000m: 0.05 percent of turnover.
> Companies with turnover above €5,000m: 0.05 percent of turnover.

IFRS place significant emphasis on the disclosure of high-quality comparable accounting information (Tendeloo and Vanstraelen 2005). They favor the disclosure of a set of performance measures rather than of a single performance measure for the description and evaluation of a firm's financial situation (Leuz and Verrecchia 2000; Bushman and Smith 2001). IFRS seek to inform investors and other stock market participants about firms' behavior, strengths, weaknesses, and internal and external financial environments. Hence, a major objective of IFRS is to reduce the scope of earnings manipulation and allow investors to assess firms' performance using valid and reliable information (Kasznik 1999; Leuz 2003). Therefore, the adoption of IFRS would be expected to reinforce stock market efficiency and attract domestic and foreign capital and investments (Botosan and Plumlee 2002). It follows that the correct and faithful implementation of IFRS and their incorporation in company accounting practice and policy would be likely to have a favorable impact on the relation between managers, investors, and other stakeholders. In contrast, the disclosure and use of inaccurate accounting information would lead to inefficient decision making and to stock returns not reflecting firms' true financial picture and expectations.

REFERENCES

Armstrong, C., M. Barth, A. Jagolinzer, and E. Riedl. 2007. Market reaction to the adoption of IFRS in Europe. Working Paper, Harvard Business School.

Ball, R., S. Kothari, and A. Robin. 2000. The effect of international institutional factors on properties of accounting earnings. *Journal of Accounting and Economics* 29:1–51.

Beasley, M. 1996. An empirical analysis of the relation between the board of director composition and financial statement fraud. *Accounting Review* 71:443–65.

Beekes, W., P. Pope, and S. Young. 2004. The link between earnings timeliness, earnings conservatism and board composition: Evidence from the UK. *Corporate Governance: An International Review* 12 (1): 47–55.

Botosan, C., and M. Plumlee. 2002. A re-examination of disclosure level and the expected cost of equity capital. *Journal of Accounting Research* 40:21–40.

Bushman, R., and A. Smith. 2001. Financial accounting information and corporate governance. *Journal of Accounting and Economics* 32:237–334.

Carnachan, R. 2003. The case for competition between US GAAP and IFRS in US capital markets. Working Paper, Harvard Law School.

Cuijpers, R., and W. Buijink. 2005. Voluntary adoption of non-local GAAP in the European Union: A study of determinants and consequences. *European Accounting Review* 14 (3): 487–524.

Dargenidou, C., S. McLeay, and I. Raonic. 2007. Ownership, investor protection and earnings expectations. Working Paper, Paper Number: 07/07, University of Exeter.

Deloitte and Touche. 2008. *iGAAP 2009—IFRS reporting in the UK*. Deloitte and Touche, UK.

Evans, J., and S. Sridhar. 1996. Multiple control systems, accrual accounting and earnings management. *Journal of Accounting Research* 34:45–65.

Fama, E., and M. Jensen. 1983. Separation of ownership and control. *Journal of Law and Economics* 26:301–25.

Financial Reporting Council. 2008. *Combined code on corporate governance*. Financial Reporting Council, UK.

Hail, L., and C. Leuz. 2007. *Capital market effects of mandatory IFRS reporting in the EU: Empirical Evidence, Report made available by the Netherlands Authority for the Financial Markets.* http://www.afm.nl/corporate/default. ashx?DocumentId=10519 (accessed 5/9/2010).

Holthausen, R., D. Larcker, and R. Sloan. 1995. Annual bonus schemes and the manipulation of earnings. *Journal of Accounting and Economics* 19:29–74.

Institute of Chartered Accountants in England and Wales. 2007. *EU implementation of IFRS and the Fair Value Directive.* Institute of Chartered Accountants in England and Wales, UK.

Kasznik, R. 1999. On the association between voluntary disclosure and earnings management. *Journal of Accounting Research* 37:57–81.

Lawrence, S. 2002. Convergence of UK GAAP to IAS: Part 1. http://www.acca-global.com/archive/2888864/568644 (accessed 5/5/2010).

Leuz, C. 2003. IAS versus US GAAP: Information asymmetry-based evidence from Germany's new market. *Journal of Accounting Research* 41 (3): 445–72.

Leuz, C., and R. Verrecchia. 2000. The economic consequences of increased disclosure. *Journal of Accounting Research* 38:91–124.

Ormrod, P., and P. Taylor. 2004. The impact of the change to international accounting standards on debt covenants: A UK perspective. *Accounting in Europe* 1:71–94.

Peasnell, K., P. Pope, and S. Young. 2005. Board monitoring and earnings management: Do outside directors influence abnormal accruals? *Journal of Business Finance and Accounting* 32 (7–8): 1311–46.

PricewaterhouseCoopers. 2007. *IFRS and UK GAAP—A comparison.* PricewaterhouseCoopers, UK.

Ramond, O. 2007. Usefulness and relevance of reporting comprehensive income under international GAAPs: Insights from major European financial markets. Presented at the 30th European Accounting Association Annual Congress, Lisbon, Portugal.

Schipper, K. 1989. Earnings management. *Accounting Horizons* 3:91–102.

Tendeloo, B., and A. Vanstraelen. 2005. Earnings management under German GAAP versus IFRS. *European Accounting Review* 14 (1): 155–80.

Watts, R. 2003a. Conservatism in accounting Part I: Explanations and implications. *Accounting Horizons* 17:207–21.

———. 2003b. Conservatism in accounting part II: evidence and research opportunities. *Accounting Horizons* 17 (4): 287–301.

Weisbach, M. 1988. Outside directors and CEO turnover. Journal of Financial Economics 20:413–60.

Contributors

Dr. Aubert earned his PhD in Accounting at the University of Auvergne (France) in 2005 where he is currently serving as an Associate Professor of Accounting. He is a Faculty Affiliate at EM Strasbourg Business School and ESC Clermont as well. He was a Visiting Fulbright Scholar at University of Illinois at Urbana-Champaign and San Diego State University in 2006–2007. He was the French PhD student-representative at 2004 KPMG-EAA Doctoral Colloquium in Mostov. His teaching and research interests lay in the area of financial reporting, international accounting and financial analysis. He recently published two papers in the *Journal of Accounting and Taxation* and one co-authored with Prof. Gary Grudnitski in the *Journal of International Financial Management and Accounting*. Also, Dr. Aubert is invited to the University of Oklahoma to teach accounting classes (IFRS and Financial Statement Analysis) at both undergraduate and graduate levels (MBA, master's in Accounting) as a Visiting Assistant Professor.

Dr. Ervin L. Black, PhD, is a Professor in the School of Accountancy at Brigham Young University. His research is primarily in the financial accounting and international accounting areas, with emphasis on examining the usefulness of firm financial characteristics in different settings. Journals in which Professor Black has published include *Accounting Review*, *Journal of Accounting and Economics*, *Accounting Organizations and Society*, *Journal of International Financial Management and Accounting*, *Journal of Business Finance and Accounting*, and the *Journal of the American Taxation Association*. Professor Black is active in the International and Financial Reporting Sections of the American Accounting Association, currently serving as the president of the International Accounting Section. Dr. Black teaches undergraduate and graduate courses in international accounting, financial statement analysis, advanced financial accounting, and professional research methods.

Dr. F. Greg Burton, PhD, CPA, is the Deloitte and Touche Fellow and an Associate Professor of accounting at Brigham Young University in Provo, Utah, where he teaches auditing, risks and controls, and international accounting at both the undergraduate and graduate level. He has been honored with several teaching awards, and has published in journals such as *Review of Accounting Studies, Contemporary Accounting Research,* and *Accounting Organizations and Society*. His research spans fraud, auditing, market behavior, and international accounting. He was appointed the 2008–2009 Academic Fellow in the Division of Corporation Finance at the Securities and Exchange Commission. In addition to his academic qualifications, he has professional experience with KPMG, most recently as a senior manager. He has recently given presentations in Brazil, China, Croatia, Czech Republic, England, France, Germany, Hong Kong, India, Ireland, Malaysia, Mexico, Singapore, Sweden, Thailand, and the United Arab Emirates.

Dr. Elena de las Heras is a lecturer at Universidad Autónoma de Madrid. Elena has made visits to the universities of Lancaster (UK), Porto (Portugal), and Zurich (Switzerland) and participates in several research projects. Her research focuses on international accounting and enforcement. Her work has been presented in different congresses, has received several awards, and has been published in Spanish journals.

Dr. Pascale Delvaille, Associate Professor at ESCP Europe in Paris, teaches primarily International Financial Reporting courses for master's degree programs, MBA, and executive education programs. She is a member of the School's Educational Committee. Her research includes the application of IFRS by listed companies and the IFRS convergence process in European countries.

Dr. Wolfgang Dick is Teaching Associate Professor at ESSEC Business School and co-director of the ESSEC-KPMG Financial Reporting Institute, and an expert in IFRS. He co-authored textbooks about IFRS in French and English and also published articles in various academic and professional journals. In addition to his academic work, Wolfgang Dick served for almost three years for PSA Peugeot-Citroen as Head of Accounting Studies and Methods and was in charge of preparing the groups first-time adoption of IFRS (2002–2004).

Dr. Roberto Di Pietra is a full Professor in Accounting and Business Administration (ABA) at the Department of Business and Social Studies, University of Siena, Italy. He received a PhD in ABA from the University of Pisa in 1997; he has also received a specialization in Banking in 1993. Di Pietra's main research interests are in International Accounting, Auditing, and Accounting History.

Dr. Holger Erchinger is an audit partner with KPMG LLP in New York with 17 years of experience in public accounting serving different clients on audit, audit-related, and consulting engagements. He has taught IFRS, International Auditing, and Corporate Governance at different business schools and published about forty articles in various journals.

Dr. Gary Grudnitski is currently Professor of Accounting in the Charles W. Lamden School of Accountancy at San Diego State University. He received his doctorate from the University of Massachusetts (Amherst) and has taught previously at the University of Texas at Austin. Professor Grudnitski's research interests are in the area of accounting and information systems. He has published in the *Accounting Review, Journal of Accounting and Public Policy, Journal of Management Information Systems,* and *Journal of Futures Markets.*

Gabriela Gueifão graduated in General Management and mastered in Accountancy. Working as a CPA in financial departments of medium-size companies along with teaching general management and accountancy subjects gave her a broad idea of the business world plus the academic one. All her teaching career, she has always had a very profound view of what academia tells and what business does. Living and working between these two worlds gave her a different sight and experience regarding accountancy and hence financial management and reporting. This is her first experience in writing about accountancy, truly enjoyed, with the aim of publishing. All her books are published inside the schools she worked for, as manuals, so have not been for the public.

Dr. Mohamed Azzim Gulamhussen—Department of Accounting and Finance, Lisbon University Institute (ISCTE Business School), Portugal. Dr. Gulamhussen teaches international finance and accounting. He was, until recently, a president of the Finance Research Center and director of the Doctoral Program of the University. He has published in the *Journal of Multinational Financial Management, International Business Review, Management International Review, Management Accounting Research, International Journal of Accounting,* and other journals.

Dr. Axel Haller holds the Chair of Financial Accounting and Auditing at the College of Business of the University of Regensburg, Germany. His research and teaching interests are comparative international accounting, IFRS, and sustainability reporting. He has taught at a lot of business schools in Europe, US, and Australia and published more than one hundred papers and monographs.

Dr. Niclas Hellman is Associate Professor at the Department of Accounting at Stockholm School of Economics, Sweden. His research covers international accounting and IFRS adoption, auditor–client interaction, and the impact of financial information on analyst and investor behavior. Dr. Hellman is a member of the Swedish Accounting Standards Board.

Dr George Iatridis is an Assistant Professor of Accounting and Finance at the University of Thessaly, Greece, and a research fellow at the University of Lancaster, UK. Dr Iatridis is a member of the Accounting and Auditing Oversight Board, Ministry of Economics, Greece. He is a member of the working group for the preparation of the new GAAP for the Greek public sector. Dr. Iatridis has worked as a Lecturer in Accounting and Finance at the University of Manchester, UK, and has also taught at the University of Manchester Institute of Science and Technology (UMIST). He holds a PhD in Accounting and Finance from the University of Manchester.

Dr. Victoria Krivogorsky is a faculty member in the Charles W. Lamden School of Accountancy at San Diego State University, US. Her international research and teaching experience includes serving on the faculty at ESSEC-Paris, France, and ESCP-EAP European School of Management, Paris, France, as a Visiting Professor. Her research interests rest in the areas of international accounting and corporate governance. Her research efforts resulted in numerous academic publications. She has presented the results of her research efforts at business schools in France, Netherlands, Switzerland, Portugal, Finland, Poland, and Russia. She is a director of International Business Economics Accounting Collaborative Network (iBEACON).

Dr. Begoña Navallas is a chartered accountant and has been working as an auditor for the last ten years. Since 2006 she has been a teacher of accounting at Universidad Autonoma de Madrid, and participates in different research projects. She has been working mainly in disclosure decisions, developing some research papers about voluntary disclosure and segment disclosure. Additionally, she has focused her research on auditing and corporate governance, presenting her work at certain international congresses.

Spencer H. Paul is a second-year Master of Accountancy (Tax) student in the School of Accountancy at Brigham Young University. He previously worked as a speechwriter for the Parliament of Scotland in Edinburgh, UK, and for Patricia Gibson, Scottish National Party candidate for the House of Commons. He has also written course materials on International Financial Reporting Standards for the Brigham Young University School of Accountancy.

Dr. Chiara Saccon is Professor of International Financial Accounting at Ca' Foscari, Venice University, MSC International Accounting and Finance (London School of Economics and Political Sciences), PhD Business Administration (Venice University). Research interests include: Financial Reporting, International Comparative Accounting, and Convergence Processes in Accounting and Auditing Regulation. Saccon has published books on Comparative Group Accounting and European Harmonization.

Dr. Jose Luis Ucieda has been Associate Professor of Accounting at the Universidad Autonoma of Madrid since 2006. He is Chair of the Accounting Department, and Director of International Programs for the US, Canada, Australia, and New Zealand. Research interests include: financial accounting, international accounting, IFRS, and teaching. He has published in international and national journals and participated in international and national conferences.

Martin Wehrfritz—Research Assistant at the Department of Financial Accounting and Auditing, University of Regensburg, Germany. Mr. Wehrfritz studied Business Administration and received his Master of Science at the University of Passau, Germany, and his MBA at the University of Cincinnati, Ohio. His research interests are in the area of international comparative accounting.

Index